MW00560548

Praise for *Safe & Simple Food All...*

"Finally, a complete, up-to-date, evidence-based resource for starting solids, baby-led weaning, and reducing the risk of food allergies, all in one place. Malkani blends the art of cooking with the science of food allergy prevention in this easy-to-follow infant feeding guide and cookbook that will infuse family mealtimes with everything parents need to grow adventurous, healthy eaters."

Kelly Fradin, MD, pediatrician, speaker, consultant, and author of *Advanced Parenting*

"Introduction of solid foods and food allergens are important milestones in infancy and early childhood. This book includes useful tips for introducing solid foods and food allergens, while following principles of baby-led weaning."

Carina Venter, PhD, RD, professor of pediatric allergy and immunology, internationally recognized allergy dietitian, coauthor of the *Health Professional's Guide to Nutrition Management of Food Allergies*, and cocreator of FARE's Pediatric Food Allergy Course

"*Safe and Simple Food Allergy Prevention* is a practical and family-centered resource that can help take the guesswork out of introducing complementary foods, including common allergens. Malina builds food allergy prevention into recipes that the whole family can enjoy together."

Michael Pistiner, MD, MMSc, director of Food Allergy Advocacy, Education, and Prevention for Mass General for Children

"Featuring tummy-warming, comforting, nutrient-rich recipes, *Safe and Simple Food Allergy Prevention* transports mealtime from a chore to a chance to get the jump on food allergens, create moments for learning and bonding, and introduce your child to the joys of eating."

Maya Feller, MS, RD, CDN, registered dietitian nutritionist, founder and lead dietitian at Maya Feller Nutrition, author of *Eating from Our Roots*, and cohost of the *Well, Now* podcast

"Malina has done it again! From her early advice on 'you provide, they decide' to a step-by-step plan on how to introduce high-allergy foods, this book is a must-have for all new parents. As a pediatric gastroenterologist, I know that parents can be overwhelmed when it comes to the what, when, and how much to feed their infant. This practical guide arms parents with practical and up-to-date advice on the introduction of solids and provides a daily plan with recipes for parents to easily follow."

Anthony F. Porto, MD, MPH, associate professor of pediatrics at Yale University, board-certified pediatric gastroenterologist, and coauthor of *The Pediatrician's Guide to Feeding Babies and Toddlers*

"At last, a practical and easy-to-follow resource for both parents and professionals! It's as if the reader can feel Malina Malkani's gentle hand on their shoulder, guiding them through the 'responsive feeding' process of starting solids with an emphasis on the specific steps for introducing the top nine food allergens to keep baby safe. Packed with evidence-based instructions and loads of recipes, this book is a gem!"

Melanie Potock, MA, CCC-SLP, author of *Responsive Feeding: The Baby-First Guide to Stress-Free Weaning, Healthy Eating & Mealtime Bonding*

"As an OB-GYN for 25 years who STRUGGLED with HOW and WHAT and WHEN to feed my OWN three children—this is the book I NEEDED that did NOT exist! I am so grateful to have it as a resource for my community and patients!"

Dr. Shieva Ghofrany, OB-GYN, cofounder of Tribe Called V

"A fearless and safe approach to introducing food allergens to your baby, no matter the feeding approach or risk for food allergies. Malina simplifies the process with realistic meal plans and nutritious recipes."

Jill Castle, pediatric dietitian and author of *Kids Thrive at Every Size*

"This book is an absolute must-have for any parent starting to introduce solid foods to their baby. *Safe and Simple Food Allergy Prevention* is a simple-to-follow, evidence-based guide with the latest research on how busy parents can safely introduce their little one to top allergens. The recipes are not only delicious for your whole family, but also packed with the essential nutrients your baby needs. I can't wait to recommend this valuable resource to all my patients!"

Dr. Dina DiMaggio, board-certified pediatrician and coauthor of *The Pediatrician's Guide to Feeding Babies and Toddlers*

"*Safe and Simple Food Allergy Prevention* is an up-to-date and comprehensive guide on starting solids and introducing allergens to infants. Malina provides research-backed guidelines in easy-to-understand bites, along with practical tips and fun recipes. This book is a must-have for all families as well as all pediatric health-care providers!"

Meghan McMillin, MS, RD, IBCLC, owner of The Lactation Dietitian

"Malkani has done it again—her first book, *Simple and Safe Baby-Led Weaning*, is an incredible resource that I recommend to parents constantly. A true expert in her field, she now uses her deep expertise in pediatric nutrition, along with years of personal experience, to bring us this relatable and invaluable guide on food allergy prevention during infancy. Approachable, specific, and evidence-based, this book is an absolute must-have for anyone with questions about starting solids and preventing food allergies."

**Ginger Hultin, MS, RDN, CSO, Seattle-based anti-inflammatory expert
and author of *Anti-Inflammatory Diet Meal Prep***

"As a nephrologist who has helped patients with kidney disease adjust their diet to protect their renal function, I applaud Malina Malkani's practical, reassuring approach to baby-led feeding that underscores the joy of eating. She offers parents excellent strategies for feeding young children, including how to introduce potential allergens as described in recent research. A delight to read, the book also emphasizes that mealtimes are an opportunity to encourage autonomy, strengthen family relationships, and create healthy habits that will last a lifetime."

Julian Seifter, MD, distinguished chair in medicine at Brigham & Women's Hospital and author of *After the Diagnosis*

"Feeding babies potentially allergenic foods can be scary! Malina has done an amazing job simplifying the science—and the process—to make food allergy prevention through early infant feeding easy and doable. Practical and empowering!"

Sherry Coleman Collins, MS, RDN, LD, food allergy dietitian

"Malina is the go-to expert in childhood feeding and showcases her expert knowledge of baby-led feeding and how to approach feeding babies to help prevent food allergies. Her approaches and tips are based on the latest science and enforced with her experience with her own three kids. This book is important for any parent who is starting the feeding process with their own baby, and especially a must-have for any parent who is anxious about feeding a child with a family history of food allergies. Malkani's down-to-earth and easy-to-understand approach will help minimize the stress involved with starting to feed your baby its first solid foods."

Toby Amidor, MS, RD, CON, FAND, award-winning nutrition expert and
Wall Street Journal* bestselling author of *The Easy 5-Ingredient Healthy Cookbook

"What Malina has done is nothing short of remarkable. As a chef, I am so impressed by the creativity and ingenuity of her approach. And as a parent, I am so grateful for her diligence and forethought. Mostly, I am amazed at Malina's ability to synthesize her knowledge and experience into a single resource that functions both as a primer on all things allergy and as a healthy, modern cookbook. This belongs on the shelf of anyone who cooks for young children."

Gabriel Frasca, owner and fish chef at Straight Wharf Restaurant

"Malina is the premier child feeding, allergy, and nutrition expert in the country, and there is no one I trust more for advice on the topic. Not only is her book, blog, and social media content thoroughly researched and grounded in the latest science, but it's also approachable, easy to understand, beautifully curated, and entertaining. I will be recommending this fabulous book to all parents and practitioners who work with children!"

Mascha Davis, MPH, RDN, author of *Eat Your Vitamins*

"This book is a must-have for any parent wanting realistic, up-to-date information on starting solids, specifically with a focus on how to introduce allergens. Malina provides the perfect balance of practical tips and evidenced-based information in a judgment-free way for parents to feel empowered in starting solids with their little ones."

Leah Hackney, RD, LD, CSP, @kids.nutritionist on Instagram and chief operating officer of BLW Meals App

"Is there a National Book Award for the Best in Parental Stress Reduction? If not, there needs to be to honor this clear, easy-to-follow, up-to-the-minute, and mind-easing work of science and writing art. No new parent should miss this book. Kudos to you, Malina. You continue to improve the lives of parents and children with your outstanding writing and educating."

Michael D. Wolf, PhD, former professor at New York University, author of six fitness books, and 10-year contributing fitness editor for *SELF* magazine

"*Safe and Simple Food Allergy Prevention* is a concise, essential, and modern handbook for anyone looking to introduce solids and allergens. Malina's content is both empirical and backed by science. Her recipes are nutritious, delicious, and noncariogenic!"

Charles Yau, DDS, board-certified pediatric dentist

ALSO BY
MALINA LINKAS MALKANI, MS, RDN, CDN

Simple & Safe Baby-Led Weaning:
How to Integrate Foods, Master Portion Sizes, and Identify Allergies

SAFE & SIMPLE
FOOD ALLERGY PREVENTION

A Baby-Led Feeding Guide to Starting Solids & Introducing Top Allergens

MALINA LINKAS MALKANI, MS, RDN, CDN

BenBella

BenBella Books, Inc.
Dallas, TX

This book is for informational purposes only. It is not intended to serve as a substitute for professional medical advice. The author and publisher specifically disclaim any and all liability arising directly or indirectly from the use of any information contained in this book. A healthcare professional should be consulted regarding your specific medical situation. Any product mentioned in this book does not imply endorsement of that product by the author or publisher.

The author partners with Mission MightyMe and ezpz. Neither company was involved in the writing of this book. The ezpz products featured in the recipe photographs were a gift from ezpz; the ezpz logo appears with permission.

Safe & Simple Food Allergy Prevention copyright © 2024 by
  Malina Linkas Malkani
Photographs by Malina Linkas Malkani
Illustrations by Eric March
Cover photos courtesy of the author (soy beans, tahini, salmon) and ©Adobe Stock / PhotoSG (shrimp), Viktor (cheese), Medard (peanut butter), gitusik (pasta), exclusive-design (tree nut butters), boomeart (egg), and Elena (baby)

All rights reserved. No part of this book may be used or reproduced in any manner whatsoever without written permission of the publisher, except in the case of brief quotations embodied in critical articles or reviews.

BenBella Books, Inc.
10440 N. Central Expressway
Suite 800
Dallas, TX 75231
benbellabooks.com
Send feedback to feedback@benbellabooks.com.
BenBella is a federally registered trademark.

Printed in China
10 9 8 7 6 5 4 3 2 1

Library of Congress Control Number: 2023059709
ISBN 9781637745359 (trade paper)
ISBN 9781637745366 (electronic)

Editing by Claire Schulz
Copyediting by Karen Wise
Proofreading by Lisa Story and Jenny Bridges
Indexing by WordCo Indexing Services, Inc.
Text design and composition by Tara Long
Cover design by Sarah Avinger
Printed by Dream Colour Printing Ltd.

Special discounts for bulk sales are available.
Please contact bulkorders@benbellabooks.com.

THIS BOOK IS DEDICATED

with love, gratitude, and appreciation to
Jeff Devine and Leslie Casillas

CONTENTS

INTRODUCTION **x**

PART ONE
Preparing for Solids

CHAPTER 1

Setting the Stage for Food Allergy Prevention: How Did We Get Here? **2**

CHAPTER 2

Adventures in Starting Solids: Should You Choose Baby-Led Weaning, Purees, or a Combo? **9**

CHAPTER 3

What You *Really* Need Before You Begin **20**

PART TWO
Establishing Feeding and Preventing Food Allergies

CHAPTER 4

First Foods **28**

CHAPTER 5

How to Assemble Balanced Meals for Baby **45**

CHAPTER 6

Top 12 Tips for BLF Mealtime Success **49**

CHAPTER 7

Understanding Food Allergies **58**

CHAPTER 8

Dos and Don'ts for Offering Top Allergenic Foods **64**

PART THREE

Staying Safe

CHAPTER 9

Gagging, Choking, and Food Safety: What Every Caregiver Needs to Know **86**

CHAPTER 10

Screening, Treatment, and Cures for Food Allergies **92**

CHAPTER 11

Identifying Allergic Reactions and Food Intolerances **96**

PART FOUR

Let's Eat!

CHAPTER 12

Stocking Your Kitchen for BLF **106**

CHAPTER 13

9-Day Allergen Introduction Plan **112**

CHAPTER 14

8 Weeks of Allergen Maintenance Meal Plans **119**

CHAPTER 15

Recipes for Baby and Family **129**
 Breakfast **130**
 Lunch **153**
 Dinner and Sides **174**
 Dessert **226**

SIGNING OFF **235**
ALLERGEN SWAPS **236**
ACKNOWLEDGMENTS **239**
NOTES **241**
INDEX **249**

INTRODUCTION

If it's almost time for your baby to begin eating solid foods, or if you've started offering purees and feel that your baby is ready for table foods and allergen introductions, let me start by welcoming you into this new, often hilarious, deeply satisfying phase of parenting. You and your baby are in for such a treat!

Let me also reassure you that while food allergies themselves (and the words "food allergy prevention") can sound complicated, reducing the risk of food allergies and feeding babies, in general, doesn't have to be. In fact, it can and should be pretty simple, but even many of the most well-intentioned pediatricians are not often up to date on the latest infant feeding guidelines and recommendations, which can lead to a great deal of confusion. My goal with this book is to translate the latest research on reducing the risk of food allergies into a stress-free feeding guide with practical tips and family-friendly recipes that will make your baby's feeding journey safe, easy, and delicious.

About Me
(and Why I Wrote This Book!)

As a licensed pediatric registered dietitian and the author of *Simple & Safe Baby-Led Weaning: How to Integrate Foods, Manage Portion Sizes, and Identify Allergies*, I run a small, New York–based nutrition practice that treats mainly infants, toddlers, and children. I also founded Malina Malkani, LLC, a nutrition consulting company that produces a top pediatric nutrition blog (MalinaMalkani.com/blog) and educates an audience of over 140,000 followers every day about infant and child feeding on my Instagram, TikTok, and YouTube accounts, which share the handle @healthy.mom.healthy.kids. My mission is to help parents and caregivers raise healthy, intuitive, adventurous eaters, always with an eye toward reducing as much parental stress around food and feeding as I can. And let me tell you, there's a lot of it!

But in addition to working in the infant and child feeding space, I am also a single mom of three kids who were born within three and a half years of each other. In other words, I've spent a *lot* of time in the weeds feeding my own babies.

During those early years, I was a parent who was stressed out about feeding, and overwhelmed by the many nutrition-related challenges we faced, including intractable thrush during breastfeeding, picky eating, food allergies that were hard to diagnose, a preterm baby who wasn't gaining weight, and more. It was hard and lonely, and as I emerged from those years, I remember thinking how much easier it would have been and how many fewer missteps I would have made if I had had access to the right guidance. That's what I hope this book will be for you: a step-by-step, baby-led approach to starting solids and preventing food allergies that is simple and safe and helps set up a positive family feeding dynamic from your little one's very first bites.

What You'll Find in These Pages

The idea for this book grew out of both my professional and personal experiences of feeding babies and navigating potential and difficult-to-diagnose food allergies in my own kids. Given the interest in food allergy prevention that seemed to flow from those who read my first book, *Simple & Safe Baby-Led Weaning,* tackling both the topic and a collection of baby-friendly food allergy prevention recipes felt like a natural next step.

While I love baby-led weaning and the many potential benefits it offers, what you will *not* find in this book is a dogmatic approach to starting solids that requires you to avoid purees and insist that your baby only self-feed. That's why I've chosen the term "baby-led feeding" instead of "baby-led weaning" (more on that later).

Research has revealed a lot in the past decade or two about food allergy prevention and infant feeding. Since I know firsthand that the last thing you have is bandwidth for complicated feeding plans, I boil it all down for you here into three simple phases that will save you time, energy, and money. I'll translate that research into foods and recipes you can feed your baby (and the rest of your family, too). And it will encourage you to take a responsive, baby-led approach to starting solids that is tailored to the needs of your unique child.

To that end, part 1 will walk you through what you need to know and do to get ready for your baby's introduction to solids—from when to begin to the essential items you'll need to get (there aren't many!) to food safety to discussing with your pediatrician your baby's level of risk for food allergies.

Part 2 will help you establish feeding and prevent food allergies from the get-go. We'll cover first foods, infant-safe food sizing and food texture, the latest guidelines on top allergen introduction, how to introduce common allergens with ease and fold them into day-to-day life, how to build a balanced baby meal, the important nutrients for infant growth and development and how to serve them, and more.

Part 3 will help you be prepared for some of the challenges that can arise. You will learn about the differences between gagging and choking, what to do in the event of each, what to look for in terms of allergic reactions, and what to do if you think your baby is having one. You will also find some basic information on how healthcare providers screen for and treat food allergies and intolerances.

Finally, part 4 will pull it all together for you with a list of helpful pantry essentials and kitchen tools, a food safety guide, meal plans, and a collection of food allergy prevention recipes that will soon become some of your baby's (and your whole family's!) favorite comfort foods.

Most of all, what I hope you'll take from this guide and recipe collection is excitement about the moments of connection, joy, and delicious sweetness that lie ahead for you and your child. Starting babies off on a positive, healthy feeding journey is one of the most loving, lifelong gifts we can give them—and mealtimes give us incredible insight into who these unique little souls truly are . . . so get your little one set for the sensory feast that lies ahead!

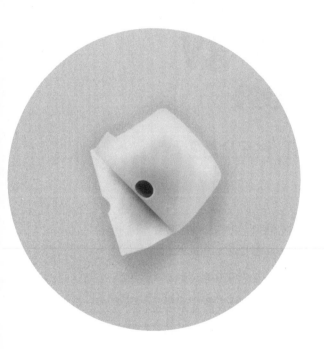

PART ONE

Preparing for Solids

Setting the Stage for Food Allergy Prevention

HOW DID WE GET HERE?

My first baby came in 2009 when I was a brand-new dietitian with almost no experience in pediatrics. Our pediatrician at the time told me to hold off on introducing top allergens, including peanuts, until after 12 months. While my daughter was not at high risk for food allergies, I was terrified. Anxiety about allergenic foods circulated constantly among my mom friends, misinformation was rampant, and there was almost no available guidance about how to introduce allergenic foods other than the American Academy of Pediatrics (AAP) recommendation to wait . . . despite the AAP having rescinded that recommendation in 2008.

On the day of my baby's 1-year well visit, I packed a little peanut butter toast, drove to the pediatrician's office, and (shaking) fed it to her in the parking lot. My thinking was that if I had to do this without guidance or reassurance, the safest place to do it would be near the doctor's office where I could find an EpiPen and knowledge about how to use it. It was a relief to find that my daughter ate the peanut butter without any adverse reaction, but the entire experience left my heart pounding and my stomach tied in knots.

Unfortunately, this is not a unique story—even today! In fact, the longer I've worked in pediatric nutrition, the more often I've heard similar versions of it from parents struggling with the same anxiety and lack of guidance around top allergen introduction. If the following sentence makes you uneasy, you are not alone:

• • •

**Offering common allergens like peanut and egg
early, often, and consistently during infancy
(starting at about 6 months of age when babies
are developmentally ready for solid foods)
helps reduce the risk that babies will develop
food allergies.**

• • •

Talking about feeding common allergens to young babies can be unsettling—even more so if you are a new parent getting advice and support from well-meaning family or friends who haven't stayed current on changes in infant feeding guidelines.

Did you know that many babies are not actually born with food allergies? Food allergies can develop over time, affect 8 percent of children, and are a common cause of strain and stress on families.[1] So, if this resonates with you, know that you are not alone! One recent study found that 81 percent of parents of children with diagnosed food allergies reported clinically significant worry, while 42.3 percent had posttraumatic stress, and 39.1 percent had moderate to extremely severe anxiety.[2] Further, the anxiety is not limited to parents who have children with food allergy diagnoses. A cross-sectional study that surveyed randomly selected parents found that more than a third of parents had avoided introducing certain foods in their baby's diet due to fears of allergy or hypersensitivity.[3] Food insecurity (heightened during the COVID-19 pandemic and disproportionately affecting Black, Hispanic, and Native American communities) places an even greater burden on families of food-allergic children who are faced with increased costs of food allergy–related medical care and dietary restrictions.[4] In other words, food allergies are worth preventing.

Unfortunately, the guidance on when and how to introduce the top allergenic foods in a baby's diet has changed no less than four times over the past two decades. There haven't just been small shifts in the guidance on allergens during infant feeding—we're talking about a 180-degree turnaround.

In 2000, the AAP recommended delaying the introduction of common allergens until 1, 2, and even 3 years of age in high-risk children, but this guidance wasn't based on clear, science-backed evidence and (although we do not know for sure) may have contributed to the dramatic 50 percent increase in the prevalence of food allergies in American children between 1997 and 2011.[5]

We need more research to fully understand what causes the development of food allergies and why there has been such a sharp increase. But thankfully, we now have a better understanding of how to reduce the risk from landmark studies like the 2015 Learning Early About Peanut Allergy (LEAP) randomized trial, which showed that early, frequent exposure to peanut in high-risk babies reduced the risk of peanut allergy by 86 percent, and the 2017 Prevention of Egg Allergy with Tiny Amount Intake (PETIT) trial, which was stopped early because it so successfully reduced the risk of egg allergy.[6]

In response to this growing body of research, recommendations from major health organizations have shifted away from avoidance to early and frequent feeding of common allergens as a way to reduce the risk of food allergies. In fact, the 2020–2025 Dietary Guidelines for Americans issued by the United States Department of Agriculture (USDA) and United States Department of Health and Human Services (HHS) for the first time offered specific recommendations for babies and toddlers and emphasized the importance of introducing allergenic foods early and often.

In practical terms, this means offering top allergens like peanuts and egg in baby-friendly forms, starting for most babies at about 6 months of age, when they are developmentally ready for solids (and potentially as early as 4 months, depending on a number of factors, which we'll cover). If the allergens are tolerated, they should be offered regularly and frequently, in keeping with the family's cultural dietary practices, to help maintain the baby's tolerance.

Early, consistent introduction and exposure to peanuts during infancy is a successful food allergy prevention intervention in babies of different races and in babies at all levels of risk for food allergies.[7] However, feeding babies peanuts and other common allergens like egg and fish still has not become a widely accepted practice, even among pediatricians.[8]

In my private practice and in interactions with parents on my social media accounts, some of the main barriers I see to the early and frequent feeding of allergens include the following:

- Anxiety about potential allergic reactions
- Nervousness about starting solids in general (mainly due to fear of choking)

The Top Nine Allergens

Peanuts

Eggs

Cow's Milk

Fish

Tree Nuts

Wheat

Soy

Shellfish

Sesame

- Confusion about how to prepare top allergenic foods in baby-safe and developmentally appropriate forms

- Lack of awareness about the importance of early and frequent allergen exposures

- The cost of foods containing common allergens

I get it. Food is expensive and costs continue to rise. You're now supposed to feed your precious new baby a bunch of foods that pediatricians used to recommend delaying? Knowing that much of it will end up on the floor or in the bin? It all seems even harder when misinformed family, friends, and even health professionals tell you you're wrong and going to hurt your baby, perhaps because the last time they fed a baby was 15 or 20 years ago or more, and they were warned to avoid feeding common allergens until well into toddlerhood.

Case in point: from the time my babies started coming, I trusted my mom to care for them in many ways—feeding included. She's generally calm and confident around babies, but I'll never forget traveling with her to another state and leaving my oldest in her care (age 11 months) to go to a wedding. I gave the baby dinner (mashed potatoes, broccoli, and scallops, all of which she had eaten before) and headed out for the event. The baby vomited not long after I left. After receiving a series of utterly panicked phone calls from my mom, who, not being able to reach the pediatrician, had taken her immediately to the emergency room, I left the ceremony and headed to the hospital. Four hours later, the ER doctors told me the baby was fine, but scolded me for feeding her shellfish, then apologized when they realized I am a dietitian and admitted they really weren't sure what foods infants should have. Everyone was confused! Should we not have given her scallops? Was she allergic to scallops? Was the vomiting due to something else? (It turns out she's not allergic to shellfish, but she still—at age 14—chooses to avoid scallops.)

I have heard many similar stories from clients and followers. And part of what inspired me to write this book is this type of confusion—because as new research emerges and we learn more about food allergy prevention and starting babies off on a successful and positive feeding journey, there is so much comforting information I will share here to make this part of your parenting journey pleasurable rather than scary, joyful rather than confusing, and life-affirming rather than anxious.

Now here's the tough part! If you introduce all nine top allergens carefully and feed them early and often throughout early childhood, is it guaranteed that your child will not develop any food allergies? No. I wish it were! (And if you happen to have food-allergic older children and are currently carrying around any amount of shame or guilt about the way they were fed as infants, I hope it releases you to hear that their food allergies are *not* your fault.) Pediatric allergists and food allergy experts emphasize that everything in food allergies is nuanced and nothing is 100 percent certain. Many babies without any risk factors develop multiple food allergies and other high-risk babies whose blood tests show that they are sensitized to peanuts can eat a whole piece of peanut butter toast without reacting.

Although we can't guarantee that early, consistent, frequent allergen introduction will definitely prevent food allergies, what we do have is research that guides us on how to feed babies in a practical way that *reduces the risk* of food allergies and increases the likelihood that babies will accept a wider variety of foods and flavors as they grow. In fact, starting solids and preventing food allergies can be quite safe and simple, but there is a critical, short window of time during the first year of life, between about 4 and 7 months, in which both are most effective.

If you've ever read anything by Michael Pollan, you might be familiar with his ability to deftly translate the titanic science of nutrition into a mere seven words to live by: "Eat food. Mostly plants. Not too much."[9]

So here is my take on feeding babies à la Michael Pollan—pretty much everything you need to know to take a baby-led approach, feed with confidence, lower the risk of food allergies, and grow a healthy, adventurous, intuitive eater without overthinking it:

• • •

Eat together.
You provide, baby decides.
Offer real foods in safe sizes and textures.
Feed allergens early, often, and consistently.
Variety is key!

• • •

Adventures in Starting Solids

SHOULD YOU CHOOSE BABY-LED WEANING, PUREES, OR A COMBO?

You may have heard the saying "Food before one is just for fun." Indeed, breast milk and/or formula will continue to be your baby's main source of nutrients throughout the first year of life. And starting solids *is* fun! (Some of my most precious memories of each of my infant daughters happened during their early experiences with solid foods and have stayed with me ever since. My middle, her huge brown eyes trained hungrily on the bowl of fresh mango coming toward her, the delight dancing across her face in response to that first juicy bite. And my youngest, fastidiously pincering every crumb with her thumb and forefinger so as not to miss a single taste of a food she liked. Priceless!)

But starting solids is about more than just fun. It provides precious moments of connection with caregivers, nutrition needed for growth, and opportunities to develop large and fine motor skills, expand the palate, and of course, help reduce the risk of food allergies.

Still, please don't let all of that overwhelm you! One of the advantages of taking a baby-led approach is that most of the wonderful benefits of solid foods for babies happen naturally when you simply draw your baby into family meals and eat together.

Rest assured, after reading this book, you will know everything you need to know to safely start your baby on solid foods and enjoy stress-free, joyful, often hilarious mealtimes with your child—and you'll be ready to dive into the recipes in part 4, which are designed to help you nourish your family while reducing your baby's risk of food allergies.

So take a deep breath and get ready to experience the immense satisfaction of introducing your baby to one of the most pleasurable parts of life.

> " My little guy loves eating and usually we have just the happiest, sweetest mealtimes. Now that I've mostly moved past fear of choking, allergic reactions, etc., it is such a fun time for us! "
>
> JESSICA, MOM OF 9-MONTH-OLD LOGAN

You Have Options!

Contrary to what many folks will tell you, there is no one "right" way to start a baby on solid foods, and no one feeding model that works for every family. Like so many other aspects of parenting, we may have an idea of how we want to introduce solids, but every baby is different. The more we recognize and respond to a baby's unique needs during the process of starting solids—especially as those needs shift and progress throughout the hours, days, and weeks of infancy—the more positive that process will be.

The good news about starting solids is that you have options, all of which are compatible with allergen introduction and can follow a baby-led approach. And you don't have to choose just one. Many babies will even make the choice for you!

Methods to consider:

1. **Baby-Led Weaning (BLW)**, which involves offering a baby **appropriately sized and textured finger foods** from the family table for self-feeding, starting at about 6 months of age when the signs of readiness for solids are present (we'll cover what these signs are in chapter 3).

2. **A conventional approach to starting solids**, which typically refers to the parent-led **spoon-feeding of purees** and can begin as early as 4 months.

3. **A combined approach**, sometimes called "modified baby-led weaning" or "baby-led feeding," which involves offering **finger foods for self-feeding as well as purees and mashes**, ideally beginning at about 6 months of age with signs of readiness for solids.

Let's take a closer look at each of these.

Baby-Led Weaning

The term "baby-led weaning" is a bit of a misnomer in that it's not actually about transitioning away from breast milk and/or formula, as we define "weaning" here in the US. Baby-led weaning was first popularized in the UK, where the term "weaning" simply means starting to offer solid foods. While BLW has been steadily gaining in popularity over the last couple of decades (starting with the groundbreaking book *Baby-Led Weaning* by Dr. Gill Rapley), it's nothing new.

Baby food in the form of smooth, uniform purees became popular in the early 1900s when doctors, not understanding the importance of breastfeeding on demand to establish and support milk supply, started providing misguided advice to mothers that they should breastfeed on a strict schedule; as a result, breast milk production decreased, babies were hungry, and cereal-based early foods were introduced to infants as young as 2 months.[1] This necessitated spoon-feeding and a cultural assumption that spoon-feeding was the only way to start infants on complementary foods, but as far as we know, for most of human history, people fed babies from the family table with some minor modifications, and that's pretty much what BLW is. So, while BLW might be seen as trendy, it's really a return to a time-tested practice.

Many caregivers are attracted to BLW because the baby eats what you eat, so there's no need to prepare two separate meals. This saves time, money, and energy, and helps foster a healthy rhythm of family meals enjoyed together. Self-feeding also provides daily opportunities for babies to practice and hone both oral motor and fine motor skills and offers regular exposure to a variety of stimulating shapes, colors, textures, and flavors. And research has found that when caregivers are educated about how to provide balanced baby meals in infant-safe forms, BLW babies can get the nutrients they need to thrive and are no more likely to choke than spoon-fed babies.[2]

Research suggests that compared with spoon-fed infants, BLW babies are started on solids a bit later (closer to 6 months—see the next chapter for more information on determining when your baby is ready to start solids).[3] They are also drawn into family meals earlier and more often, given freedom and autonomy at meals to decide whether and how much to eat, and offered exposures to a greater variety of foods and textures, including vegetables and proteins. Some studies show that BLW babies demonstrate more adventurous eating and less food fussiness while others do not.[4] In any case, doing BLW doesn't guarantee that you will end up with a child who isn't ever picky.

However, what I love most about BLW is that responsive feeding and the honoring and strengthening of a child's internal cues for hunger and fullness are built right into mealtime. This sets the stage early on for families to follow the "Division of Responsibility" between parents and children coined by Ellyn Satter, an internationally recognized dietitian, family therapist, and authority on eating. Satter describes how the feeding relationship tends to thrive in most families when caregivers decide the what, when, and where of meals, and children are allowed to decide whether and how much to eat.[5]

Spoon-Feeding with Purees
(a.k.a. Parent-Led Weaning)

Although BLW has its advantages, parent-led spoon-feeding of purees (which has been the conventional approach to introducing solids for many years) has its place. Some caregivers opt to start solids using parent-led spoon-feeding because it tends to be less messy. Studies show that spoon-feeding may also result in greater infant weight gain, which is desirable in some situations, such as when there are concerns about growth velocity or when a baby is showing a dramatic drop in growth rate and falling off their growth curve.[6]

BLW is also not the best fit for every baby. Those who may tolerate purees better than finger foods include the following:

- Some preterm babies
- Babies with specified medical conditions or developmental delays
- Babies who need oral or sensory assessments before finger foods can be considered safe

Further, for babies at high risk for food allergies whose allergists have recommended very early introduction of peanut and egg as a preventative measure starting at around 4 months of age, spoon-feeding is necessary because babies don't yet have the motor skills or coordination to self-feed.

During those first few initial feedings of top allergenic foods, spoon-feeding also makes it easier to feed your baby without allowing the allergens to routinely touch the baby's skin or face, which is important in higher-risk babies with eczema—more on this in chapter 7. (Pro tip: If your baby has eczema, applying a layer of an ointment on the skin before meals can help create a protective barrier.)

❝

Around 2½ years ago, I sent you a video of my then 6½-month-old enjoying some sauerkraut. Well, now she's a 3-year-old, who kept saying how much she loves it while eating dinner! As we start BLF now with her little sister, I'm a little nervous (mostly about the mess!) but so much better equipped thanks in large part to you.

EVE, MOM OF
LYLA AND HARPER

❞

Modified Baby-Led Weaning (a.k.a. Baby-Led Feeding)

Your approach to feeding your baby doesn't have to be strictly BLW or strictly purees. A combined approach, sometimes called modified BLW or baby-led feeding (BLF), involves offering finger foods for self-feeding as well as purees and mashes on a preloaded spoon and/or responsively spoon-fed by a caregiver. In other words, BLF enables your baby—and you!—to get the best of both worlds:

- Plenty of exposure to different flavors, foods, and textures—including purees

- Early involvement in family meals

- Easier transitioning between feeding at daycare, home, and with other caregivers who may not understand or be comfortable with BLW

- More feeding options that allow you to better tailor feeding to your unique baby and to roll with your baby's moods, needs, teething discomfort, and/or illness

- Ease of feeding while traveling

BLF also has benefits for food allergy prevention. BLF makes it easier to serve top allergenic foods while trying to avoid routine skin exposure during the first few feedings (though note that getting some food on a baby's skin and face is somewhat inevitable—a little spoon-feeding early on just makes it easier to accomplish the goal of getting more of the food *in* than *on*). Once tolerance to allergens has been established, BLF offers a way to keep consistently serving allergens that may be challenging to work into an infant-friendly finger food. In general, spoon-feeding also helps contain particularly messy foods that are beneficial for your baby, but that you might be less likely to serve if your baby is self-feeding.

Why Choose Baby-Led?

There's too much noise and binary thinking in the baby-feeding space. I find that people get so concerned about choosing and following a particular method that they forget what's really important, which is feeding responsively, or letting your baby lead.

My two cents? Take the pressure off yourself to join Team BLW or Team Purees and instead, choose baby-led.

In my experience, our babies benefit the most in both the short and long term when we let them and their needs guide the process of early feeding and focus on three main things: (1) responsive feeding, (2) prioritizing nutrient density and diet diversity in the foods offered, and (3) building top allergens into the diet early, often, and consistently to help prevent the development of food allergies.

What Is Responsive Feeding and Why Is It the Best Path Forward?

Responsive feeding is the cornerstone of a joyful, connected baby-feeding journey (and perhaps the most underappreciated concept in infant feeding). Responsive feeding happens when, instead of shoveling a bite of food into a baby's mouth when the baby is distracted or uninterested in eating, a caregiver reads the baby's cues for hunger and fullness and responds to them immediately and warmly.

> " Because I followed your advice and have never pressured or bribed her with eating, my 2½-year-old has so much trust in me. Does she tell me, "Don't like it" sometimes? Sure. But she'll take a bite of most things I put in front of her.
>
> JEN, MOM OF EMMA "

Dispelling the Myth About Combo Feeding

There is no evidence that a combined approach to starting solids that involves offering both finger foods and purees is detrimental for babies or increases choking risk, and most babies have no problem switching between pureed and finger food textures. Purees are a food texture like any other, and an important one for babies to learn because we continue to eat purees throughout life in the form of foods such as yogurt, mashed potatoes, and applesauce. Wondering how to use a "baby-led" approach while offering purees? Simply preload the spoon with puree, turn it around, and hand it to your baby to self-feed.

While responsive feeding techniques can and should be used when spoon-feeding purees, they are naturally built into BLW as well, because babies are self-feeding, and therefore responding to internal hunger and fullness cues on their own. Why is this so important? Responsive feeding strengthens a baby's own internal self-regulation system from the first few bites—something many people struggle with even into adulthood. When we ignore a baby's cues for fullness and continue to passively spoon-feed, we teach them to ignore their own satiety cues and keep eating when they are full.

Responsive feeding takes trust, which isn't always easy. During moments when you are tempted to sneak another bite into your little one's mouth to make sure they are full, keep in mind that babies are incredible at meeting their needs and self-regulating their intake when we allow them to decide how much to eat.

How Do Babies Tell Us They Are Hungry and/or Full?

Babies communicate hunger and fullness in their own unique ways. A lot of responsive feeding comes down to trusting yourself to recognize when your baby is communicating a need, and trusting that your baby will tell you when they are hungry or full.

When she was hungry, my oldest daughter would crawl over to my feet, look up at me, open her mouth as wide as she could like a little baby bird, and hold it wide open until I did something about it. An Instagram follower of mine shared a video of her 9-month-old son, who would communicate fullness by taking whatever he was eating and placing it on top of his head with a sly grin.

Common signs of hunger in babies

- Mouthing the fist
- Opening the hands and/or mouth
- Pointing or gesturing toward food
- Leaning in toward food
- Becoming more alert and active
- Reaching for spoons or bowls
- Getting excited at the sight of food
- Using words or vocal sounds to communicate readiness to eat

Common signs of fullness in babies

- Closing or pursing the lips
- Turning the face away
- Shaking the head no
- Spitting out food
- Throwing food or pushing it away
- Signaling the desire to get out of the highchair

I used to marvel at how my babies could one minute be happily shoveling pasta shells into their mouths and the next, flinging food across the room and scrambling to escape the highchair because they were full. Baby sign language is particularly helpful during mealtimes when you can teach your baby how to communicate "milk," "more," and "all done" before the meal goes south.

> "Our biggest struggle was trusting him to eat the amount his body needed, but you helped me push past that. We still get nervous even now (he's 3), but allow him to eat as much or as little of what we offer and he's doing great."
>
> GRACE, GRANDMOTHER OF CADEN

Milk: Repeatedly open and close your fist—think milking a cow.

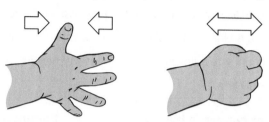

All done: Hold up your hands with your palms facing you, then turn your hands so your palms face out.

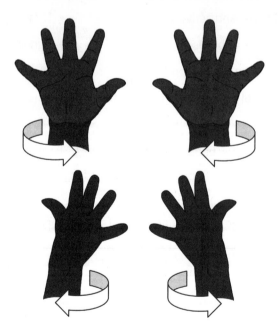

More: Bring your fingers and thumbs together on both hands, then tap your fingertips together a few times.

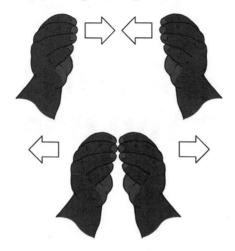

I love the way my friend and colleague, feeding therapist and pediatric speech language pathologist Melanie Potock, describes the responsive feeding relationship:

• • •

Like learning to dance, the first few steps may feel awkward and require a lot of concentration to make sure they're in the right sequence, but soon, everyone is dancing in sync and having a lovely time.[7]

• • •

No matter how you choose to feed your baby, let responsive feeding be your North Star throughout the process. Now that you are more familiar with how to approach the feeding relationship, let's talk about a few things you need to get started.

What You *Really* Need Before You Begin

When I was pregnant with my first baby and my friend offered to throw me a baby shower, I did some research on baby-care "essentials" and enjoyed adding items to my registry. But when it came time to start solids, we ended up using very few of those items I'd registered for. Looking back, here's the advice I wish I had received about what is truly essential, which feeding-related items would most likely sit unused in the cupboard, and which ones I needed in order to begin. You really only need a handful before you start (and some aren't even things you can buy).

A Conversation with Your Child's Healthcare Clinician

Before starting your baby on solid foods, talk to the pediatrician and get the go-ahead that your child is ready. Even better—have a conversation with your pediatrician about your baby's level of risk of food allergies at around the 2- or 3-month checkup. (In chapter 7, we'll cover risk factors and how babies are identified as higher risk, so you'll know what to look for.)

All babies need to start allergen introduction early, but if your baby is high-risk, your healthcare clinician may recommend even earlier introduction of foods like peanut and egg between 4 and 6 months of age, as babies at higher risk for food allergies stand to benefit the most from these early introductions. Note that these early conversations before you start solids are a great time to speak with your doctor about how the practice handles communication about potential allergic reactions. This way, if you think your baby is having a reaction, you will already know exactly how and to whom you should reach out.

If you have specific concerns after starting solids, you can always contact your pediatrician or pediatric dietitian for guidance. Happily, there are usually seven recommended doctor visits throughout a baby's first year, which provide plenty of opportunities to check in about feeding.

A Baby Who Is Ready to Start Solids

Guidelines have changed a lot over the past several decades, and people have widely different opinions on this, but experts generally agree that there are risks associated with starting solids too early (before 4 months, which include an increased risk of type 1 diabetes, celiac disease, obesity, and food allergies) or too late (after 7 months, which include an increased risk of food allergies and feeding difficulties such as texture aversions and delayed oral motor function).

At this point, most major health organizations recommend starting solids at around 6 months of age, once the baby is showing the developmental signs of readiness—not necessarily on the baby's

> "Our little guy started solids at 6 months, and we jumped right in. The most challenging part is the fear of choking, especially when bigger is better for younger babes. He's 16 months now and has the most unbelievable relationship with food—so the early exposure to new textures, tastes, spices really worked!"
>
> JORDAN, MOM OF TEDDY

Flavor Training

You may have heard about a trend in infant feeding called flavor training. This happens between 4 and 6 months, which is when research shows that a baby's palate is particularly open to the flavor of vegetables.[2] Flavor training is not about starting solids, but rather involves offering babies little licks of pureed vegetables during the sensitive window of time between 4 and 6 months as a way to increase familiarity with vegetable flavors.[3] It seems that the more babies experience new tastes during this period, the more likely they will be to accept those vegetables and flavors down the road.[4] You can do this with your baby too, however often you'd like. Simply cook whatever vegetables you'd like until tender, puree, add a bit of breast milk or formula to thin the puree, and then place a small lick of puree on your baby's lips or tongue.

✳ **Fun fact:** Flavor training happens through breastfeeding too, as flavors from Mom's diet pass into breast milk.

6-month birthday and sometimes a bit earlier (but not before 4 months—see previous page).[1] For preterm babies, it's important to consider "corrected" (or "adjusted") age, when figuring out when to start offering solid foods. Corrected age is calculated by subtracting the number of weeks the baby is born prematurely from the baby's chronological age. During the first two years of life, a baby's corrected age can give you a better sense of when to expect common developmental milestones, including signs of readiness for solids.

Signs of Readiness

Below are the developmental signs that indicate readiness for solid foods. Notice if your baby is showing all of the following signs:

- Can sit upright with minimal support
- Has good head and neck control
- Can push upright with straight elbows when lying face down
- Grasps larger objects and brings them up to the mouth, chews on hands
- Shows an interest in food

If your baby is 6 months old and you are not seeing these signs, it's fine to wait a few days and reassess; babies develop so rapidly at this stage that even a single day can make a world of difference. This will not delay your baby or cause significant long-term deficits in their eating journey.

✽ **Fun fact:** The presence of teeth is not a sign of readiness for solids. Contrary to popular belief, babies don't need teeth to start eating soft finger foods.

Short List of Key Feeding Essentials

Many brands and companies will work hard to convince you that you need a big collection of their feeding-related items in order to successfully feed your baby. You don't. When it comes to starting solids, the most important tools a baby needs are hands, and there are only a few other truly necessary items. Here is a short list of feeding essentials that help make mealtimes more successful and easier to manage.

Highchair with a Footrest

If you're going to invest in any one item, let it be your highchair. You'll use it multiple times every day, and your baby's level of comfort while eating will influence how they feel about food and feeding. The best highchairs are easy to wipe clean and fully adjustable, support upright sitting with knees and hips at 90-degree angles, and have an adjustable footrest. Don't skip the footrest, if at all possible. Having a stable place to plant the feet helps improve a baby's trunk stability, focus, and coordination during mealtimes. It can even help reduce the likelihood of mouth stuffing, food and highchair refusal, and lack of interest in food. I love the Stokke Tripp Trapp because it grows with your child all the way up through preschool. The IKEA Antilop is considerably cheaper and also a great choice, but you'll need to purchase a separate footrest, and the chair won't be usable for most babies beyond age 2.

"We went from a highchair that didn't have an adjustable footrest to one that did and wow—huge difference! Baby went from slouching (what we didn't want with her torticollis, which we've spent a lot of PT time and money improving) to sitting upright with feet planted."

ROMAN, DAD OF 10-MONTH-OLD ANNA

Spoons with Short, Wide Handles

When serving mashes and purees, you'll need some short, thick-handled spoons that are easy for your baby to grasp and that have small, flat spoon bowls that fit easily into the baby's mouth. Silicone is best, as it's a safe, easy-to-clean material that is gentle on the gums. Some spoon bowls are designed with ridges that "grab" the puree, increasing the likelihood that it will stay on the spoon even when your baby is waving it around. I love ezpz's spoons, which are designed with sensory bumps at the base of the spoon bowl to help babies quickly learn how far to put the spoon into the mouth before it causes a gag (ezpz gifted me several spoons and feeding sets that are featured in my recipe photos, so you can take a look). Have a few spoons handy during meals so that if they get dropped or your baby doesn't hand them back to you right away for preloading, you have a couple of others ready to "trade."

Suction-Bottom Bowls and Plates

Look for some strong, shallow, suction-bottomed bowls and plates that are easy to clean and help cut down on food and plate throwing. Serving food in a shallow bowl or on a plate also helps support self-feeding and makes foods easier for babies to grasp because they can brace their hands against the sides when picking up food.

Open Cups and Straw Cups

Once babies are able to sit upright independently, they can (and should) start learning how to use an open cup. Open-cup drinking is an important milestone that helps strengthen the muscles needed for speaking, chewing, and swallowing. Straw cups are helpful for babies' development as well, cut down on spills, and are great for on-the-go. Drinking from open and straw cups are skills that can take some time to master; given that the AAP recommends weaning from bottles between 12 and 18 months (ideally closer to 12), getting an early start on these skills makes it much easier to transition away from bottles when the time comes. In general, it's best to skip hard- and soft-spouted sippy cups, which may delay oral motor and speech development and can lead to tooth decay.

Mess Control: Bibs, Splat Mats, and Soft Washcloths

One of the biggest barriers to baby-led feeding (and starting solids in general) is the mess! Bibs with a front pocket help catch falling food (and/or vomit), while long-sleeved cover-all bibs help protect clothing. Alternatively, you can always strip your baby down to a diaper for meals, but be sure first that the temperature is warm enough that your baby will be comfortable without clothing. A clean splat mat under the highchair can help collect (and even allow you to repurpose) fallen food, and soft, reusable washcloths dunked in warm water help make postmeal cleanup more comfortable for your baby, which can help build positive associations with feeding.

Some parents swear by "nice-to-have" feeding tools, like lidded snack containers (helpful during toddlerhood) or toy straps to keep cups and spoons from falling (or being thrown) from the highchair tray. If you have the means and find these tools helpful, that's fantastic, but it's also fine to keep things simple and stick to the essentials only.

Speaking of essentials, the above list includes the important BLF feeding tools, but not the actual ingredients you'll need to prepare meals. If you're wondering about what to keep on hand for easy BLF meal prep, keep an eye out for lists of helpful BLF pantry, freezer, and refrigerator staples in part 4.

PART TWO

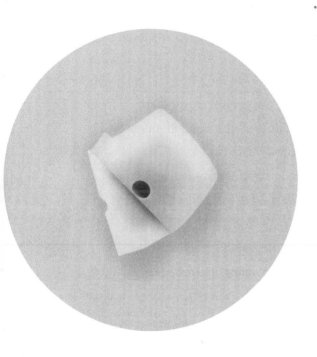

Establishing Feeding and Preventing Food Allergies

4

First Foods

You've been given the go-ahead by your pediatrician to start solids and your baby is showing all the signs of readiness for solid foods . . . so now what?

Many new parents I speak with agonize over which food to offer first, searching for that perfect combination of infant-safe, delicious, and nutritious—and fearful that if they don't find just the right food, their baby will not take to solids.

Don't get derailed. It's likely that your baby won't actually ingest much at first. Early meals are often more about exploring, squishing, smelling, smearing, and dropping foods, and many babies don't end up doing a whole lot of eating.

And, anyway, there's no such thing as a "perfect" first food.

Instead, it can help to think about a collection of nutrient-rich early food options that you can use to invite your baby into the world of solids and establish feeding before jumping into allergen introduction. Establishing feeding first is important because it helps prevent us from confusing a teething or other feeding issue with an allergic reaction (we'll cover common issues and reactions in part 3).

Above all, don't let any of this stress you out! Take comfort in the built-in insurance policy you have, which is that breast milk and/or formula will continue to be your baby's main nutrient source for now.

Size and Texture of Finger Foods for BLW

Babies can eat a surprising number of foods during infancy, but some require a few minor modifications to make them safe and easy to self-feed. The texture of finger foods should be soft and easily squishable between your thumb and forefinger so that your baby can use their gums to mash down or "chew" before swallowing.

When it comes to food sizing, match the size of the food to the type of developmental grasp your baby is using. Most 6-month-olds use a palmar grasp to palm foods up to the mouth and don't have the dexterity yet to access the portion of food inside their fists. For this reason, it's helpful to offer pieces of food that are the size of an adult finger, or even larger. Soft-cooked green beans and the top halves of asparagus spears are great examples of foods that work well for babies using a palmar grasp.

Usually at around 9 months of age (although every baby develops at their own rate), babies develop a pincer grasp, which enables them to pick up small objects with the thumb and forefinger. When the pincer grasp begins to emerge, it's time to start cutting soft foods into small pieces about the size of a chickpea or Cheerio. As the pincer grasp develops, you can offer both some stick-shaped foods and small chickpea-sized bites so that your baby gets to practice using the pincer grasp without getting too frustrated.

As you work your way through the recipes in this book, adapt the size of the foods you offer to match your baby's developmental stage and grasp, and continue to upgrade the textures you offer as your baby's feeding skills advance.

How do you know when your baby is ready to advance to a new texture? Observe carefully as your baby gains experience with chewing and swallowing. In the early stages when babies have not yet learned to chew, swallow, and/or spit out foods, serve soft, squishy foods that are easy to mash down with gums. Babies each advance at their own rate along this timeline, but usually somewhere between 6 and 12 months, they learn to chew and swallow or chew and spit out foods. As you notice this happening, you can slowly start to offer firmer foods that can be easily gummed.

What you *don't* want to do is start your baby on solids with purees and *not* advance to lumpier textures and finger foods by 9 or 10 months, as waiting too long to progress can lead to less food acceptance and more feeding problems down the road.[1] Use your intuition—if a certain food or texture makes you nervous or seems to cause more gagging and difficulty for your baby, wait a week or so, then gradually build it into the rotation again.

Key Nutrients for Babies

Learning to eat is a skill that develops over time. Because babies are still learning how to eat, have small stomachs but high nutrient needs for growth and development, and don't usually ingest much at one sitting, it's important to maximize the nutrition in every bite of food we can. Choose nutrient-rich early foods strategically to help meet your baby's needs and teach them early on to accept and enjoy foods that provide the nutrients they need for growth and development—especially foods that are rich in key nutrients for babies: iron, zinc, docosahexaenoic acid (DHA) omega-3, choline, fat, and vitamin D.

Why these nutrients in particular?

Iron

Most full-term babies start to show signs of readiness for solids at around the same time that they have exhausted the stores of iron they built up in utero and need to start getting iron from complementary foods.

Iron is an essential growth nutrient that plays an important role in the formation of hemoglobin, the part of the red blood cell that carries oxygen throughout the body. It also plays a crucial role in the development of the growing brain and immune system.

We want to be strategic about choosing iron-rich foods for babies and offering food combinations that maximize a baby's iron absorption, as many babies end up deficient in iron regardless of the method used to start them on solid foods.[2] No need to count milligrams or overthink it, though! By offering a balanced, varied diet and including an iron-rich protein food, a fruit or vegetable, and a high-energy food at meals, we can support adequate iron intake.

Here are some of the top iron-rich foods for babies (served in modified, baby-friendly forms):

- Meat
- Poultry
- Fish and shellfish
- Beans
- Lentils
- Tofu
- Green leafy vegetables
- Nuts and seeds (finely ground or pureed into a butter and thinned with liquid)

Cooking in cast-iron pots and pans is another great way to boost your family's iron intake. Iron leaches into the food you are cooking, especially if the food is acidic.

Breast milk is notoriously low in iron, so exclusively breastfed babies are at higher risk for iron deficiency than formula-fed babies. **What does this mean for you?** If your baby is breastfed, talk to your doctor about the potential need for an iron supplement starting at 4 months. And whether your baby is breastfed, formula-fed, or both, be sure to prioritize those iron-rich early foods starting at about 6 months. (See more about iron-fortified foods on page 37, "What About Infant Rice Cereal?") Given that all babies will eventually wean from formula and/or breast milk, helping them acquire a taste early on for foods that contain iron helps build healthy habits that support growth through the transition from mostly milk to mostly solids.

�֍ **Fun fact:** Vitamin C helps boost the absorption of iron from plant foods. You can help maximize your baby's absorption of iron from foods like beans, nuts, and seeds by serving them along with a fruit or vegetable high in vitamin C.

Zinc

Zinc is an essential mineral that plays an important role in overall growth as well as the development and function of your baby's immune system. A great way to support your baby's immune health is to build plenty of food sources of zinc into meals. Fortunately, many protein-rich iron foods (and some top allergenic foods!) that work well for babies also contain a good amount of zinc, including beans, meat, fish, shellfish, eggs, nuts, and poultry (you will find recipes that include all of these foods in part 4).

✖ **Fun fact:** What has more zinc per serving than any other food? Oysters! (Note: Hold off on serving raw fish or raw shellfish to infants, as babies are at higher risk for foodborne illness, and keep in mind that cooked oysters should be finely chopped before serving to a baby to help reduce choking risk. Check out my Oyster Noodle Casserole recipe on page 187.)[3]

DHA

During the first two years of life, DHA omega-3 fatty acids play a critical role in brain and eye development, as well as the development of the central nervous system. DHA is primarily found in cold-water fatty fish (such as salmon and sardines, which are great choices for babies!) as well as seaweed and algae, but other types of seafood, fortified eggs, and fortified milk are good sources as well. Note that not all US infant formulas contain DHA omega-3 fatty acids. (In Europe, infant formulas are required to include DHA.)

Choline

Choline is an underappreciated nutrient that plays a crucial role in brain development, cell membrane structure, and brain function. It aids in the synthesis of fats and helps transport DHA throughout the body (not unlike a "DHA delivery truck"). Eggs are one of the best sources of choline (and there is no limit or restriction on how many eggs a baby can have per week), but you can also find this nutrient in beans, beef, fish, and soybeans.

�֍ **Fun fact:** When it comes to eating eggs, don't skip the yolk! The egg yolk is where almost all of the nutrition (including choline) in eggs is concentrated.

Fat

Babies need plenty of fat for energy, brain development, and overall growth. Don't be afraid to be liberal with fat when cooking or preparing food for your baby—the AAP does not recommend restricting fat for babies under the age of 2 years. Include full-fat versions of dairy products like yogurt and cheese and choose fats from a variety of different sources, including olive and avocado oils, ghee, nut and seed butters, coconut milk, avocado, and ground nuts and seeds in baby-safe forms (more on this in part 4).

Note: If you can't find or don't have access to full-fat versions of dairy products like yogurt and cheese, there are still benefits to offering low-fat versions, and you can include enough fat in your baby's diet by serving other fat-rich foods listed above.

Vitamin D

Sometimes referred to as the "sunshine vitamin," vitamin D helps an infant's body absorb calcium, aids in bone mineralization, supports immune health, and aids in the prevention of many chronic diseases. There may be a relationship between vitamin D and food allergy prevention when babies receive adequate (although not excessive) amounts, but research in this area is mixed and currently inconclusive.[4] In any case, it's important to meet a baby's needs for vitamin D, and supplementation is required for all breast- and formula-fed infants under 12 months, unless they are drinking 1 liter of formula per day, as sunlight is not a reliable source given the use of sunscreen and sun-protective clothing, time spent indoors, and other variables including altitude, weather, pollution, and skin color. There aren't many natural food sources of vitamin D, but once babies start eating solids, foods like salmon, egg yolks, and fortified milk can also contribute to vitamin D needs.

What About Protein?

You may have noticed that protein is not included in this list of key nutrients for babies. While protein is a critical nutrient for growth and regulating many important body processes, babies don't need as much as we tend to think they do (only 9 to 11 grams per day during the first year of life), and babies who drink enough breast milk and/or formula typically get more than enough protein to meet their needs.

10 Ideal First Foods for Babies

Here are some great first food options to consider. Keep in mind that there is no right or wrong food to start with (although I'm partial to the first four on the list because they are iron-rich). In any case, the sooner you can build a variety of different foods into your baby's diet, the better, so don't get hung up on any one food. If your baby doesn't take to it right off the bat, try again on another day.

Self-feeding tip: If you find that your baby is struggling to pick up a piece of food, try handing it to them in the air at chest level.

1. **Steak:** Offer an adult-finger-length strip, cooked medium-well to well-done, cut *with the grain*, about 1 inch wide; your baby should be able to suck out the iron-rich juices without breaking off a smaller piece of meat from the strip. Alternatively, you can offer a piece of steak on the bone after removing any protruding smaller pieces of meat or fat. Once babies can tear off chunks of steak from a strip, it's best to cut beef into tiny, chickpea-sized bites to help reduce choking risk.

2. **Chicken or turkey:** Offer a finger-length strip of dark meat, which tends to be richer in iron and more tender than white meat. Alternatively, you can offer a chicken or turkey drumstick after removing the skin and any protruding smaller bones and pieces of gristle. Younger babies may not accomplish much more than mouthing the meat and sucking out those iron-rich juices, but both are beneficial.

3. **Lamb:** Cook ground lamb and puree using a bit of breast milk, water, or formula to thin the mixture out, and spoon-feed or serve on a preloaded spoon.

> "The first couple of times I made shrimp when my 10-month-old was eating our food, she wouldn't touch it with a 10-foot pole! I just made it again (about a month later) and she ate five pieces!
>
> RORY, MOM OF RHYS"

A finger-length, 1-inch-wide strip of cooked steak, cut with the grain

A skinless chicken drumstick with any protruding smaller bones and pieces of gristle removed

Half of a banana, with the
top half of the peel cut away

A wedge of ripe avocado with half of
the peel left on for easier gripping

A crinkle-cut stick of
cooked sweet potato

A tender-cooked broccoli floret with
stem for easier gripping

A peeled mango pit with most
of the flesh removed

4. **Beans:** Mash or puree soft, cooked beans (cannellini, great northern, and kidney beans all work well); if needed, thin out the mixture with a bit of breast milk, formula, or water, and spoon-feed, serve in a bowl for scooping with hands, or offer on a preloaded spoon.

5. **Green beans:** Serve them whole, trimmed, and tender-cooked. Add a bit of olive or avocado oil for easier swallowing.

6. **Banana:** Before peeling, wash a ripe banana, then cut in half crosswise. On one half, gently cut away about half of the peel so that the banana flesh is left exposed; this creates a natural "handle" your baby can use to hold the banana and munch away.

7. **Avocado:** Cut ripe avocado into a wedge, leaving half of the peel on for easier gripping. Or roll wedges of peeled ripe avocado in iron-fortified infant cereal, chia seeds, or ground flaxseeds for easier gripping and a nutrient boost.

8. **Sweet potato:** Peel and slice into an adult-finger-length stick; use a crinkle cutter to make sticks easier for baby to grip, then steam, bake, or air-fry until soft.

9. **Broccoli:** Trim into florets, leaving some of the stem available for your baby to use as a "handle," then steam until tender and toss with olive or avocado oil for easier swallowing.

10. **Mango pit:** Peel and cut away most of the flesh from the pit, then hand your baby the mango pit to mouth and chomp on.

The More Flavor, the Better!

A common (and unfortunate!) feeding myth is that food served to babies should be bland. This leads many parents to offer a steady stream of mainly refined, processed carbohydrate foods, which can prime a child's palate to prefer only a limited number of flavors as they grow. Studies show that offering a variety of flavors and textures during infancy may reduce the likelihood of picky eating behaviors and lead to greater acceptance of a variety of different foods and flavors later in life.[5] One study found that babies pre-exposed to carrots prenatally (in amniotic fluid) and postnatally (in breast milk) behaved differently when introduced to carrot-flavored cereal than those who were not pre-exposed; mothers also reported that pre-exposed infants seemed to enjoy the flavor of carrot-flavored infant cereal more than plain, unflavored cereal.[6] And certain flavors in a mom's diet (such as garlic, anise, carrot, and more) have consistently been found to transfer to and flavor both amniotic fluid and breast milk.[7] So you can feel confident about bringing on the flavor! Don't be afraid to build familiarity with a variety of tastes by seasoning foods for your baby with spices and herbs such as ginger, garlic, turmeric, basil, thyme, dill, cinnamon, and nutmeg.

What About Infant Rice Cereal?

Did you notice that rice cereal is not on my list of first foods? It has been the cultural norm in the US for many decades to offer rice cereal as a first food starting at around 4 months of age, the rationale being that infant rice cereal helps with weight gain and is fortified with iron and unlikely to cause an allergic reaction. Rice cereal is also accessible and affordable, and families who are economically challenged and/or feeding on a tight budget need convenient, iron-rich food options.

For high-risk babies under 6 months of age who are not ready for finger foods but need very early exposure to foods like peanut and egg, rice cereal can serve as a convenient vehicle into which an allergen can be mixed.

However, while occasional rice cereal is OK, I don't recommend it as an early food. First, it's nutrient-poor (aside from iron), bland, and uniform in texture, and we know now how important it is to offer a variety of flavors and textures early on.[8] It's also filling and can end up replacing more nutrient-dense options in a baby's diet, and contrary to popular belief, adding rice cereal to a bottle to encourage longer periods of sleep is not recommended. But perhaps the most compelling reason that rice cereal is not an ideal food for infants is that because of the way rice grows, rice and rice-based foods have been found to contain elevated levels of inorganic arsenic, a toxic metal and known carcinogen.[9] Babies are especially susceptible to the higher levels of arsenic in rice-based foods because their bodies are so small.

Other grain-based infant cereals are not necessary early foods in general, but if you want to use one (I used them from time to time with my babies), or if you are looking for an iron-rich food that is affordable, convenient, and easy to find, healthier options without the higher risk of toxic metal content are baby cereals made with whole grains like oats, amaranth, barley, quinoa, and buckwheat.

A Word on Sodium

The National Academies of Sciences, Engineering, and Medicine sets the daily sodium limit for 7- to 12-month-old infants at 370 mg per day, but there isn't much available research to back up the recommendation, or even much science about the topic at all.[10] The bottom line is that in the context of food, we don't really know how much sodium is too much for babies. What we do know is that about 70 percent of the sodium in the American diet comes from packaged, processed, and restaurant foods.[11] So, in my opinion, if you're mostly serving your baby minimally processed foods cooked at home, it's not necessary to count milligrams of sodium or stress about your baby's sodium intake. It can help reduce stress about sodium to consider your baby's sodium intake over the course of a week rather than from meal to meal. If you notice that your baby eats a particularly salty meal, just dial back on the higher-sodium foods throughout the rest of that day and week.

Here are some other easy ways to help keep your baby's sodium intake in check:

- Serve fresh, whole foods as much as possible.
- Choose low-sodium or no-added-salt versions of the processed foods and ingredients you buy—unsalted butter, low-sodium soy sauce, low-sodium jarred tomato sauce, low-sodium canned beans and legumes, etc.
- Drain and rinse canned beans before use.
- Skip salting the water when cooking pasta.

You can also choose to reserve a portion of the foods you cook for your baby before adding the salt, but it's also fine to skip that step and use just a small amount of salt or salty condiments during the cooking process.

Babies and kids (and adults!) are more likely to eat foods that taste good to them. I don't know about you, but I'd rather see a baby enjoy and benefit from the nutrients in some buttered and lightly salted steamed broccoli than refuse to eat plain steamed broccoli because it isn't yummy.

Foods to Avoid During the First Year of Life

While people are often surprised at how many foods babies can actually eat during infancy, some foods are important to avoid:

- **Honey (raw, cooked, and/or baked into recipes):** Honey can be tainted with a toxin that causes infant botulism. While the risk of infant botulism is extremely low, it is still considered dangerous for babies under 12 months. Throughout the first year of life, the risk continues to decrease as a baby's digestive system matures, so that at 1 year of age, their bodies can handle the bacteria before it would cause harm.

- **Cow's milk as a beverage:** When used as an ingredient in recipes like oatmeal or pancakes, cow's milk is fine and even recommended, but cow's milk should not be offered *as a beverage* during infancy. We don't want it to end up replacing any of the breast milk and/or formula in a baby's diet before age 1 for a variety of reasons. Unlike breast milk and infant formula, cow's milk is difficult for babies to digest in large amounts and doesn't contain enough of the key nutrients babies need. In fact, too much cow's milk in a baby's diet can inhibit iron absorption and irritate the lining of the stomach and intestines. However, for babies who tolerate cow's milk protein, offering it early and often as an ingredient in recipes (such as oatmeal, muffins, puddings, pancakes, and egg dishes) and in foods like yogurt and cheese may help reduce the risk of milk allergy.

- **Cheese and dairy products made with unpasteurized milk:** These products can contain a germ that flourishes in refrigerator-like temperatures and causes a serious bacterial infection called listeria.

- **High-mercury fish:** Avoid serving large-prey, higher-mercury fish (such as shark, king mackerel, swordfish, tilefish from the Gulf of Mexico, bigeye and albacore tuna, orange roughy, and marlin, per the CDC), as overexposure can be harmful to a baby's developing brain and nervous system.

- **Sugary and/or caffeinated beverages like soda, juice, and sweet tea:** Again, we don't want to replace any of the breast milk and/or formula in your baby's diet—especially with something that may mess with sleep!

- **Choking hazards:** The following foods increase the risk of choking during infancy. I have included tips on how to modify to make them safer, if possible. Otherwise, avoid.

  - Hard candies: Avoid.

  - Whole grapes, cherry or grape tomatoes, cherries, and other hard round fruits: Cut lengthwise into quarters.

  - Whole nuts and large seeds: Finely grind in a nut grinder or food processor.

  - Nut and seed butters in globs: Spread a thin layer on toast, stir into oatmeal, or thin out using a little breast milk, formula, or water.

- Stone fruits: Remove the pit and slice into soft, ripe wedges or small chickpea-sized bites.

- Any coin-shaped, hard and/or chewy, round foods that are shaped like a windpipe, such as hotdog or sausage rounds or raw carrot rounds: Avoid.

- Moist white breads: Lightly toast to remove moisture so that they are less likely to form a gummy ball in the mouth.

- Hard, dry crackers, tortilla chips, and potato chips: Avoid.

- Popcorn: Avoid.

- Dried fruits: Soften in hot water for at least 5 minutes, then chop into small bites.

- Raw apples, carrots, and other hard fruits and vegetables: Steam, bake, or boil until tender; to serve raw, peel, then grate or shred.

Does It Have to Be Organic?

Have you wondered whether the food you feed your baby should be organic? When my first baby came, I was determined to feed her only "clean" (whatever that means . . . which is actually nothing), organic, nutritious foods. I wanted every morsel she ate to help her grow healthy and strong because I was a new mom and wanted to do everything "right." But the cost of organic groceries added up quickly and by the time my second and third babies came, I had done more digging into pesticides and whether organically grown foods are actually more nutritious than nonorganic.

The topic continues to be debated, but current research does not suggest that organic food offers significantly more nutrition than foods produced conventionally.[12]

Does eating organic food lead to better health outcomes in people? Some observational studies show a correlation between modest health benefits and eating organic foods.[13] But how can we figure out whether those health benefits come from organic food or from the lifestyle habits that people who prioritize and can afford to eat organic food tend to adopt? Or something else?

Eating organic foods may reduce exposure to pesticide residues and antibiotic-resistant bacteria.[14] However, while high levels of exposure to pesticides have been shown to have negative effects on neurodevelopment, tolerances for pesticide residues in conventionally grown foods have legal limits that are strictly regulated by the Environmental Protection Agency and include strong provisions for protecting infants and children, and it's not clear whether the tiny differences in pesticide exposure from organic versus conventionally grown produce have an impact on human health.[15]

Many people believe strongly that organic farming is more sustainable for the environment and in many ways, it is—it doesn't cause the soil erosion, lack of biodiversity, pesticide runoff, or water pollution caused by some types of conventional farming.

However, organic farms do use pesticides (types that are naturally derived, such as biological pesticides) and sometimes in larger quantities than the synthetic pesticides used in conventional farms, since naturally derived pesticides are not always as effective against certain insects and fungi. Organic farming has also been criticized for requiring too much land to grow too few crops, which contributes significantly to higher greenhouse gas emissions.

What does this mean for you? Whether to buy organic is a personal decision, like just about everything else in nutrition. Where organic and nonorganic foods definitely differ is in price. If you prefer the taste and texture (some people do) and can afford it, organic food is an excellent choice for you and for your babies and kids. (That said, I might argue for choosing local over organic to help reduce the carbon footprint. Planting a home garden with your little ones is even better!)

If you have limited resources or prefer not to spend the extra money on organic food, please know that conventionally produced foods are an excellent choice too. You can always reduce the pesticide residue on conventionally produced foods by washing, peeling, and cooking fruits and vegetables, and trimming the skin and fat from meat, poultry, and fish. **In general, diets that include a wide variety and greater quantity of conventionally grown fruits and vegetables are healthier than diets that include a limited amount of organic produce.**

What About Added Sugars?

The AAP, American Heart Association, and the 2020–2025 Dietary Guidelines all recommend avoiding added sugars in a baby's diet throughout the first 2 years of life. Not to be confused with natural sugars found in foods like fruit and dairy products, added sugars are added to foods during processing for a variety of different reasons, like extending shelf life and improving taste.

It's smart to limit the added sugars in a baby's diet for a few different reasons, one being that babies are already familiar with sweet flavors from birth, as breast milk, formula, and even amniotic fluid are all slightly sweet. A taste preference for bitter and sour flavors is learned over time and with repeated exposures during infancy when a baby's palate is open, which is why repeatedly offering a variety of vegetables is recommended. But we don't need to teach babies to like sweet foods, nor is it helpful to condition their palates to expect and prefer everything to taste sweet by only offering sweet foods.

Added sugars are also nutrient-poor and there isn't room in a baby's diet for foods that don't contribute to their high nutrient needs, given how tiny their stomachs are and how little can fit in them.

All this being said, unlike avoiding honey before age 1, avoiding added sugars before age 2 isn't a hard-and-fast rule, and a little taste here and there is OK—especially if the added sugar–containing food delivers other beneficial nutrients, flavors, and textures.

The majority of the recipes in this book do not contain added sugars. However, as a mother of three, I've found that "No added sugar before age 2" is a great goal, but one I was able to accomplish only with my firstborn—not my second and third once we hopped on the birthday party train. As more children are added into the mix and family meals become larger, sometimes a little sugar added to certain recipes means the difference between a family meal no one eats and a family meal everyone enjoys.

What does this mean for you? You can absolutely choose to omit ingredients like brown sugar, maple syrup, BBQ sauce, or chocolate chips from the handful of recipes in this book that do contain them if you prefer, or feel free to use the suggested sugar-free alternatives. Do what works best for you and your family and know that above all, balance and variety are key.

5

How to Assemble Balanced Meals for Baby

When baby-led weaning started gaining in popularity, people were concerned that babies who self-fed would not be able to take in enough nutrients to meet their needs.

Happily, research has found that while there are some minor potential differences in estimated nutrient intake between self-feeding and spoon-fed babies, both can be nutritionally adequate if caregivers are educated about nutrient density, iron- and zinc-rich foods for babies, and how to build balanced baby meals.[1]

Balanced meals are key—and not just for babies, by the way! Rather than focusing on the amount your baby eats, offer a variety of foods from different food groups. This gives the body an array of the nutrients it needs to function, grow, and thrive while training the palate to accept a wide range of flavors.

Plus, diet diversity may offer protective effects against the development of food allergies, decreasing the odds of developing one during the first decade of life by a third.[2] A triple win! How do you ensure that your baby is eating a diverse diet? Offer at least one new food per day as often as you can.

According to the 2015 BLISS Study published in *BMC Pediatrics*, balanced meals for babies include one of each of the following:

- An iron-rich protein food (e.g., meat, poultry, beans, eggs, tofu, fish, chickpea pasta)

- An energy-dense food, preferably with healthy fats (e.g., avocado, full-fat yogurt, pancake with butter, toast with cream cheese)

- A vegetable or fruit, preferably high in vitamin C (e.g., broccoli, green beans, tomato sauce, strawberries, cantaloupe, watermelon)[3]

As best you can, build meals for your baby around the iron-rich protein food first, then add an energy-dense food and a vegetable or fruit.

Portion Sizes

How much of each food should you serve? **Given the size of their stomachs, it's reasonable to expect that babies can eat about 1 tablespoon per year of life of each food offered at each meal, but that doesn't necessarily mean they will.** Babies' appetites can vary depending on many factors that you might not even be aware of.

So start with small portions—maybe three or four pieces of finger foods. This makes mealtime less intimidating to your baby and can help reduce food waste. If your baby seems to want more and more is available, feel free to offer more and allow your baby to decide when they are done.

Balancing Breast Milk and/or Formula with Solid Foods

Balancing breast milk and/or formula with solid foods can be confusing at first! Here are some tips to keep in mind while you navigate.

When you're first getting started, try to time solid food meals for when your baby is not too tired and only slightly hungry—not so hungry that they are heading into meltdown territory. Every baby is different, but for 6- or 7-month-olds, it's reasonable to start with one or two solid food meals per day and continue with four to six bottles or nursing sessions.

As far as when to offer solid foods versus when to offer breast milk or formula, do what seems to work best for your baby. Many parents find that feeding milk after meals helps babies learn that solid foods will satisfy their hunger.

> " I struggle with worrying that my babies are eating 'enough' and trusting them to follow their appetites. And not passing along messed-up food issues my husband and I got from our parents. It's freeing to learn that when we feed responsively, babies are great at eating as much as their bodies need."
>
> ANJALI, MOM OF 11-MONTH-OLD NAVI AND NAYA "

Usually at around 8 or 10 months, the gagging reflex subsides and self-feeding skills start to really take off (more on gagging in chapter 9). At this point, you can start offering three solid food meals per day. The number of bottles or nursing sessions varies, but most formula-fed babies will still take 24 to 32 ounces per day. This is usually around the time that milk intake also begins to decrease because they are eating more food, and you may notice that your baby naturally drops a bottle or nursing session.

As babies grow, it's OK to let them go longer between their meals and milk feeds so that they build up a little more hunger in between.

By 11 or 12 months, most babies are taking three solid food meals per day and a varying number of milk feeds, often dropping to 18 to 24 ounces per day.

In general, between the ages of 6 and 12 months, the only "snack" babies need between solid food meals is breast milk and/or formula. Solid food snacks once in a while are fine, but too many can compromise breast milk and/or formula intake, which is your baby's most important nutrient source during the first year of life.

6

Top 12 Tips for BLF Mealtime Success

As your baby's feeding journey begins, here are some top tips for a smooth introduction to solids and successful meals from the start. The simple tips in this chapter will help you avoid some of the feeding pitfalls that can end up complicating mealtimes down the road.

1. Wash both your hands and your baby's hands before eating—and make sure the dog hasn't helped you with the washing! (Your baby's canine sibling will undoubtedly be hanging around the highchair with his own ideas about how the meal will go.) If it's challenging to reach those little arms under the running water at your sink, a faucet extender (a flexible faucet attachment that funnels the flow of water closer to the front of the sink) can be a game-changer and costs less than $10 for a pack of two.

2. Use a safe seating environment. The best, safest highchairs are easy to wipe clean and have a fully adjustable footrest, safety straps, and a supportive, upright back that encourages hips, knees, and ankles to bend at 90-degree angles.

> **Baby girl is 15 months old and I still plan messy dinners on bath days. I let her eat and then immediately get her into the bathtub. Saves my sanity.**
>
> SARA, MOM OF SERENA

> **My biggest struggle with starting solids is getting used to embracing the mess for this short period of time. And making sure no one has big reactions when he doesn't eat something, throws the food, or starts playing with it.**
>
> PETE, DAD OF 7-MONTH-OLD CHARLIE

3. Always supervise carefully at mealtimes and never leave your baby unattended with food—not even for a minute.

4. Eat with your baby as often as possible—the same foods if you can. It's tempting to feed babies first and then enjoy your meal later (and fine to do sometimes, especially during the earlier weeks if and when your baby's meal consists mostly of purees). But babies learn to eat by mimicking and will benefit from every family meal and opportunity they are given to eat along with a caregiver. Put away screens and other distractions so you can connect with your baby and role model the process of eating. The benefits of these precious moments are lifelong, and while these months of meals with baby can be challenging, they fly by like lightning.

5. Bring joy to mealtimes! Keep meals as positive and stress-free as you can, saving uncomfortable topics of conversation for later so that your baby learns to associate feeding with pleasure. My kids and I each love offering up one "rose and thorn" from our day during dinnertime. When they were small, the older two would make up a rose and thorn for the baby too, drawing her into their conversation.

6. Although it's not always possible, try to time meals for when your baby is not too tired, hungry, or full. For many, this means serving solids about an hour or so after milk, while some fare better when milk comes right before or after solids. The schedule that works best for your baby will emerge with time.

7. Check the texture and temperature of foods before you serve them. Finger foods should be easy to squish between your thumb and forefinger, and warmed foods should feel uniformly lukewarm rather than hot.

8. Start with small portions and follow your baby's cues. If they seem to want more of a food and more is available, offer more.

9. Offer a small amount of water in an open or straw cup at meals only. Babies get all of the hydration they need from breast milk and/or formula. However, open-cup drinking is an important skill for babies to learn because it helps strengthen oral motor development and the muscles needed for speaking, swallowing, and chewing. While it's important to limit water for 6- to 12-month-olds to 4 to 8 ounces per day to help protect their intake of breast milk and/or formula, offering a little water in an open cup during meals helps babies learn this valuable skill, eases swallowing, and can help relieve constipation associated with starting solids. Skip the sippy cups, which may delay oral motor development, as well as juice, which is not recommended for babies under the age of 1 (unless clinically indicated).

10. Embrace the mess! Many parents feel compelled to clean up during the meal and wipe a baby's hands and face throughout or catch falling puree on the face by scraping it from the cheeks and chin with the spoon—I know I did! But exploring food with hands is part of how babies learn to eat, and overcleaning or face-scraping with the spoon during meals can be so uncomfortable for some that it leads to negative associations

> 66
> My daughter hated Brussels sprouts at first. She would put a bite in her mouth and then spit it out, but I've kept offering them. Last night, I tried for the fourth time, but sliced differently, and she grabbed it out of her bowl and ate it!
>
> TAMIRA, MOM OF 11-MONTH-OLD NIA
> 99

SAFE & SIMPLE FOOD ALLERGY PREVENTION

> **"** We started solids about a week ago. He had been doing fab at self-feeding, but started feeling sick yesterday and wasn't excited for his meal after nursing like he has been. So I stopped and gave some snuggles instead. Amazing how well they know their bodies and show what they need and want!
>
> JESSIE, MOM OF
> 6-MONTH-OLD JORDAN **"**

with feeding and even highchair refusal. Instead, wait to clean your baby until the meal is done, take the activity of cleaning away from the highchair, and gently wash over at the sink, tub, or another neutral area.

11. Don't give up on a food if your baby rejects it—keep building it into your meal rotation. It can take an average of 15 exposures before a baby will accept a new food, so don't assume that if your baby didn't eat that broccoli the first time you served it, they won't learn to like it if you offer it on another day.[1]

12. Make accommodations when your baby seems to need them. Your little one may not want to eat when teething or fighting a cold or illness. During these periods, focus more on hydration and breastfeed and/or offer formula more often while you ride it out.

How to Approach BLF at Daycare

If your baby attends daycare or has another regular caregiver, it's important to open up the lines of communication about feeding as you get ready to start your baby on solids. Some daycares are familiar with a baby-led approach and happy to offer finger foods during meals, but most prefer traditional spoon-feeding for at least the first few months. Whether your daycare will be open to offering finger foods to your baby depends on the facility and its policies.

If you feel strongly that you want your child to continue with baby-led feeding at daycare or with another caregiver, starting the conversation gently and with a low-pressure approach can help. Explain how you feed your baby at home, what seems to be working best, and what your goals are for the meals your baby eats under their care. Showing a video of how your baby or another baby explores finger foods is a helpful, nonthreatening way to introduce the concept of BLF to caregivers who might be unfamiliar with it.

Caregivers may be curious, surprised, concerned, or enthusiastic. If they are open to more information, you might try offering a clear, evidence-based guide they can use to learn more about BLF. (I have a free guide to BLW at Daycare available on my website that offers printable, clear instructions on how to safely offer finger foods and reduce choking risk—understandably one of the biggest barriers to BLW at daycare.)

When you feel ready, ask about offering finger foods to your baby at daycare. Some may say yes, especially if you are the one preparing and packing foods (since they may not be familiar with safe food sizes and textures of finger foods for babies). However, if a daycare refuses and insists on spoon-feeding purees, don't sweat it. There is no evidence that a combination of two feeding models—spoon-feeding at daycare and offering finger foods at home—is confusing, detrimental, or bad for babies, as long as caregivers are using responsive feeding techniques, feeding without pressure, and responding to the baby's cues for hunger and fullness.

Different daycares have different policies about allowing common allergens like peanuts and tree nuts in their facilities. A baby's first introduction to a top allergenic food is best done at home so that you can watch for any potential reactions. So if your baby is in daycare 5 days a week, it may work best to introduce them on the weekends (more on introducing allergens in chapters 7 and 8).

If you find that your baby tolerates allergens like egg and cow's milk, daycare meals can be a great place for your baby to continue getting exposure to these common allergens in their regular diets, in foods like hard-boiled eggs and plain yogurt.

Setting Your BLF Expectations

As your baby begins eating solid foods, lean into your parental role in the responsive feeding relationship. Rather than focusing on how many bites your child eats and whether they finish the portions you offer, remember that it's not your job to get your child to eat. It's your job to offer a variety of foods in baby-safe forms, role model eating, and coach your baby to chew and swallow (which you can do by exaggeratedly role modeling the process of chewing and swallowing, narrating what you're doing in simple terms, and cheering your baby on when they mimic you). Feeding is most often successful—in both the short and long term—when we trust our babies to decide whether and how much to eat.

> My now 8½-month-old was being a lazy eater for a while at first, yawning during meals with a little gag here and there, but she's now scarfing down food as soon as it hits her tray!
>
> SOPHIE, MOM OF ELLE

What can you expect during the early days of baby-led feeding? Lots of exploring, squishing, dropping, and spitting out of food! Perhaps a few bites here and there, but usually not much actual ingesting until your baby is closer to 9 months (although all babies develop at their own rate).

You'll probably see some interesting faces in response to new flavors, which doesn't necessarily mean your baby doesn't like the food! So many times, I can remember my girls making "yuck" faces when trying a new food for the first time, and then immediately going back in for another bite.

Get ready for big changes to your baby's stool when solid foods are introduced. Some of those colorful diapers after meals that include foods like blueberries, carrots, spinach, or beets can be downright alarming. I can't even tell you how many parents see banana shreds in their baby's stool and panic that they are seeing worms! You may notice differences in the frequency, color, texture, and smell, as well as bits of undigested food in your baby's poop—all totally normal.

Some constipation is also common—signs include straining to poop, being fussier than usual, spitting up more than usual, and passing unusually hard stools. Here are some natural constipation remedies for babies:

- Offer 1 to 2 fluid ounces of water with meals.

- Offer 1 ounce of 100% apple, prune, or pear fruit juice for every month of life for babies up to 4 months of age.[2] (Juice usually isn't recommended for babies younger than 12 months, but when a baby is constipated, the sugar in juice can help by causing more water to enter the bowel, which helps loosen stool.)

- For babies older than 4 months, offer 2 to 4 ounces of diluted apple, prune, or pear juice (dilute with water in a 1:1 ratio).

- Offer the "p" foods that help manage constipation (pureed or softened and chopped prunes, pears, peas, peaches, and apricots).

While we're on the topic of baby poop, we might as well address baby gas, as most infants tend to have a good amount of it! Gas happens when babies swallow air while crying, drinking, eating, or sucking on a pacifier. Viruses and digestive issues like constipation can make it worse, as can the process of starting solids and experiencing new foods.

Gas, while irritating to some babies, is a normal part of infancy. In fact, baby gas is considered a temporary, usually minor, symptom rather than a medical condition. However, some babies can seem restless, uncomfortable, or even extremely upset until it passes. If your baby has recently started solids and you are concerned about an increase in gas that seems to be disrupting sleep or causing your baby discomfort, here are some tips that will help:

- Gently bicycling your baby's legs, massaging the belly, giving warm baths after meals, and encouraging tummy time can all help alleviate both gas pains and constipation. When my youngest baby seemed to be restless and struggling with gas, I remember walking around holding her feet and resting her little baby belly firmly on the edge of my shoulder, which seemed to help. The disproportionately loud sounds she made certainly indicated that she was getting some relief!

- Higher-fiber foods, including some vegetables, beans, whole grains, lentils, cabbage, broccoli, cauliflower, stone and citrus fruits, bran, and oats help bulk up the stool and keep things moving, but they may also cause a greater amount of gas. Gas tends to resolve with time as a baby's digestive system matures and gets used to processing different types of food. Instead of eliminating these foods, keep in mind that avoidance doesn't always help reduce gas, and your baby can still benefit from these types of nutrient- and fiber-rich foods if you offer a little less of each and increase portion sizes slowly over time.

- If you still feel concerned, keep track of the foods your baby eats that seem to cause more gas than others and discuss them with your healthcare provider (see chapter 11 for guidance on how to create an easy food/reaction tracker). In some babies, excessive gas can be a sign of food intolerance or sensitivity.

- Excessive gas that is accompanied by a fever of 100.4°F or more, vomiting, constipation, bloody stools, or extreme fussiness warrants a call to your pediatrician, as gas can occasionally indicate a more serious digestive issue needing medical attention.

The Power of Family Meals

When it comes to starting solids, one of the best parts of a baby-led approach is that it draws babies into family meals earlier and more often than conventional spoon-feeding, perhaps because everyone in the family is eating the same thing.[3]

Don't get me wrong, the frantic pace of our day-to-day lives makes it challenging to gather families regularly at mealtimes. That said, throughout my mothering journey, whenever I have found myself tempted to throw in the towel on the effort it takes to get dinner on the table and then round everyone up to eat it together, one look at the statistics on the short- and long-term benefits of family meals is all it takes to remind me why it is so wise to make frequent family meals a priority whenever possible.

You may already have noticed that for babies, family meals offer invaluable opportunities to connect with you, see what solid food is for, mimic mealtime behaviors, and learn self-feeding skills.

What you may not know is that the frequency of family meals has been shown to help improve the social and emotional well-being of parents as well.[4] This is perhaps partly because including the baby in family meals saves you time, energy, and money by having to prepare only one meal at a time, rather than buying or preparing something different for the baby and feeding them separately.

But even more compelling is that as babies grow into toddlers, children, and teenagers, the benefits of regular family meals reach further into areas that involve nutrition, as well as other aspects of holistic health that may seem unrelated. For example, a 2011 review in *Pediatrics* showed that kids and teens who share meals with their families at least three times per week are more likely to experience the following benefits:[5]

- Better relationships with parents
- Better academic performance
- Greater sense of self-esteem and resilience
- Lower risk of depression
- Greater likelihood of choosing a healthier dietary pattern and falling into an optimal weight range
- Lower likelihood (about 35 percent!) of disordered eating behaviors
- Lower likelihood of engaging in risky behaviors like alcohol, drugs, and sexual activity
- Bigger vocabulary (in preschoolers)
- Less picky eating[6]

7

Understanding Food Allergies

Now that you know more about your role and your baby's role in the feeding relationship, as well as how to prepare for your baby's introduction to solid foods and how to get solid food feeding off the ground, we're ready to dive into the food allergy prevention part—my favorite!

The ironic thing about the top nine allergens (peanut, egg, cow's milk, fish, tree nuts, wheat, soy, shellfish, and sesame) is that despite the fear around introducing them, they are all nutrient-dense, minimally processed foods that show up frequently in popular American dishes and contain many important nutrients for babies.

My best advice? Don't delay! Once your baby has had a few early foods (avocado, banana, oats, and sweet potato are my usual go-tos) and seems to be more or less enjoying the process, tolerating the texture, and taking a bite or two here and there, start introducing common allergens. Research shows that the prevention of a peanut allergy is most effective when it begins between 4 and 6 months of age and that its efficacy decreases with every passing month.[1] The earlier and faster you introduce allergens, the more at ease you'll be and the wider the range of family food choices you'll have. While there are many ways to go about allergen introduction (and no one "right" way), it's satisfying to see the sense of relief, accomplishment, and forward motion in the parents I work with who move quickly through this phase of starting solids.

First, for context, let's explore answers to some frequently asked questions about food allergies.

What Is a Food Allergy?

A food allergy happens when a person's immune system misinterprets a component of a food (most often a protein) as dangerous and responds with an adverse reaction. Typically, immunoglobulin E (IgE) antibodies trigger the release of chemicals in the body (such as histamines), which can cause hives, vomiting, swelling of the lips and throat, wheezing, and other symptoms associated with food allergies.

During a food-allergic reaction, any of the following four organ systems can be affected: the gastrointestinal tract, respiratory system, cardiovascular system, and/or skin. Neurological changes are also possible during a reaction, including inconsolability and lethargy. A true IgE-mediated food allergy is reproducible, meaning that a reaction will happen whenever the offending food is eaten. Symptoms range from mild to severe and in some cases can be life-threatening, usually taking place within a few minutes of when the food was eaten, although some reactions can take up to 2 hours to emerge and, in rare cases, longer.

Conversely, non-IgE-mediated food allergies are not typically life-threatening; they trigger other parts of the immune system, often causing delayed reactions that happen within a few hours of having eaten the food, as opposed to minutes. We'll explore non-IgE-mediated food allergies more in chapter 11.

How Do Food Allergies Develop?

Food allergies develop over time and can theoretically develop at any point in life, although most food allergies emerge during infancy or childhood. What we don't know is exactly *how* they occur.

Some researchers speculate that the skin may act as a shield against food allergens in the environment. When the skin barrier is affected by eczema, it seems that the skin's immune cells are more exposed to proteins from food in the environment and can become the route of sensitization, setting up the development of a food allergy. This "dual exposure hypothesis" theory, developed by Dr. Gideon Lack, suggests that food allergens entering the body through broken skin are more likely to make the immune system react than if the first exposures to those same food allergens happen through the mouth/digestive tract. This may explain why the early, frequent, and consistent *oral* introduction of top allergenic foods during infancy seems to be protective against food allergies (especially in babies who have moderate to severe eczema and are already at increased risk).[2]

What Are the Top Nine Food Allergens?

While over 170 foods are known to cause food allergies, any food can theoretically cause one. That being said, only eight foods are responsible for triggering over 90 percent of all food allergies.[3] Sesame recently joined the list as the ninth major food allergen in the US as a result of the Food Allergy Safety, Treatment, Education, and Research (FASTER) Act of 2021. American food labels for processed foods are required to disclose if any of these foods are intentionally included in a packaged product, although precautionary labeling (such as "may contain xyz") is voluntary and not regulated. According to the Food Allergen Labeling and Consumer Protection Act (FALCPA), these are the top nine allergens:[4]

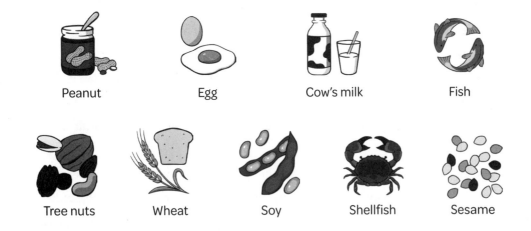

Peanut · Egg · Cow's milk · Fish

Tree nuts · Wheat · Soy · Shellfish · Sesame

Who Is at Higher Risk for Food Allergies?

As of now, there is no internationally agreed-upon set of characteristics that define infants at high risk for developing food allergies. However, in a 2020 consensus document updating their current approach to food allergy prevention, the American Academy of Allergy, Asthma, and Immunology (AAAAI); American College of Allergy, Asthma, and Immunology (ACAAI); and Canadian Society of Allergy and Clinical Immunology (CSACI) agreed on the following:

1. **Severe eczema is the strongest risk factor for food allergies.**

2. Babies with mild to moderate eczema, a family history of allergic disease in one or both parents, or a known, previously diagnosed food allergy are all considered to be at some increased risk.

   The "Guidelines for the Prevention of Peanut Allergy in the United States" from the National Institute of Allergy and Infectious Diseases (NIAID) defines high-risk babies as those with severe eczema and/or existing egg allergy.[5]

If your baby has any of the above risk factors, start talking with your pediatrician early about the potential for food allergies. But even if your baby has no eczema and no other obvious risk factors, it's important to note that food allergies often develop in babies who have no identifiable risk factors.[6] In fact, the majority of the burden of peanut allergy comes from kids with no eczema or mild eczema! **This means that early, frequent, consistent exposure to common allergens is important for all infants, regardless of their level of risk.**[7]

Ironically, while there is no evidence that the sibling of a peanut-allergic child is at increased risk of also having a peanut allergy, caregivers with one peanut-allergic older child often delay or avoid peanut introduction with younger children, which increases the younger child's risk of developing peanut allergy.

Highest risk for the development of food allergies

Babies with severe eczema

Babies with another diagnosed food allergy

Babies with mild to moderate eczema

Babies with a family history of allergic disease in one or both parents

Babies in the general population

Standard risk for the development of food allergies

Adapted from Fleischer et al., "A Consensus Approach to the Primary Prevention of Food Allergy."[8]

While the prevalence of food allergies has been steadily increasing in all children, minority populations and children from families of lower socioeconomic status have been disproportionately affected, and food allergy rates are significantly higher in nonwhite infants.[9] A recent meta-analysis showed that early and consistent introduction to peanut foods was successful in babies of both European and non-European descent, indicating that early introduction works universally.[10] But almost 21 percent of families burdened with food allergies are also food insecure, which makes the cost of food allergy–related dietary restrictions an even greater challenge, and studies show that nonwhite infants and infants from families of lower socioeconomic status are less likely to receive early, frequent, and consistent exposure to top allergenic foods.[11]

These unfortunate and unacceptable disparities highlight the importance of addressing barriers to food allergy prevention, such as making common allergens like peanut butter, eggs, tahini (sesame paste), yogurt, mixed nut butters, seafood, and tofu (made from soy) more affordable and accessible through federal assistance programs and food pantries.

Speaking of potential allergens, you might have some questions about the safety and practicality of these foods and how to offer some of them in baby-safe forms. Chapters 8 and 13 will walk you through the process of how to prepare and serve top allergens simply and safely to your baby, and provide answers to common concerns and questions you may have about allergenic foods.

Dos and Don'ts for Offering Top Allergenic Foods

When it comes to food allergy prevention, there's a lot we know and a lot we don't. In the US, the official guidelines we have on food allergy prevention are from the AAAAI in 2013 and NIAID's "Addendum Guidelines for the Prevention of Peanut Allergy" in 2017. However, the consensus report from the AAAAI, ACAAI, and CSACI released in 2020 expanded upon and updated these guidelines based on an exhaustive review of the research in food allergy prevention and best practices in infant feeding.[1] This chapter outlines some key points from both.

What to Focus On:

- Start solids when developmental signs of readiness are present at around 6 months—sometimes a bit earlier, but not before 4 months.

- Know that there is debate about whether to screen high-risk babies before allergen introduction; see chapter 10.

- Prioritize the introduction of peanut and egg at home in baby-friendly forms at around 6 months (but not before 4 months), in keeping with your family's cultural dietary practices. I'll show you how in chapter 13.

- **Once peanut and egg have been introduced and tolerated, continue offering both a few times per week going forward to help maintain tolerance.** The recipes in this book will help make this part easier on you!

- **Don't delay the introduction of other common allergens, including cow's milk, tree nuts, soy, wheat, fish, shellfish, and sesame, and once you've introduced them, keep offering them regularly.** There is no evidence that introducing them is harmful and good evidence that **diet diversity is protective against food allergies.** Plus, these are nutritious foods that provide great nutrition for babies.

- If your baby is introduced to and tolerates a cow's milk–based formula at any point during infancy, keep offering it—regular ingestion of it (as little as 10 mL, or about 2 teaspoons, daily) has been shown to help prevent loss of tolerance.[2]

- Work toward feeding your baby a diverse diet as quickly as possible—that is, introduce and include as many different foods and food groups to your baby as you can. This may help promote food allergy prevention and provides a range of other nutrition-related benefits as well.[3]

What to Ignore

The broad guidelines I just outlined are basically all you have to keep in mind. Other than this, there's a lot of bogus advice floating around out there that you can safely ignore.

Don't overthink it. You don't need to take special precautions if you have a low-risk baby.

The most important things for caregivers of low-risk babies to focus on are (1) introducing top allergens into your baby's diet early and often in age-appropriate forms that fit in with your family's culture and culinary preferences; and (2) helping your baby eat and learn to accept a wide variety of different foods, flavors, and textures. Part 4 of this book will make this easier for you. In other words, feel free to feed!

You don't need to introduce allergenic foods in any particular order.

While we prioritize introducing peanut and egg early and often because these are the most well-researched allergens for food allergy prevention, there is no evidence that new foods must be introduced in a specific order. What's more important is offering a commonsense progression of food introductions that meet your baby's nutrient needs in forms they can manage and that work within your family's cultural dietary preferences.

You don't need to introduce new foods singly or pause for a certain number of days between common allergen food introductions.

Pediatricians used to recommend single food introductions for all foods (not just major allergens) and waiting 3 days before introducing another. There is no evidence behind this recommendation, and it is now considered outdated advice, causing unnecessary stress on caregivers and hampering our ability to feed babies a variety of different foods early on, which offers a potential protective effect against food allergy development.[4] Feel free to ignore it, unless your doctor has recommended otherwise for a specific reason.

That said, pausing for 3 days between single food introductions of the top nine allergenic foods is a conservative approach to allergen introduction that, in the event of a reaction, may make it easier to determine which food is responsible. However, it's not necessary or recommended to wait 3 days before introducing a new top allergen. It's simply an option. Take it or leave it!

Don't overstress about getting a certain amount of each allergen into your baby.

We learned from the LEAP study that 2 teaspoons of peanut butter or peanut powder fed three times per week is protective against peanut allergy in high-risk babies, from the Enquiring About Tolerance (EAT) study that 2 teaspoons of peanut foods per week is protective in the low-risk population, and from the Consensus Guidelines that about one-third of a cooked egg fed two or three times per week is beneficial for the prevention of egg allergies, so it's wise to **aim for about 2 teaspoons of peanut foods and 2 teaspoons (or one-third of an egg) at least twice per week, as best you can.**[5] Lower amounts of these foods might also be protective, but we don't know yet what that lower limit is. We know less about other allergens, although as I mentioned previously, research suggests that once cow's milk–based formula has been introduced and tolerated, regular exposure to cow's milk protein (at least 10 mL per day) helps maintain tolerance to cow's milk.[6] In any case, it seems that **regular exposure to an allergenic food may be more impactful on preventing allergy development than consuming a specific amount of the food.** This is comforting when you consider how much infant appetites can fluctuate and how often babies refuse certain foods! In the recipes in this book, I specify how many grams of each allergen are found in each serving of the dish in case you are curious—but it's often impossible to know just how much food made it into baby's tummy and how much is in their hair, on the floor, or in the family dog's tummy. So, instead of feeling pressure to get a certain number of grams into your child, focus instead on offering a reasonable amount of each allergen a couple of times a week in foods your baby seems to enjoy, and leave it at that.

> " It made this mama's heart so much lighter to hear that breastfeeding may not prevent food allergies. I couldn't breastfeed for a bunch of different reasons and was really beating myself up about the food allergy prevention part until I saw your post.
>
> DARLA, MOM OF 2-YEAR-OLD JACOB "

Don't rely on breast milk for food allergy prevention.

Breast milk is the gold standard of nourishment for babies up to 6 months old, provides a wide range of health benefits for both baby and mom, and is recommended up to age 2 years and beyond if it's working for both the baby and the family. However, there is currently no conclusive evidence that breastfeeding prevents food allergies specifically.[7] There are a million different reasons why breast milk may not be an option (all of which are valid, in my opinion). So, if you feed your baby formula and have been carrying guilt over a perceived food allergy prevention benefit of breast milk that your baby isn't getting, I hope it will be a relief to read this!

Don't use a hydrolyzed or specific formula as a way to help prevent the development of food allergies.

Hydrolyzed infant formulas have also not been shown to protect against food allergy development or food sensitization, so there is no need to use one from a food allergy prevention perspective unless, of course, your baby needs it for another clinical reason.[8]

Don't stress about excluding or including certain foods and/or supplements during pregnancy or breastfeeding as a way to prevent food allergies and food sensitization.

There is currently no conclusive evidence that including or excluding certain foods during pregnancy or breastfeeding prevents or contributes to the development of food allergies. Some babies with diagnosed food allergies may react to food proteins in breast

Why Not Just Use a Commercial Multiple-Allergen Product?

There are several commercial products currently available that aim to make early and frequent introduction of top allergens easier on caregivers. Some include multiple allergens in a puff, cracker, or bar that can be fed directly, or a powder that can be mixed into a puree or liquid. Products range in price; those containing multiple allergens can cost as much as $67 for a 1-month supply.

If cost is not a deterrent, you may appreciate the convenience of one of these products. But if we rely entirely (or even mostly) on a powder or commercial product for allergen introduction, it's easy to overmedicalize the process of starting solids.

For now, none of these products have been endorsed by any of the major allergy organizations, and while the results of one blind randomized controlled trial suggest that multiple-allergen products are safe and well tolerated, there are currently no peer-reviewed studies showing that they are effective.[9] Some products contain smaller amounts of allergenic proteins than doses used in research. This is highlighted in a study showing that nine children who were dosed with early allergen introduction products experienced allergic reactions after eating larger portions of the same common allergens to which they had theoretically already been exposed multiple times.[10]

My two cents? Stick with mostly real foods for both food allergy prevention and nourishment purposes, and if you like offering your baby puffs, look for the ones from Mission MightyMe, which offer the same baby-friendly meltable texture as regular puffs, but with a research-backed, recommended number of grams of peanuts and tree nuts in each serving, making it easier to keep these allergens in your baby's diet consistently.

Fun fact: I am a Mission MightyMe brand partner, and part of what draws me to the company is the fact that their puffs were developed by a team that includes Dr. Gideon Lack, the allergist behind the groundbreaking LEAP study.

milk from the mother's diet, but that is a separate topic. In a 2018 systemic review and meta-analysis in *PLoS Med*, researchers found that probiotics taken during pregnancy and breastfeeding may reduce the risk of eczema and sensitization to cow's milk.[11] (If a person is "sensitized" to a food, it basically means that their body is primed—although not guaranteed—to develop an allergy to it). Similarly, the World Allergy Organization recommends probiotics for pregnant and breastfeeding mothers at high risk for allergy in their children due to the potential net benefit related to eczema prevention, but eczema prevention doesn't necessarily guarantee food allergy prevention, as about a quarter of children diagnosed with food allergies never had eczema. Also, omega-3 fatty acids taken during pregnancy and lactation may reduce the risk of sensitization to egg, but remember that sensitization does not necessarily mean that a baby is and/or will become allergic.[12]

Should You Introduce Animal-Based Top Allergens If You Are Vegan or Vegetarian?

There is no clear-cut, easy answer to how families should approach the introduction and inclusion of animal-based top allergenic foods in their children's diets—especially when the choice to be vegan or vegetarian is rooted in strong ethical or moral feelings about living a plant-based lifestyle. The best we can do as caregivers is examine and understand the available options and make a fully informed decision about how to proceed. Here are some things to consider:

- About half of the top allergenic foods in the US (egg, cow's milk, fish, and shellfish) are animal-based.

- A growing body of research suggests that introducing egg early and frequently during infancy is protective against egg allergies; we have less conclusive evidence about early introduction of cow's milk and fish and even less about shellfish, but good reason to think future studies might suggest that offering these foods early and often is protective too.

- Particularly for babies who are at high risk for food allergies, there may be a meaningful safety benefit to introducing top allergens early and often during infancy.

- Observational data suggest that delaying the introduction of common allergens increases the risk for food allergies.[13]

- As caregivers, our children's diets are within our control for only a handful of years; as they grow, make friends, go to birthday parties and sleepovers, and explore the world on their own, the risk of accidental and/or purposeful exposure to different foods grows as well.

- Not knowing their allergy status could become a significant source of stress.

- Learning about a food allergy later in childhood without the guidance of an allergist and an individualized allergy action plan in place could be dangerous.

There are different ways to arrive at the best approach for you and your family. For example, I follow a mostly plant-based diet but made an informed decision to introduce all of my girls to all foods early on—mostly to encourage adventurous, flexible eating habits and give them a chance to experience a wide variety of foods and flavors while benefiting from the range of nutrients in all the food groups.

A pediatrician colleague of mine, Miles, is a lifelong vegetarian who introduced eggs and milk to his three children during infancy but decided not to introduce fish and shellfish. His rationale was that his children were at lower risk for food allergies, he and his wife have never consumed or prepared fish or shellfish for themselves and find both pretty easy to avoid, and he doesn't feel comfortable cooking or ordering seafood from an ethical standpoint. However, he makes a compelling point you might want to think about, too, regarding accidental exposures down the line: "Even if my wife and I were vegan, we still would have fed our babies eggs and milk because we would have been worried about the kids eventually being exposed accidentally or purposefully to these foods at a friend's house, birthday party, or other social event down the road."

There are no right or wrong answers here! Only what is best for you, your family, and your baby.

How to Offer a Top Allergenic Food for the First Time

> **Introducing top allergens has been the hardest for me! I like doing BLW and don't freak out very much. But the top allergens are scary even though no one in my or my husband's family has allergies.**
>
> RORY, MOM OF 7-MONTH-OLD JACKSON

Let's set the scene. Your baby is showing developmental signs of readiness, you've gotten the green light from your pediatrician to start your baby on solids, and you've offered a few non-top-allergenic foods— maybe some banana, sweet potato, and avocado if you're offering finger foods. Perhaps some applesauce, oatmeal, and pureed butternut squash if your baby is doing better with purees. It seems to be going well. Now what? It's time to start offering the top allergenic foods.

If your baby is high-risk and/or you are nervous about allergen introductions and prefer to take a more conservative approach, the following steps outline a simple way to introduce common allergens for the first time that makes it easier to identify the responsible food, should your baby have a reaction. And remember that if your baby is low-risk, it's totally fine to be much more casual about the process!

Here's a simple, step-by-step guide on how to introduce each new top allergen:

1. Take a moment to check in with your baby. It's best to start with a healthy, happy baby so that we don't confuse a potential virus or teething issue with an allergic reaction.

2. If it works in your schedule, pick a weekday morning, a couple of hours before your baby's next nap, when you can be fully attentive for at least 2 hours. This is because most allergic reactions occur within a few minutes to 2 hours of when the food was eaten, so we want to be able to monitor while your baby is awake. (Doing this on a weekday morning makes the pediatrician easier to reach should their guidance be needed, but if work, daycare, or other scheduling issues make that impossible, weekends are fine too. Just be sure to introduce the allergen a couple of hours before your baby usually goes to sleep.)

3. While not necessary, consider offering the top allergenic food alone or as a part of a meal that includes foods the baby has had and tolerated before so that if there is a reaction, it's easier to determine which food is responsible.

4. Start by offering a tiny bite on the tip of a spoon, then wait 10 minutes and observe. If there is no reaction, offer the rest and allow your baby to finish the portion, but don't worry if they don't. There is no need to pressure or force your baby to eat the allergen—or any food, for that matter!

5. Feel free to introduce a new top allergenic food each day or every other day. As mentioned previously, waiting 3 days before introducing the next top allergen used to be recommended but is now considered unnecessary, even in high-risk babies.[14]

6. Don't forget that introducing major allergens is only one piece of the food allergy prevention puzzle: frequency is important, too. Once a new top allergenic food has been introduced and tolerated, it should stay in your baby's diet regularly (a couple of times a week).

Allergen FAQs

The 9-Day Allergen Introduction Plan in chapter 13 concisely lays out how to safely serve each allergen for the first time, but if you are curious, here are answers to several of the most common questions and concerns about allergens that come up again and again in my practice. Let's take a closer look at how to safely approach these foods during allergen introduction and beyond.

In What Forms Can I Offer Peanuts to My Baby?

As you might guess, whole peanuts and globs of peanut butter are choking hazards for babies and must be modified (finely ground or processed into a nut butter and thinned with liquid) before serving. You'll want to use smooth peanut butter or peanut powder as opposed to crunchy peanut butter. My favorite peanut butters for babies contain only one ingredient—peanuts—but any smooth peanut butter will work. Aim for 2 teaspoons of peanut butter or peanut powder two or three times per week for the purposes of peanut allergy prevention.

Another easy way to consistently keep peanuts in a baby's diet is to offer Proactive Peanut Butter Puffs from Mission MightyMe, cofounded by Dr. Gideon Lack of the LEAP study. One small bag of these baby-friendly puffs per week delivers 6 grams of peanut protein in a meltable texture.

If a Baby Is Allergic to One Tree Nut, Will They React to All Tree Nuts?

Tree nuts are recommended early foods for babies because they offer lots of important nutrients, including plant-based protein, iron, magnesium, and zinc. According to Food Allergy Research and Education (FARE), cashews, pistachios, walnuts, hazelnuts, pecans, and almonds are the most allergenic of all tree nuts. Having an allergy to one tree nut does not necessarily mean that a person will also react to other tree nuts. However, certain tree nuts have proteins that are closely related to another specific tree nut, like cashew with pistachio, or pecan with walnut, and an allergy to one means an allergy to the other is more likely.

As with peanuts, don't forget that tree nuts must be modified (finely ground or processed into a nut butter and thinned with liquid) to reduce choking risk.

Tree nuts are a particularly tricky top allergen because there are so many of them. The early and frequent introduction of tree nuts has not yet been studied enough for us to make concrete recommendations on how much and how often tree nuts should be served. Until more research is available, it's reasonable to assume that, like peanut and egg, 2 grams (about 2 teaspoons) of allergenic protein per week from each introduced nut is protective. As a result, recommendations on tree nut portion sizes for babies are based on amounts that fit into a healthy eating pattern for babies, leaving room for a variety of different foods from all the food groups while aiming for roughly 2 grams of each introduced nut protein per week.

Introduce specific tree nuts that you eat as a family and that your child is more likely to encounter as they grow. Once introduced, aim to keep those nuts in the diet consistently, serving your baby about 2 teaspoons of each nut per week. Or you can offer about 1 tablespoon per week of a mixture of tree nuts.

In case you are curious, coconut is not a tree nut. It is technically classified as a fruit and not included among the top nine allergens. While coconut allergies can happen, they are rare, and even most people with tree nut allergies can safely enjoy coconut foods.

As a reminder, if your baby is at high risk for food allergies, talk to your pediatrician about how and when to introduce tree nuts. If low or moderate risk, there's no perfect way to introduce, and people take different approaches.

A conservative approach (helpful particularly in higher-risk babies) is to offer each type of nut on its own or along with foods that have been tolerated before, which makes it easier to determine which nut is responsible if there is a reaction. A less conservative approach, which is more appropriate for lower-risk babies, is to offer a group of tree nuts together all at once, using either a mix of ground nuts or mixed nut butter. Do what works best for you.

What does this look like in daily life? Nut butters are particularly convenient because they can be added to pancake or muffin batter, drizzled over cooked veggies, swirled into yogurt, thinly spread on toast, or thinned with water or milk and served on a spoon or as a dip. You can use commercially made mixed nut butters (Costco's Kirkland brand and Target's Good & Gather brand offer smooth mixed nut and seed butters with no added sugar and minimal sodium) or make your own by processing about 1 cup mixed nuts with ¼ cup neutral oil (such as avocado or canola oil) in a high-speed blender until smooth. Be sure to refrigerate nut butters to prevent spoilage.

Another of my favorite ways to keep tree nuts consistently in the diet is to make a soup or stew, transfer about 1 cup of the broth to a blender, and blend with about ½ cup nuts until smooth, then stir the puree back into the soup. Raw cashews work especially well for this and produce a very creamy, rich broth.

Another convenient, affordable approach to making sure all these nuts stay in rotation is to finely grind 1 cup mixed nuts into a powder, store it in the freezer, and serve about a teaspoon or so three times per week sprinkled into fruit puree, as a nutrient-rich coating for slippery fruits, mixed into yogurt, or added on top of cooked vegetables or pasta. The Proactive Nut Butter Puffs from Mission MightyMe are another option; these include a combination of the most important nut allergens in a baby-safe texture that makes it easy to offer 2 grams of each nut protein per week without overthinking things.

What's the Best Way to Serve Eggs to My Baby?

Be sure to fully cook eggs before serving to your baby (no runny yolks, as raw or undercooked eggs carry a higher risk of foodborne illness and may be more likely to cause a reaction than eggs that are fully cooked). Scrambled and hard-boiled eggs tend to work well.

Be sure to serve both the egg white and yolk and aim for your baby to eat about one-third of a cooked egg two or three times per week for the purposes of egg allergy prevention.

Can I Give My Baby Yogurt?

When it comes time to introduce cow's milk protein to babies during infancy, yogurt is an easy and popular first exposure. Once introduced and tolerated, yogurt becomes a great way to introduce other new foods because it mixes well with different flavors and textures.

When you're buying yogurt, check the labels and look for brands that are fortified with vitamin D and carry the "Live Active Cultures" seal, which indicates the presence of gut-friendly probiotics. Buy plain yogurt, preferably full-fat. See chapter 4 for information on why cow's milk is not recommended as a beverage for babies under 12 months; the same is true for plant-based milk alternatives.

What Are the Best Cheeses for Babies?

Pasteurized cheeses that are lower in sodium are another great option. Babies using a pincer grasp can get lots of practice using their fine motor skills when you offer shredded cheeses on the tray or on a plate. When shopping, look for full-fat, lower-sodium, pasteurized cheeses that are soft in texture, aiming for 50 to 100 mg sodium per serving since some cheeses (I'm looking at you, feta, halloumi, asiago, pecorino, and cotija!) can be excessively high in sodium.

Softer cheeses that have ideal textures for babies (like full-fat ricotta, fresh mozzarella, quark, paneer, cream cheese, créme fraîche, labneh, and low-sodium

Butyrate Who?

Stay with me here, I'm about to get sciencey on you, but for a good reason! When we eat certain dietary fibers (called "prebiotics") found in foods like legumes, whole grains, nuts, and fruits, short-chain fatty acids (SCFAs) are produced in the colon when the fibers are fermented by our intestinal microbes (or "friendly bacteria" in the gut). Butyrate is one of the SCFAs that show up in our colon as a result of the fermentation process of prebiotic fibers, but we can also increase the butyrate in our diets by eating foods that contain it, such as cheese, butter, and especially ghee (or clarified butter). High levels of butyrate at one year of age are associated with a reduced risk of allergic disease, and in one recent study, kids with the highest butyrate levels were less likely to be diagnosed with a food allergy.[15] More research is needed on butyrate for the prevention of food allergy, but it's hopeful to think that the fiber-rich foods and food sources of butyrate we offer to babies may have a positive impact on food allergy outcomes.

�֍ **Fun fact:** This is partly why I include ghee in many of my recipes! Ghee can be used interchangeably with butter in a 1:1 ratio, but it has more butyrate than butter. I also love that it has a higher smoke point than butter because the milk solids are strained out. With ghee, you get the versatility of coconut or avocado oil with a yummy flavor similar to that of browned butter.

The price of prepared ghee at many grocery stores can be prohibitive. However, it's very simple to make your own! Start with 1 pound unsalted butter (European-style is best because it contains less moisture and therefore yields more ghee, but any type of butter will work). In a medium saucepan, melt the butter over medium-high heat. Turn the heat down to low and gently simmer *without stirring*; you will see foam appear then start to clear (this is the process of the milk solids forming and then falling to the bottom of the pan). Continue allowing the ghee to simmer until you see a fine foam with tiny bubbles appear on the surface. The entire simmering process should take about 25 minutes total. Turn off the heat and allow the ghee to cool for about 5 minutes so more milk solids can fall to the bottom of the pan. Strain into a pint-size jar using a fine-mesh strainer lined with a coffee filter, piece of cheesecloth, or even a paper towel, then discard the milk solids in the strainer. Cover the jar tightly and store your ghee in the refrigerator for up to 6 months.

cottage cheese) tend to be lower in sodium than hard cheeses, although Swiss cheese is generally low in sodium too and works well as a finger food when sliced into paper-thin strips. Limit the higher-sodium cheeses mentioned above (a little here and there is fine as long as it's pasteurized) and avoid all unpasteurized, mold-ripened cheeses as well as any cheeses made with raw milk (including Gorgonzola, Brie, Camembert, Roquefort, queso fresco, queso blanco, and goat cheese).

What Are the Best Breads for Babies?

You're not alone if you get overwhelmed in the bread aisle at the grocery store. It's hard enough selecting a bread for yourself, let alone one for your baby, but toasted bread strips are a great early finger food and an ideal vehicle for all sorts of nutritious spreads. Here are some tips to help make it easier for you to choose a baby-friendly bread, since there are so many available options:

- First, there is no perfect bread, so don't let the search for one stress you out—just try to find the best option you can.

- Look for lower-sodium breads (aim for no more than 100 to 150 mg sodium per slice) without added sugars, but don't sweat it if you can't find one. If you have to choose between bread that contains honey or bread with excess sodium, choose the one *without* the honey. Remember, babies shouldn't have honey during their first year of life (see page 40).

Toast Toppings!

Here are some ideas for toast toppings:

- Mashed avocado + hemp hearts
- Cream cheese + mashed berries
- Ricotta cheese + mashed mandarin oranges
- Thin layer of peanut, almond, cashew, or another nut butter + mashed berries or banana
- Thin layer of tahini + chopped herbs
- Bean dip + sliced tomato
- Tomato sauce + melted cheese
- Hummus + chia seeds
- Mascarpone cheese + banana slices

- Avoid breads containing large pieces of nuts, seeds, or dried fruits, which increase choking risk. Whole oats, chia seeds, hemp hearts, and/or millet in bread are fine because they are so small.

- Sprouted whole-grain breads are usually more digestible since the sprouting of the grain releases enzymes that help break down the grains; they also tend to be lower in sodium.

- Try to avoid white bread, which tends to form a gummy ball in the mouth and can increase choking risk.

- To avoid bread that falls apart easily into a squishy mess in baby's hands, lightly toast whole-grain bread or offer baby the heel of a loaf of whole-grain peasant bread, which will hold its shape and allow baby to gnaw on and suck off small pieces.

Once wheat has been introduced and tolerated, you can offer strips of lightly toasted bread topped with nutritious spreads. This adds a nutrient boost and makes the bread easier for babies to swallow and manage in the mouth.

What Are the Best Types of Fish for Babies?

Fish offers many important nutrients for babies and kids alike, including iron, zinc, protein, choline, vitamins B_{12} and D, and brain-building omega-3 fatty acids. Introducing fish to babies on the earlier side (between 6 and 8 months) may be more impactful for food allergy prevention than waiting to introduce it after 9 months.[16] Once seafood has been introduced and tolerated, aim to offer a 1-ounce serving two to three times per week going forward. Choose small-prey fish that are highest in omega-3 fatty acids and lowest in mercury. Great choices for babies include the following:

- Sardines
- Salmon (particularly wild-caught Alaskan salmon)
- Flounder

- Steelhead trout

- Haddock

Before serving to babies, cook fish thoroughly and be sure to remove any bones. When shopping for canned fish, look for BPA-free packaging and choose brands labeled "low salt" or "no salt added."

Some types of fish contain higher levels of mercury than is ideal for small bodies, and too much mercury in the diet can have negative effects on a child's developing nervous system. As mentioned previously, avoid larger-prey fish like king mackerel, swordfish, tilefish, and shark, and limit tuna to no more than twice per week (if at all). If you're choosing canned tuna for babies, I recommend canned light tuna, rather than albacore or bigeye, which are higher in mercury.

Our Family Doesn't Eat Shellfish.
Does My Baby Have to Have It?

Whether early introduction of shellfish specifically reduces the risk of shellfish allergy is not yet well researched; if shellfish is not already a part of your family's diet, it's OK to ignore it. But, if shellfish *is* something you eat and enjoy as a family, it's a good idea to introduce it to your baby early on. Shellfish allergies that emerge in childhood tend to be lifelong, and many shellfish allergies develop in adulthood.

When offering shellfish to a baby, keep in mind that the texture generally tends to be rubbery, which increases choking risk, so it does need to be modified before serving. Also, most types of shellfish are naturally high in sodium, so on a day when you serve shellfish to your baby, try to keep sodium levels low in whatever else you serve throughout the rest of the day.

What types of shellfish are best? Whatever you like, as long as it's fully cooked! Shrimp, crab, and lobster work well for babies when cooked and shredded or finely chopped. Once shellfish has been introduced and tolerated via spoon, keep it in the diet by adding it to fritters, sauces, patties, or something similar to a crab cake. Less commonly eaten forms of shellfish are clams, scallops, mussels, oysters, squid, and octopus; of these choices, squid and octopus are the lowest in sodium and work well for babies when finely chopped and added to fritters or fish cakes.

Is Soy Safe for Babies?

In general, soy is a fantastic source of plant-based protein, fiber, and many essential micronutrients, including iron, zinc, and calcium. It's also a great source of antioxidants. However, myths and misinformation about soy continue to circulate, including fears that soy-based infant formula may negatively affect brain, sexual, thyroid, or immune development in babies, and that soy isoflavones may reduce the production of the male hormone testosterone and/or raise the risk of breast or endometrial cancer in women.

These concerns are not supported by sound science.[17] Studies actually show that soy-rich diets may be protective throughout the life cycle against certain types of cancers, improve heart health, support fertility, and lower blood pressure, blood sugar, and cholesterol levels.[18]

So, how to offer soy to a baby? Firm or extra-firm tofu works nicely as a finger food for babies, and its versatile, mild taste blends well with a variety of different flavor profiles. You can offer sticks of raw or cooked tofu, sticks of cooked tempeh, or grated cooked tempeh; cook the tempeh in a generous amount of fat for easier swallowing.

You can also offer plain, unsweetened soy yogurt or use plain, unsweetened soy milk to make oatmeal, chia seed pudding, muffins, or pancakes. Like cow's milk, soy milk should not be served as a beverage to babies before age 1.

Mashed edamame (with the skins removed for easier swallowing—they slip off easily when boiled or steamed) is another great option that babies can scoop with their hands for self-feeding, or eat from a preloaded spoon.

What's the Best Way to Serve My Baby Sesame?

Sesame seeds are bursting with important minerals for babies, including iron, zinc, and calcium, as well as healthy fats, protein, and fiber, but the nutrients in sesame seeds aren't as easily absorbed by the body when the seeds are consumed in their whole form.

Serving sesame to babies in the form of tahini (sesame paste) makes the nutrients more bioavailable, but like other nut and seed butters, tahini served in globs is a choking hazard and it must be spread thinly or thinned with liquid before serving to an infant.

Once sesame is introduced and tolerated, keep it in your baby's diet consistently by spreading tahini in a thin layer on teething crackers or toast strips, stirring it into familiar fruit purees, using it as an ingredient in hummus, or drizzling it over cooked vegetables.

• • •

I hope all of this talk of delicious, nutritious food is getting your creativity and excitement flowing. Soon your littlest eater will be able to share some of your favorite dishes right along with you! But first, let's get on the same page in part 3 about how to keep your baby safe during the process of learning how to eat.

PART THREE

Staying Safe

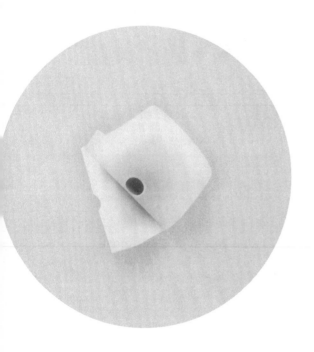

9

Gagging, Choking, and Food Safety

WHAT EVERY CAREGIVER NEEDS TO KNOW

When it comes to starting solids, the biggest source of stress among caregivers I see in my work is fear of choking. If you feel this way too, you're not alone. After feeding your baby an entirely liquid diet for months, offering solid foods is an enormous shift that can feel scary.

The best way to lower the risk of choking and reduce your own stress is to learn about these topics:

- The differences between gagging and choking

- What to do in the event of each

- Which foods, food shapes, and textures increase choking risk (see chapter 4)

- How to prepare the safest food sizes and textures for babies (see chapter 4)

Learning to eat is a brand-new experience for babies that involves chewing, swallowing, and breathing all at the same time. It takes time to master. Gagging is a normal, noisy part of learning to eat. However, I'm with you if you think it can sound and look alarming. My own usually relaxed mother used to panic every time one of my baby girls would start to gag during a meal. I'll never forget one dinner time when my oldest was crawling around the kitchen after a meal and gagged on a teething toy she had found under the table. Bless her heart, my mom dove under in a flash and scared the heck out of the baby, who was *not* choking. It took some time afterward to console them both! But it can take experience and education to understand that gagging is actually nothing more than a built-in safety mechanism and a way to bring food forward that the baby isn't ready to swallow. In other words, it's a good thing!

> " I've been loving this journey of exploring new foods with Zach, even though it raises my blood pressure at times. Learning the difference between gagging and choking has been critical for us.
>
> TAMAR, MOM OF 9-MONTH-OLD ZACHARY "

Gagging can sound like gurgling, sputtering, or coughing, and babies will often open their mouths and thrust their tongues forward during the process. Sometimes it even results in vomit, which is another defense against choking and usually not a concern.

When babies are around 6 months old, the gag reflex is strong and very far forward in the mouth, toward the front of the tongue. Over time and with practice eating and mouthing objects, it shifts farther back into the mouth, and by around 10 months (and especially if a baby has had plenty of practice eating), the gagging usually subsides.

A common misconception is that gagging during infancy is bad, and that if babies gag on a food, it means they are not yet ready for that type of texture. On the contrary, it actually helps to take advantage of that gag reflex earlier on, during the time between 6 and 10 months of age when the reflex is strong and more protective of a baby's airway. This way, babies can build sensory knowledge of the insides of their mouths, learn how to manage different textures, and take appropriately sized bites before the gag reflex shifts farther back into the mouth and becomes less protective.

The best thing you can do to help your baby during a moment of gagging is to stay calm and positive and not intervene. You can coach your baby, encourage the baby to chew, mimic the action of chewing, and offer a little water in an open cup to wash things down afterward. But do your best to let your baby work it out without panicking. This is because babies are like sponges—they absorb our emotions. When we react with alarm, this can cause us to take a sharp intake of breath. When babies see us do that and panic in the same way, it can suck food toward the throat and turn a gagging event into a choking event.

Do not reach into your baby's mouth to try to remove the food during gagging—this can actually end up pushing food into the airway.

If after your baby has had a month or two of practice with solid foods and gagging still seems excessive or seems to be causing your baby stress, vomiting, or tantrums at most meals, talk to your pediatrician and see if a referral for a feeding therapist is indicated.

Choking Is Very Different from Gagging

Choking is a mostly silent, serious event that happens when a piece of food or object gets lodged in the airway and blocks it. When choking, babies may become distressed but unable to cry, experience changes in skin color (blue, purple, ashen), and grab at the throat—but no air is passing through, so there may be high-pitched sounds or none at all. Intervention is usually needed to force the food out of the baby's airway.

The best defense against choking is knowing which foods are choking hazards (find a list on page 41), avoiding and/or modifying them, and offering finger foods that are sized and textured appropriately.

And the best way to reduce stress about choking and keep your baby safe is for you and anyone else who will be caring for your baby to take an accredited training course in infant CPR and first aid.

In the meantime, familiarize yourself with the steps involved in responding to a choking event:

1. Stay calm.

2. Notice if your baby is forcefully coughing and/or crying, both of which indicate that some air is passing through; if yes, do not administer first aid—if something is partially blocking the airway, crying and coughing can help push it out.

3. Call 911 on speakerphone while administering first aid.

4. Sit down and lay your baby face-down across your thighs.

5. With your nondominant hand, firmly and securely hold your baby's jaw and tip the head down so that it's lower than your baby's torso.

6. Deliver five firm, quick back blows between your baby's shoulder blades with the heel of your dominant hand.

7. If the object does not dislodge, turn your baby face-up along your lap, supporting the head and keeping it below the torso.

8. Deliver a series of five quick, smooth chest thrusts, compressing the breastbone about ½ inch in the middle, just below the nipple line.

9. Repeat the five back blows and five chest thrusts until the object becomes dislodged or the baby loses consciousness.

10. If your baby loses consciousness, shout for help, continue cardiopulmonary resuscitation (CPR) for 1 minute, then follow the 911 operator's instructions.

11. If your baby is unconscious and you can see the object blocking the airway, try to remove it with your fingers, but never try to grasp and remove an object lodged in the throat if your baby is alert.

I know, choking is terrifying to think about, but don't let fear prevent you from moving forward with solids. And if fear of choking is causing you to rethink finger foods, keep this in mind: It's possible for a baby to choke on any type of food (including purees). Recent studies have found that BLW is not associated with an increased risk of choking. In fact, a 2017 study published in the *Journal of Human Nutrition and Dietetics* found that babies who were offered finger foods the least often had the highest frequency of choking episodes, and a 2016 study in *Pediatrics* found that by the time they reach the age of 8 months, BLW infants gag less frequently than spoon-fed infants.[1]

Perhaps this is because babies who self-feed have more early opportunities to develop oral motor skills through mouthing, gumming, and chomping on resistive foods that don't break off in the mouth (like mango pits, corn cobs, chicken drumsticks, and spare ribs).

In any case, your baby will learn with time, patience, and practice under your careful supervision.

Food Safety 101

According to a 2011 report by the CDC, an estimated one in six Americans gets sick and 128,000 are hospitalized each year as a result of foodborne illness.[2] Anyone can be affected, but certain groups of people are more likely to get sick from contaminated food and more likely to experience serious effects from foodborne illness. Babies and children under age 5 are among the more vulnerable groups who are more susceptible because their immune systems are still developing. The best way to protect your baby against foodborne illness is to always practice proper food safety guidelines when handling their food.

If you're not familiar with food safety guidelines, here are nine top tips to help educate you on the basics and make food safety a consistent part of your routine as you prepare meals for yourself and your baby:

1. Before preparing or handling any food, wash your hands with soap under warm running water for at least 20 seconds. Be sure to always wash again after handling raw eggs, seafood, or meat.

2. Avoid cross-contamination by thoroughly washing and disinfecting any cutting boards, surfaces, or utensils that come in contact with raw meat and/or eggs before using them again to prepare ready-to-eat foods.

3. Wash fruits and vegetables thoroughly before prepping, even if you don't plan on eating the skin, so that nothing from the outside contaminates the inside flesh during peeling and slicing.

4. Defrost frozen foods safely overnight in the fridge—never on countertops or in the sink.

5. Keep cold foods cold and hot foods hot. The temperature danger zone is between 41°F and 135°F—foods that remain in this zone for more than 4 hours can start harboring pathogenic microorganisms and should be thrown out. Perishable leftovers kept at room temperature for more than 2 hours should be tossed as well.

6. When in doubt, throw it out.

7. Raw flour that has not been cooked can contain germs that cause foodborne illness, including *E.coli*; avoid serving your baby or anyone else foods that contain raw flour that has not been heat-treated.

8. Use a dial or digital food thermometer to confirm that you are cooking animal proteins to the USDA's Recommended Safe Minimum Internal Temperatures: 145°F for steak, veal, lamb, and seafood; 160°F for ground beef, pork, and egg dishes; and 165°F for all poultry.

9. When reheating leftovers, bring all foods to an internal temperature of 165°F.

Screening, Treatment, and Cures for Food Allergies

If your baby is at high risk for food allergies, it's important to establish your child as a patient right away with a board-certified allergist who can discuss any need for screening on an individual basis. That being said, while the NIAID suggests pre-screening depending on a baby's level of risk, more recently published consensus guidelines from allergy organizations around the world suggest that **routine screenings before allergen introduction are not generally required or recommended in high- or low-risk babies.**[1]

Here's why: the information allergists can gather from pre-screening tests—which include skin prick tests (SPTs) and allergen-specific immunoglobulin E (sIgE) tests—is limited. Remember that the symptoms of a food allergy happen as a result of the interaction between a food allergen and IgE antibodies. During an SPT, an allergist will check for the presence of IgE antibodies for a specific food by placing a small drop of the allergen on the arm or back and using a small needle to scratch the surface of the skin, allowing the allergen to enter so that the allergist can look for signs of a reaction. A sIgE test is a blood test that measures the amount of IgE to a specific food in the blood. Both tests are known for poor specificity and a high rate of positive test results that may not be clinically relevant. These tests can help allergists diagnose a food allergy in combination with the clinical history and can indicate whether a person is sensitized to a specific allergen. But keep in mind that you can have a positive sIgE or SPT without symptoms of food allergy. While being sensitized means that your immune system will form allergen-specific IgE antibodies when exposed to a specific food, it doesn't necessarily mean that you will experience an allergic reaction or become allergic. **People who are sensitized to certain foods may be more primed to develop a food allergy to those foods, but not all will.**

SPTs and sIgE tests can be useful in ruling out a potential food allergy. They can also help allergists determine a child's baseline numbers after a food allergy has been diagnosed. Tracking SPT and sIgE test results and watching how they change over time can help indicate whether it's time to offer a food challenge and determine if a child has outgrown a food allergy.

But the danger of leaning on SPTs and sIgE tests as a guiding factor in whether to *introduce* a food is that a positive test may lead to avoidance of a food to which your baby is sensitized but not allergic—and this avoidance during infancy can subsequently increase the risk that your baby develops an allergy to it. For this reason, and because severe reactions to new foods in infants are extremely rare, routine screening tests before food introductions are not required or recommended per the 2020 consensus prevention guidelines from the AAAAI, ACAAI, and CSACI (along with the UK Department of Health and Social Care, the British Society for Allergy and Clinical Immunology,

> **"** Introducing allergens early and often was one of the best things we did during BLF. I had so much more confidence and felt better about feeding our son a variety of different foods once he'd already been exposed to all the top allergens.
>
> DAVID, DAD OF
> 11-MONTH-OLD ROWAN **"**

the Australasian Society of Clinical Immunology and Allergy, and the European Academy of Allergy and Clinical Immunology), which recommend "early introduction of selected high-risk foods without any pre-introduction screening."[2]

That being said, whether to screen for sensitization to peanut before introduction continues to be an area of some debate among medical professionals. The AAP supports the NIAID Addendum Guidelines, which suggest that healthcare providers consider screening in high-risk children before oral introduction. Some families also feel strongly about wanting pre-screening tests and/or feel extremely uncomfortable about introducing a food at home without supervision. In these cases, the AAAAI, ACAAI, and CSACI recommend that if screening is performed, most babies who are sensitized to a particular food should follow up as soon as possible with an in-office oral food challenge (OFC) (or, even better, skip the screening tests altogether and go straight to the in-office OFC), where the child is fed the allergenic food under office supervision to verify the presence or absence of an allergy. In most cases, this is a better option than delaying the introduction of foods like peanut and egg or relying on SPTs or sIgE tests, which may get it wrong.[3]

The problem is that OFCs are expensive and sometimes hard to schedule. You may not be able to get an appointment for weeks or months and end up missing the window of time when the introduction of peanut and egg is most effective at reducing a child's risk of food allergy development.

Bottom line: it can feel scary for some to introduce allergens with or without pre-testing. But sometimes in parenting, the scary thing is the best thing we can do for our babies. Talk it over with your doctor, insist on shared decision-making with your healthcare providers, and decide on the best path forward for your baby and for you.

Can Food Allergies Be Outgrown?

In most cases, yes! By the age of 5, most children will outgrow IgE-mediated food allergies to milk, egg, wheat, and soy, although some outgrow food allergies as late as adolescence. Only about a quarter of children with allergies to peanut and slightly fewer with allergies to tree nuts will outgrow their allergies. Food allergies to shellfish tend to be lifelong.[4]

Is There a Cure for Food Allergies?

As of now, there is no known cure for food allergies.

Treatment for Food Allergies

For the majority of food allergies, the only current management strategy is strict avoidance of the offending food. However, there have been some exciting advances in the areas of reaction prevention and oral immunotherapy (OIT) , and research is ongoing.

In February 2024, the FDA approved Xolair® (omalizumab) for both children and adults as the first medication to help reduce allergic reactions to multiple foods after accidental exposure. While not a cure for food allergies, Xolair helped 68 percent of people avoid a severe allergic reaction in clinical trials.

The FDA approved an OIT for peanut allergy called Palforzia in January 2020. Palforzia and other OITs involve exposing an allergic person every day to small, increasing amounts of the allergen as a way to help modify the person's immune response to the allergen.[5] OIT is not a cure, nor will it definitely eradicate a food allergy. The goal of treatment is to help keep food-allergic people safer by reducing the likelihood of a severe reaction if the allergen is ingested accidentally.

As existing research and development increase the availability of these treatment options, there is a great deal of hope that omalizumab, OIT, and others will help improve the lives of more food-allergic people in the future.

11

Identifying Allergic Reactions and Food Intolerances

While most babies won't have an allergic reaction to new foods, it's wise to become familiar with the signs and symptoms before introducing common allergens. This also reduces stress and helps everyone feel more confident during mealtimes.

In babies, the most common symptoms of food allergy are rash and vomiting. But vomiting is tricky because while it can be a symptom of food allergy, babies vomit for a whole host of other reasons as well, such as overfeeding, an overactive gag reflex, viruses, and reflux.

Another lesser-known cause of vomiting is food protein–induced enterocolitis syndrome (FPIES), a severe, non-IgE-mediated condition based in the gastrointestinal tract and sometimes referred to as "delayed food allergy" because it can cause severe vomiting 1 to 4 hours after a trigger food is ingested. Common trigger foods are cow's milk, soy, rice, and oat. FPIES often develops during a baby's first year of life during the process of starting solids, and most children outgrow the condition by age 3 or 4.

The severity of IgE-mediated food-allergic reactions can range from mild to severe and be difficult to predict. Most appear within a few minutes of consuming the food. Here's the good news, which I hope you find as comforting as I do:

• • •

Severe allergic reactions in infants are extremely
rare. And the smaller the amount of allergen eaten,
the smaller any potential reaction is likely to be.

• • •

That's why when we are offering a new top allergenic food for the first time, it's wise to start with a tiny amount on the tip of a spoon.

Signs and Symptoms of an Allergic Reaction

Common symptoms of food allergy can surface alone or in combination in one or more of the following ways:

Mild to Moderate Symptoms
- A few localized hives (red, warm, raised welts) or itchiness around the mouth or face

- Nausea and vomiting

- Diarrhea

- Repetitive coughing

- Stomach pain

Severe Symptoms

- Generalized hives that are widespread on the body

- Swelling of the lips, tongue, and throat that blocks breathing

- Loss of consciousness

- Difficulty swallowing or breathing

- Sudden tiredness, lethargy, weakness, and confusion

- Drop in blood pressure

- Anaphylaxis (a potentially life-threatening allergic reaction that can impede breathing and send the body into shock and that affects more than one organ system—such as vomiting accompanied by hives)

If you think your baby is having a mild or moderate allergic reaction, stop feeding the allergen right away and contact your pediatrician, who may refer you to an allergist for further evaluation. In the event of a mild reaction, your pediatrician will take your child's medical history into consideration and guide your next steps. Some recommend watching and waiting, others recommend cetirizine (sold under the brand name Zyrtec), and others recommend diphenhydramine (sold under the brand name Benadryl), although Benadryl is recommended much less frequently these days because it can cause drowsiness, and in the event of a mild reaction, we want a baby to stay awake so that we can monitor closely. In any case, do not administer any medication to your baby unless your doctor recommends it, and be sure to follow your doctor's dosing recommendations.

If you see any signs of a severe allergic reaction or multiple signs of an allergic reaction that affect different parts of the body, call 911 and request an ambulance with auto-injectable epinephrine. Epinephrine is the only medicine that can treat anaphylaxis and it must be administered rapidly. **Neither cetirizine (Zyrtec) nor diphenhydramine (Benadryl) or will treat anaphylaxis.**

Should you keep any medications on hand during this process, just in case? It depends, but probably not. Talk to your pediatrician about it if you are concerned. Although severe reactions are uncommon in infants, they can occur. In rare cases, an allergist may identify a child as high risk for anaphylaxis and prescribe an EpiPen to ease symptoms in the event of an emergency—a great reason to get an early start on those conversations with your pediatrician about your baby's level of risk for food allergies.

One tip that will help prepare you for a food allergy reaction and any other medical emergency is to gather a few pieces of information about your child on a card, keep it up to date, and stash copies in the diaper bag, your wallet, on the fridge, and anywhere else that can be easily and conveniently reached by you and your baby's caregivers. If you ever do need to call 911, the operator may ask about your baby's birth date, current weight, medical history, address, and insurance information, and it will be helpful to have this information readily accessible.

If your baby is diagnosed with a food allergy, that food must be avoided unless and until your allergist tells you otherwise. Work closely with your allergist and/or pediatrician, who will follow your little one over time and determine the best plan of action going forward.

Importantly, if you notice a reaction to any food in your baby, talk to your doctor about how to proceed, but **never try to diagnose the reaction as a food allergy yourself**. This can lead to the unnecessary elimination of healthy foods from your baby's diet and may prevent your baby from eating foods during infancy that help reduce the risk of food allergy. A board-certified allergist will consider several different factors and rule out other unrelated health conditions before making a diagnosis.

> **"** I focused on egg first and then peanuts. I had anxiety about those two foods and would feed him allergens at my parents' house, because they live closer to an emergency room, but then we got the hang of it and I was able to relax." **"**
>
> VANESSA, MOM OF
> 1-YEAR-OLD TOMAS

Is It Drool Rash, Contact Dermatitis, or an Allergic Reaction?

Baby skin is sensitive. Rashes can pop up easily for a variety of different reasons, and at times it can be difficult to determine whether a baby's rash is a symptom of an allergic reaction or a harmless skin irritation. Here's what you need to know:

Contact reactions in babies are often caused by baby drool or acidic foods like strawberries and citrus fruits. You may have heard the feeding myth that strawberries are a top allergen that should be avoided during infancy. Not true! Strawberries are rich in vitamin C and actually a great early food for babies. They are not a common cause of food allergies, but they are acidic and can sometimes cause minor irritation on areas of a baby's body where the food has touched the skin (often the mouth and cheeks). This is considered a contact rash and usually consists of a simple, flat, rash that is purplish in darker skin tones and reddish in lighter skin tones. My oldest would often get these rashes on her cheeks after meals. I worried so much about it at the time, but it was harmless, and she outgrew it eventually. Drooling is another cause of this type of mild skin irritation. Both can be prevented by coating a baby's skin with a barrier ointment frequently if you have a drooler, or before feeding if your baby's skin seems to react to acidic foods. I wish I had known this when my oldest was an infant! (Note: Sometimes persistent drool rash can benefit from an over-the-counter antifungal cream—check with your pediatrician.)

On the flip side, a rash that happens as a result of a food-allergic reaction is often similarly reddish on lighter skin tones or purplish on darker skin tones, but blotchy, bumpy, and raised (sometimes similar to the look of a mosquito bite). This indicates an activation of the immune system. A baby experiencing this type of rash may seem itchy, uncomfortable, and be scratching in areas where the food did not touch the body. This type of allergic reaction can be predictable in some babies; in others, it can get worse with every exposure to the offending food. In severe cases where a rash is widespread, the baby may need immediate medical attention. If you find yourself concerned about a rash and not sure what to do, and your pediatrician's office accepts photos through their online portal, consider snapping a picture and sending it to your pediatrician or allergist's office and asking for guidance on the next steps.

How Do You Introduce a Food to Your Baby If You Are Allergic to It?

There is no right or wrong answer here and a lot depends on the severity of your allergy, how likely it is that your child will come in contact with the food going forward, and/or whether other children in your home are allergic to it as well. The highest-priority foods for early and frequent introduction during infancy are peanut and egg. If you are allergic to either or both of these foods and uncomfortable having them in your home or feeding them to your child, you may want to enlist family, friends, or other caregivers to help you feed your baby a couple of times a week so that your child can hopefully avoid the development of the same food allergy.

Some of the families I work with ask a friend, family member, or babysitter to feed certain foods to their baby when at the park, outside, or just out of the house so that they don't have to worry about cross-contamination at home. Some allergic caregivers feel comfortable preparing their offending allergen-containing foods and feeding them to their babies a couple of times a week as long as they are taking care to thoroughly wash hands and surfaces that were touched by the allergen after meals.

If you have food allergies to top allergens other than peanut and egg, know that as of yet, and as mentioned earlier, there is no conclusive evidence that feeding them during infancy will help prevent a food allergy from developing (although we have good reason to think it might). Whether it is motivating enough to feed these foods early and often to your baby when you are faced with the extra challenge of managing a food allergy in yourself or another family member comes down to personal choice and individual circumstances.

Food Intolerances and Other Types of Food-Related Reactions

You might have heard about other food-related conditions and have questions about those as your baby starts eating solids. There are too many to cover in this book, but the following will hopefully give you somewhere to start in case you suspect a problem.

Unlike food allergies, which involve an immune response, food intolerances are usually caused by an inability to digest certain foods, which leads to symptoms involving the gastrointestinal system, such as bloating, diarrhea, constipation, cramping, gas, and nausea. For example, lactose intolerance (which is rare prior to puberty) can cause loose stools, gas, bloating, and cramping and happens when the body lacks an enzyme that is needed to digest lactose, a natural sugar found in cow's milk.

Celiac disease is a lifelong hereditary autoimmune disease triggered by a food protein that causes people with the condition to experience small intestine damage, inflammation, and malabsorption of nutrients when they eat gluten, a natural protein found in wheat, barley, and rye grains.

Food Protein-Induced Allergic Protocolitis (FPIAP) is a non-IgE-mediated food allergy that is common in young babies and characterized by blood in the stool. FPIAP often presents during the first few weeks of life as rectal bleeding in an otherwise healthy baby and is outgrown by the baby's first birthday. The most common triggers are cow's milk and soy proteins, and symptoms resolve when the offending protein is removed from the diet.

Oral allergy syndrome (OAS) is a condition in which eating certain raw fruits and vegetables causes itchiness in the mouth and throat. OAS is non-life-threatening and caused by an IgE-mediated food allergy to the cross-reactive pollen in the offending produce. Those with OAS can usually tolerate the fruits and vegetables that bother them as long as they are cooked first.

If you have concerns about a potential food allergy, condition, or intolerance but are unsure how to interpret what you're noticing, it will be of enormous help to your pediatrician and/or allergist to track and take note of any signs and symptoms you think may be related to certain foods.

You can **create a simple food/reaction tracker** by keeping a small notebook handy (or by using a notes section in your phone) and recording the following:

1. Date/time

2. Description and duration of the reaction

3. What and how much your child ate (especially of any foods you suspect might be the culprit)

4. How long it took for the reaction to emerge after eating the food

5. Whether it was a first-time reaction—if not, note similarities and differences compared to previous reactions and their surrounding circumstances, how you managed previous reactions, and whether it helped

Here's an example:

Jan. 25, 12:30pm

- Jessie had a few hives around the mouth that stayed localized to that one area and went away within about 4 hours.

- She had eaten half a plain, full-fat yogurt mixed with ~2 tablespoons applesauce and ~2 teaspoons ground walnuts; she's eaten yogurt and applesauce many times before without a problem, but this was the first time she tried walnuts.

- Hives happened within about 5 minutes of her eating the walnuts.

- This was a first-time reaction to (I think) walnuts.

- On Thanksgiving, she had a small bite of my pecan pie and broke out right away in similar hives (just around the mouth). We called the pediatrician, who said to give her an antihistamine, which helped.

Don't forget that, as previously mentioned, it's normal to see an increase in gas and changes in the frequency, color, odor, and consistency of your baby's stool when your baby starts solids. These changes don't necessarily indicate food sensitivities or intolerances and in most cases resolve over time as the digestive system matures and adjusts to solid foods. For tips on preventing and managing constipation and excess gas, see chapter 6.

OK, the tricky part is behind us. Now you and your family can get ready to enjoy some satisfying and deliciously good eats!

PART FOUR

Let's Eat!

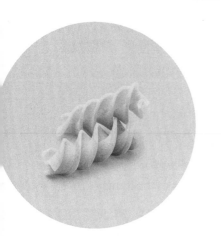
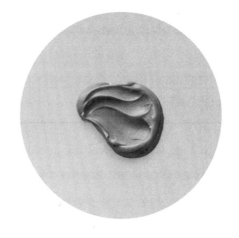

12

Stocking Your Kitchen for BLF

A little preparation up front goes a long way for BLF! During my first pregnancy, I received a "baby food cooker" as a shower gift. When it came time to start solids, I used it once and promptly gave it away because it made only tiny portions at a time (so much for family meals!) and didn't steam the food nearly as well as my good old strainer and saucepan.

When it comes to feeding babies, what you need are pantry items and kitchen tools that make the process of cooking easy and fast. You may already have many of the items listed below. If you don't, I hope this list will make it easier for you to outfit your kitchen with long-lasting essentials you'll need to prepare meals for your family—not just during your baby's infancy, but throughout the childhood and teenage years as well.

Baby-Led Feeding Kitchen Essentials

Box grater: This multiuse tool can grate harder cheeses, tempeh, and hard raw fruits and veggies like apples and carrots into infant-safe forms. I love the type with different sides for grating, shredding, slicing, and zesting, as well as a detachable container for collecting grated food.

PAGE
131

PEANUT BUTTER BANANA MINI MUFFINS

ZUCCHINI WALNUT BREAD
PAGE
132

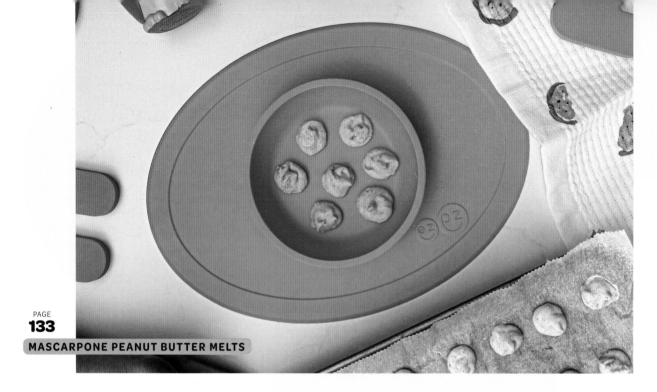

PAGE
133
MASCARPONE PEANUT BUTTER MELTS

6-ALLERGEN BLENDER PANCAKES
PAGE
134

PAGE
135

ALMOND CARDAMOM SHEET PAN PANCAKES

APPLE OAT BABY BARS

PAGE
136

PAGE
138

PEANUT BUTTER AND JELLY MUFFINS

CINNAMON OAT BREAKFAST BARS

PAGE
139

PAGE
140

STRAWBERRY MANGO CHIA SEED PUDDING

BAKED PB OATMEAL STICKS

PAGE
141

PAGE
142

BUTTERNUT APPLE MUFFIN CAKES

WALNUT-CRUSTED BUTTERNUT FRENCH TOAST

PAGE
144

PAGE
145
TAHINI DATE SHAKE

RAINBOW EGG BITES
PAGE
147

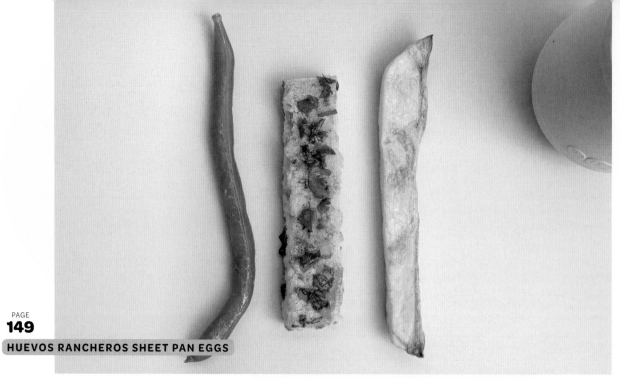

PAGE
149
HUEVOS RANCHEROS SHEET PAN EGGS

SAVORY SCONES
PAGE
150

PAGE
152
SHRIMPY GRITS

SUPER SALMON SALAD WITH PICKLED RED ONION
PAGE
155

PAGE
156
CHEESY CRAB DIP

SHRIMP AND VEGETABLE FRITTERS
PAGE
157

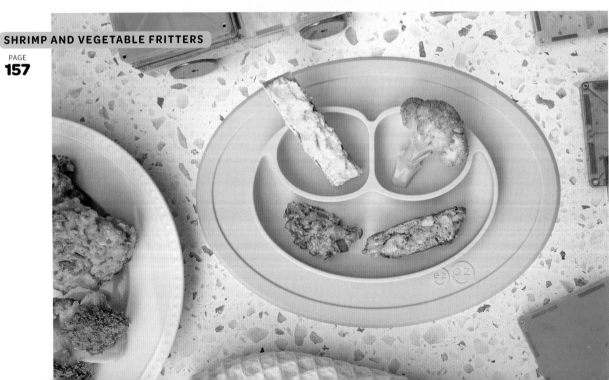

PAGE
165

ENGLISH MUFFIN BABY PIZZAS

SHELLS AND CHEESE WITH CARROTS AND PEAS

PAGE
169

PAGES
171
AND
164

PINKALICIOUS BEET HUMMUS + EDAMAME TAHINI DIP

TAHINI EGG SALAD

PAGE
172

PAGE
176
EASY SHEET PAN SALMON DINNER

COD TACOS WITH LIME SAUCE
PAGE
182

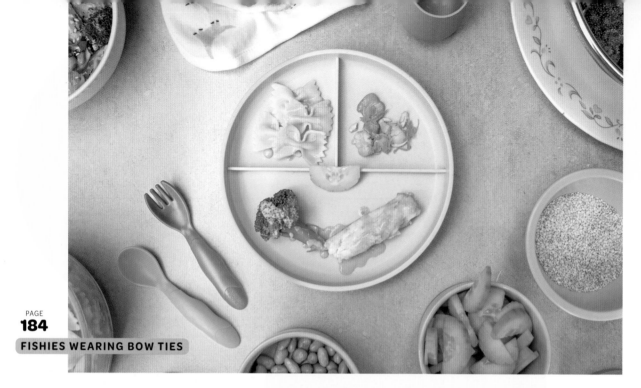

PAGE
184

FISHIES WEARING BOW TIES

OYSTER NOODLE CASSEROLE

PAGE
187

PAGE
190

CRAB LINGUINE WITH LEMON AND BASIL

SQUID STEW

PAGE
191

PAGE
192

HERBED CLAM CHOWDER

SHEET PAN ZA'ATAR CHICKEN DRUMSTICKS

PAGE
196

PAGE
200
GREEK MEATBALLS WITH TOMATO SAUCE AND ORZO

SKILLET MACARONI WITH VEGGIES AND BEEF
PAGE
208

PAGE
198
TURKEY AND TEMPEH SLOW COOKER CHILI

CAST IRON SKILLET CORNBREAD
PAGE
209

PAGE
210

COCONUT CURRY LENTIL STEW

MANY NUT PESTO PASTA + EASY FOIL-GRILLED HADDOCK

PAGES
214
AND
178

PAGE
216
MISO MUSHROOM SOUP WITH EGG

ZUCCHINI BOATS
PAGE
219

PAGE
220
SPAGHETTI SQUASH QUINOA BAKE

AFRICAN PEANUT STEW
PAGE
222

PAGE
230
CHERRY CHOCOLATE ICE POPS

CHERRY ALMOND BLF COOKIES
PAGE
227

PAGE
229

PEANUT BUTTER BANANA BABY COOKIES

PUMPKIN SPICE COOKIES

PAGE
231

PAGE
232
TOASTED COCONUT PUMPKIN PUDDING

BETTER-FOR-YOU BLACK BEAN BROWNIES
PAGE
234

Peeler: A peeler is helpful when preparing some fruits and vegetables for babies, such as apples, mangoes, and carrots.

Knives: Invest in a few good, sharp knives: a chef's knife, utility knife, paring knife, and serrated bread knife.

Kitchen shears: These are a game-changer for cutting foods like quesadillas into strips or chickpea-sized bites.

Metal strainer: You'll use this for draining pasta and washing produce, and it can also double as a steamer.

Instant-read thermometer: This gadget is key for making sure meats and leftovers are cooked to a safe internal temperature before serving to babies.

Dishwasher-safe cutting boards: Be sure to help prevent cross-contamination by using different cutting boards for produce and for raw meats, and sanitizing between uses. Popping cutting boards right into the dishwasher may be the simplest, but you can easily sanitize boards that have held raw meats, poultry, and seafood by washing them thoroughly with hot, soapy water, disinfecting with a sanitizing solution (1 tablespoon household chlorine bleach + 1 gallon water), and rinsing with clean water.

Baking pans: I find that 9 × 13-inch and 9 × 9-inch pans work well for baking most casseroles and roasting vegetables and protein foods. An 8 × 8-inch pan is also ideal for making bars.

Cast-iron skillet: Cooking in cast iron is a great way to boost your baby's iron intake—and your own, while you're at it.

Pots and pans with lids: I love having an 8-quart stockpot on hand for soups and stews, as well as 2-quart and 3-quart saucepans with lids for cooking vegetables, making sauces, and boiling eggs.

Sheet pans: A 13 × 18-inch rimmed baking sheet is great for making everything from bars to cookies to sheet pan meals. Get a couple if you can, as these will become the go-to kitchen tools you cannot live without.

Parchment paper: Lining your baking pans and sheets with parchment paper helps prevent food from sticking and makes cleanup a breeze.

Silicone ice-pop molds: These offer a perfect way to repurpose leftover smoothies or freeze pumped breast milk for teething babies. They are dishwasher-safe and often come in adorable shapes with baby-sized handles for easy self-feeding.

Blender (or even better, a high-speed blender!): My high-speed blender may get the most use out of any appliance in my kitchen. It makes preparing purees, mashes, soups, pancakes, batters, smoothies, ice pops, and sauces so much easier. A regular blender will work for the majority of recipes in this book, but investing in a high-speed blender will streamline your meal prep process further.

Food processor: A food processor will cut down significantly on time spent chopping, mincing, and grinding food for your baby. Some high-speed blenders—like the Vitamix—come with a food processor function, so you may not need both.

Slow cooker: Meats prepared in the slow cooker are excellent for babies because the slow cooking process makes them tender, soft, moist, and easier to swallow, plus there is no better feeling than filling your slow cooker in the morning and coming home to the scent of a home-cooked meal that's ready to eat.

Standing or handheld mixer: A mixer is not essential, but it can be a helpful time-saver.

Baby-Led Feeding Pantry Staples

Seeds and seed butter: Have on hand a variety, such as ground flax, chia, poppy, sesame, and sunflower seeds, as well as tahini (sesame paste).

Nuts and nut butter: Try as many as you can, especially peanut, almond, cashew, hazelnut, walnut, pistachio, pecan, and macadamia.

Canned fish: My favorites for babies are sardines in olive oil and salmon.

Canned beans: Look for low-sodium chickpeas and kidney, black, and cannellini beans.

Canned tomatoes: These are so useful in many dishes—look for low-sodium diced tomatoes and tomato paste, and tomato sauce low in sodium and added sugars.

Canned coconut milk: Look for full-fat coconut milk to use as a base for chia seed puddings and curry dishes.

Flours: Stock your pantry with almond, whole wheat, oat, all-purpose, spelt, and hazelnut flours if you can find them—Nuts.com is a great place to look, and Bob's Red Mill is available in many grocery stores.

Oats: Buy both quick-cooking oats (for fast, convenient oatmeal) and old-fashioned rolled oats (for bars and muffins).

Quinoa and farro

Breadcrumbs: I like to use both panko and regular breadcrumbs.

Pasta: Stock regular, whole wheat, lentil, and chickpea pastas, as well as egg noodles; choose larger shapes like shells, penne, or fusilli that have some texture so they're easier for babies to grasp.

Lentils: Dried lentils are easy to cook and a rich source of plant-based nutrition.

Canned pumpkin, sweet potato, and/or butternut squash: Be sure not to confuse pure pumpkin puree with pumpkin pie filling, which is often high in added sugars.

Canned or boxed low-sodium broth: Vegetable, mushroom, beef, and chicken

Boxed (shelf-stable) plain, unsweetened soy milk: This is a great way to build more soy protein into recipes for babies.

Onions and garlic

Potatoes: Any type is great, including sweet, purple, white, and yellow potatoes.

Dried spices and herbs: The more flavor, the better!

Low-sodium soy sauce

Barbecue sauce with no added sugar

Oils: Have on hand olive, avocado, coconut, canola, and toasted sesame oils.

Vinegar: I especially like to use white wine, red wine, and apple cider vinegars.

Baby-Led Feeding Freezer Staples

Fruit: Some favorites for babies include frozen strawberries, mangoes, pineapples, blueberries, raspberries, and pitted sweet cherries.

Veggies: Have on hand frozen broccoli, spinach, peas, diced carrots, green beans, asparagus, and bell peppers.

Edamame: Frozen edamame is a quick, convenient, baby-friendly protein food that makes soy introduction easy.

Bread: I always keep English muffins, sprouted whole-grain breads, and parbaked sourdough loaves in the freezer.

Whole-grain waffles: These are a convenient vehicle for top allergens like peanut butter or ricotta cheese (which contains cow's milk).

Soft corn or almond flour tortillas

Fish: Frozen favorites for babies include salmon, rainbow trout, cod, and arctic char.

Meats and poultry: Stock your freezer with ground beef, ground turkey, and chicken thighs and drumsticks.

Baby-Led Feeding Refrigerator Staples

Lemons and limes

Eggs

Mayonnaise

Fresh ginger: Store in an airtight container in your refrigerator's crisper drawer.

Dijon mustard

Tofu: Try both firm (for cooking or eating raw) and silken (for blending into smoothies and purees).

Plain, full-fat yogurt

How to Use the Recipes

Each family-focused, baby-friendly recipe in this book contains at least one common allergen (and in most cases, multiple top allergens). The recipes are either ready to be offered to babies at various stages of their solids journey, or they offer suggestions on how to deconstruct and/or modify the food so that your baby can easily join in meals right along with you and any other children you might have.

If your child has been diagnosed with a food allergy to one or more of the foods used in these recipes, there is a list of allergen swaps on page 236 that will make it easy for you to substitute the problem food wherever necessary.

Serving sizes for each recipe are calculated in terms of adult portion sizes (unless noted otherwise) to make it easier for you to serve the recipe to your whole family. When determining portion sizes for your baby, start with about a tablespoon of each food served at the meal and offer more if your baby seems to want more.

I also offer a series of meal plans, but if you're not a meal-planning kind of person, that's completely fine! Feel free to go rogue and explore the recipes on your own. Most recipes include suggestions for side dishes that you can use to help create a balanced meal. And although recipes are divided into breakfast, lunch, dinner, and dessert categories, don't feel bound by these labels. Serve recipes at whatever meal of the day works best for you and your family.

While you're exploring, you'll see that the amount of allergenic protein in each recipe is calculated for you. Many of the ingredients in the recipes contain protein, so I've separated out the amount of protein that comes from common allergens (these are the proteins that are more likely to cause a reaction in food-allergic people). Do not worry about counting grams of protein or stressing over this in any way. I did these calculations so that I could track the recipes that contain enough allergenic protein to help with food allergy prevention and thought it might be interesting to include for those who are curious about how much allergenic protein is present. If you like nerding out on science as much as I do, the information is there for you! Otherwise, feel free to ignore it.

Note: Allergen-containing ingredients that contribute a negligible amount of allergenic protein may not be particularly helpful for food allergy prevention, but they could still cause a reaction in someone who is allergic. As a result, I have noted their presence in the recipes even if their protein content is <1 g, to help those with food allergies make appropriate ingredient substitutions.

13

9-Day Allergen Introduction Plan

As I've mentioned before, there's no one right way to introduce allergens. How you choose to tackle allergen introduction depends on your baby's level of risk for food allergies, any specific guidance from your pediatrician or allergist, your own level of comfort, and your baby's developmental readiness for finger foods and multiple textures. And what matters just as much as early introduction is consistently keeping common allergens in the diet once introduced.

But when it comes to something as important as starting solids and preventing food allergies, it can be comforting if someone you trust takes the reins and just does all of the thinking and planning for you. That's what I wish I had had when my girls were babies. To that end, here are two different ways to proceed—choose what works best for you and your baby:

1. **For higher-risk babies and any caregivers who prefer a more prescriptive, conservative approach:** Introduce the top nine allergens using the following 9-Day Allergen Introduction Plan. It walks you through how to introduce each allergen via spoon (to help prevent allergens from touching the skin or face during the first few exposures), either alone or along with foods a baby has eaten before and tolerated, so that in the event of a reaction, it's easier to determine which food is responsible. Feel free to blow through it in 9 consecutive days or take a day or two off in between allergen introductions, depending on your schedule, bandwidth, and child's tolerance. If all of the foods are tolerated, use the 8 Weeks of Allergen Maintenance Meal Plans in chapter 14 to keep tolerated allergens in the diet a couple of times per week and encourage self-feeding going forward. If not all allergens are tolerated, you can still use the meal plans, along with the Allergen Swaps table on page 236 to substitute the foods to which your child is allergic.

2. **For lower-risk babies and caregivers who prefer a more liberal approach:** The risk of a reaction is low, and achieving diet diversity as soon as possible is the goal, so feel free to introduce the top nine allergens quickly, starting at about 6 months (use the following 9-Day Allergen Introduction Plan if you like). Then start exploring and feeding your baby a variety of the recipes from this book regularly, all of which contain at least one top allergen to help make it easier for you to keep allergens in your baby's diet regularly once they have been introduced and tolerated.

9-Day Allergen Introduction Plan

Quick reminder that while these foods are each considered a top allergen, they are all also flavorful, nourishing foods that contain plenty of nutrition for your growing baby. By introducing these foods early and often, you are helping reduce the risk of food allergies, while also providing variety and key nutrients to help your baby thrive. Give yourself a pat on the back!

 ## Day 1: Introduce egg.

Ideas for How to Introduce Egg

- ⅓ of a scrambled egg, cooked in olive oil, served on a spoon

- ⅓ of a fully cooked hard-boiled egg, pureed with a bit of breast milk or formula and served on a spoon

Notes:

- Fully cook eggs before serving to your baby—no runny yolks, as raw or undercooked eggs carry a higher risk of foodborne illness and may be more likely to cause a reaction than eggs that are fully cooked.

- Be sure to serve both the egg white and yolk.

- Don't expect your baby to finish an entire egg, although it's fine if they do—remember, aim for your baby to eat about one-third of a cooked egg two or three times per week for the purposes of egg allergy prevention.

- For more tips on introducing eggs, see chapter 8.

Day 2: Introduce peanuts.

Ideas for How to Introduce Peanuts
- 2 teaspoons smooth peanut butter, peanut flour, or peanut powder thinned with a little breast milk or formula and served on a spoon
- 2 teaspoons smooth peanut butter mixed with a familiar fortified infant cereal (such as oatmeal made with breast milk or formula) or familiar fruit puree and served on a spoon
- 2 teaspoons smooth peanut butter mashed with ¼ banana and served on a spoon

Notes:
- Choose smooth peanut butter rather than crunchy, which can have overly large nut pieces that increase choking risk.
- If your baby doesn't want to finish the entire portion, don't sweat it—remember, aim for 2 teaspoons peanut butter or peanut powder two or three times per week for the purposes of peanut allergy prevention.
- For more tips on introducing peanuts, see chapter 8.

 Day 3: Introduce cow's milk.

Ideas for How to Introduce Cow's Milk
- 2 tablespoons plain, full-fat yogurt served on a spoon
- 2 tablespoons full-fat ricotta, cottage, or mascarpone cheese served on a spoon
- 1 tablespoon familiar fortified infant cereal (such as oatmeal) made with 2 tablespoons cow's milk served on a spoon

Notes:
- My favorite way to introduce cow's milk protein is in the form of plain, full-fat yogurt, which is often easier to digest because of the fermentation process used to make it. For more tips on introducing cow's milk, see chapter 8.

Day 4: Introduce wheat.

Ideas for How to Introduce Wheat

- 1 tablespoon wheat germ mixed with a familiar fruit puree and served on a spoon

- ¼ cup tender-cooked wheat-based pasta tossed in extra-virgin olive oil

- ¼ cup farina or fortified infant wheat cereal served on a spoon

Notes:

- For tips on introducing wheat and choosing the best breads for babies, see chapter 8.

 ## Day 5: Introduce fish.

Ideas for How to Introduce Fish

- 1 ounce canned sardines, mashed and served on a spoon

- 1 ounce canned salmon mashed with 1 tablespoon plain, full-fat yogurt or mashed avocado, served on a spoon

- 1 ounce (a finger-sized piece) tender-cooked salmon, cod, or haddock, mashed and served on a spoon

Notes:

- Before serving to babies, remember to cook fish to an internal temperature of at least 145°F and be sure to remove any bones.

- See chapter 8 for more tips on choosing fish for babies.

Day 6: Introduce tree nuts.

Ideas for How to Introduce Tree Nuts

- 2 teaspoons tree nut butter thinned with a little breast milk or formula and served on a spoon

- 2 teaspoons ground tree nuts mixed into plain, full-fat yogurt (if tolerated) and/or familiar fruit puree served on a spoon

- 2 teaspoons smooth tree nut butter mashed with ¼ banana and served on a spoon

Notes:

- Introduce specific tree nuts that you eat as a family and that your child is more likely to encounter as they grow.

- For more tips on introducing tree nuts, see chapter 8.

 # Day 7: Introduce soy.

Ideas for How to Introduce Soy

- 2 tablespoons plain, unsweetened soy yogurt served on a spoon

- 2 tablespoons silken tofu mixed with 1 tablespoon familiar fruit puree served on a spoon

- 1 tablespoon familiar fortified infant cereal (such as oatmeal) made with 2 tablespoons plain, unsweetened soy milk served on a spoon

Notes:

- Once soy has been introduced and tolerated via spoon, firm or extra-firm tofu works nicely as a finger food for babies.

- See chapter 8 for more tips on offering soy.

Day 8: Introduce shellfish.

Ideas for How to Introduce Shellfish

- 1 ounce finely minced, cooked shrimp served on a spoon

- 1 ounce finely minced cooked shrimp or crabmeat mixed with 1 tablespoon mashed potato and served on a spoon

Notes:

- Keep in mind that the texture of shellfish generally tends to be rubbery, which increases choking risk, so it does need to be finely minced before serving.

- Most types of shellfish are naturally high in sodium, so try to keep sodium levels low in whatever else you serve throughout the rest of the day.

- See chapter 8 for more tips on introducing shellfish.

 ## Day 9: Introduce sesame.

Ideas for How to Introduce Sesame

- 2 teaspoons tahini mixed into plain, full-fat yogurt or a familiar fruit puree, served on a spoon

Notes:

- Serving sesame to babies in the form of tahini (sesame paste) makes the nutrients more bioavailable, but like other nut and seed butters, tahini served in globs is a choking hazard and must be spread thinly or thinned with a liquid before serving to a baby.

14

8 Weeks of Allergen Maintenance Meal Plans

Once a top allergen has been introduced and tolerated, don't forget to help maintain that tolerance by offering the allergen a couple of times per week going forward! The recipes in this book are designed to make this part easy. To help make it even easier, I've done all of the thinking and planning for you in the meal plan that follows.

Each meal in the 8-week meal plan contains a balance of foods (from recipes in this book, simple meal ideas, and suggestions for side dishes) that provide the nutrients babies need to thrive and grow. There are no recipe repeats. If you follow the 8-week meal plan, your baby will be exposed to all nine top allergens at least two or three times per week.

Tree nuts were a challenge when designing the meal plan, as everyone's nut preferences will be different and there are too many to incorporate every week. At least 2 grams of tree nut protein per week are present in the meal plan. Once you've selected and introduced the specific nuts you'd like to serve consistently to your baby, see chapter 8 for tips on keeping them in your rotation after these 8 weeks.

> **My biggest issue has been what to serve for each meal. I love watching other babes at the same age and what they are eating and then trying it out on my kiddo. Bonus if it's a meal I can make for everyone.**
>
> DESTINY, MOM OF
> 9-MONTH-OLD AALIYAH

When you reach the end of the 8 weeks, feel free to start at the beginning again and repeat, or branch out and try some of the other allergen-containing recipes in this book.

Each week is designed to minimize shopping and cooking; the same fruits and vegetables show up a couple of times per week so you can use them up before they spoil, and there are plenty of opportunities each week for leftovers.

When it comes to food sizing, cut foods in the meal plan to match your baby's current developmental grasp: finger-length, stick-shaped, soft finger foods for babies using a palmar grasp and small, chickpea-sized pieces for babies using a pincer grasp. When the pincer grasp starts to emerge (usually around 9 months), you can start to offer some of both shapes at meals. This will reduce some of your baby's frustration if they are hungry but can't pincer up small bites of food fast enough.

Here are a few notes on food preparation:

- **Corn on the cob:** Whole corn kernels off the cob are harder for babies under age one to chew and mash down with their gums, but corn served on the cob is great for babies from about 6 months and up. This is because the cob offers an easy-to-grasp hard surface on which babies can chomp down, get some relief from teething pain, and gnaw off bits of corn. As babies press their gums against the cob, it smashes down the corn kernels so they are less round, thereby reducing choking risk.

- **Cucumber:** Large sticks of cucumber are great teethers if teeth have not yet popped through. As teeth emerge and babies can bite off larger pieces of a whole or halved cucumber, slice cucumbers lengthwise into paper-thin strips or offer a strip of the inner, soft, seedy portion.

- As mentioned, reduce choking risk by checking that all foods you give your baby can be easily squished between your thumb and forefinger.

Week 1

Balanced, Baby-Friendly Meal Suggestions

Allergens

SUN	Breakfast	Cottage Cheese Mash + whole wheat toast strips with 2 teaspoons peanut butter	
	Lunch or Dinner	Lasagna Roll-Ups + cucumber	
MON	Breakfast	Peanut Butter and Jelly Muffins + scrambled egg	
	Lunch or Dinner	Shrimp and Broccoli Croquettes + watermelon	
TUES	Breakfast	*Leftover* Peanut Butter and Jelly Muffins + plain, full-fat cottage cheese	
	Lunch or Dinner	*Leftover* Shrimp and Broccoli Croquettes + cucumber	
WED	Breakfast	Almond Cardamom Sheet Pan Pancakes + plain, full-fat yogurt	
	Lunch or Dinner	Skillet Macaroni with Veggies and Beef	
THURS	Breakfast	*Leftover* Almond Cardamom Sheet Pan Pancakes + plain, full-fat yogurt	
	Lunch or Dinner	Super Salmon Salad + whole-wheat toast strips + tomato wedges	
FRI	Breakfast	Tahini Date Shake + oatmeal	
	Lunch or Dinner	*Leftover* Super Salmon Salad + pita bread + steamed asparagus	
SAT	Breakfast	whole wheat toast strips with tahini drizzle + thawed frozen strawberry	
	Lunch or Dinner	African Peanut Stew + steamed asparagus	

Week 2

		Balanced, Baby-Friendly Meal Suggestions	Allergens
SUN	Breakfast	Sweet Potato Almond Butter Mash + orange wedges	
	Lunch or Dinner	Avocado Crab Quesadillas + Roasted Zucchini Sticks	
MON	Breakfast	Mango Surprise Smoothie + oatmeal	
	Lunch or Dinner	Easy Foil-Grilled Haddock + steamed cauliflower + quinoa	
TUES	Breakfast	*Leftover* Mango Surprise Smoothie made into ice pop + buttered waffle strips	
	Lunch or Dinner	*Leftover* Easy Foil-Grilled Haddock + steamed cauliflower + Sweet Potato Almond Butter Mash	
WED	Breakfast	Shrimpy Grits + watermelon	
	Lunch or Dinner	Steak strip + mashed potatoes + steamed green beans	
THURS	Breakfast	Rainbow Egg Bites + *leftover* mashed potatoes	
	Lunch or Dinner	English Muffin Baby Pizzas + ripe kiwi + smashed black beans	
FRI	Breakfast	*Leftover* Rainbow Egg Bites + strips of buttered whole wheat toast + ripe kiwi	
	Lunch or Dinner	Lemon Tahini Lentil Stew + watermelon	
SAT	Breakfast	waffle strips topped with 2 teaspoons smooth peanut butter + scrambled egg + orange wedge	
	Lunch or Dinner	*Leftover* Lemon Tahini Lentil Stew + orange wedges	

Week 3

Balanced, Baby-Friendly Meal Suggestions

Allergens

SUN			
	Breakfast	6-Allergen Blender Pancakes + ripe cantaloupe	
	Lunch or Dinner	Sheet Pan Shrimp and Tofu Fajitas	

MON			
	Breakfast	Oatmeal made with whole milk + scrambled egg + thawed frozen strawberry	
	Lunch or Dinner	*Leftover* Sheet Pan Shrimp and Tofu Fajitas	

TUES			
	Breakfast	*Leftover* 6-Allergen Blender Pancakes + thawed frozen strawberry	
	Lunch or Dinner	Sesame Eggplant Dip + strips of naan bread + ripe cantaloupe	

WED			
	Breakfast	Apple Oat Baby Bars + ripe avocado + plain, full-fat yogurt	
	Lunch or Dinner	Sardine Avotoasts + tomato wedges	

THURS			
	Breakfast	*Leftover* Apple Oat Baby Bars + ripe avocado + mascarpone cheese	
	Lunch or Dinner	*Leftover* Sesame Eggplant Dip + strips of naan bread + orange wedges	

FRI			
	Breakfast	Peanut Butter Banana Baby Cookies + full-fat cottage cheese + steamed green beans	
	Lunch or Dinner	Cod Tacos with Lime Sauce + roasted sweet potato fries + steamed broccoli	

SAT			
	Breakfast	*Leftover* Peanut Butter Banana Baby Cookies + plain, full-fat yogurt + orange wedges	
	Lunch or Dinner	Coconut Curry Lentil Stew + steamed broccoli	

Week 4

		Balanced, Baby-Friendly Meal Suggestions	Allergens
SUN	Breakfast	Peanut Apple Fritters + plain, full-fat yogurt + cinnamon	
	Lunch or Dinner	Shells and Cheese with Carrots and Peas + steamed green beans	
MON	Breakfast	Nutty French Toast Casserole + ripe mango	
	Lunch or Dinner	*Leftover* Shells and Cheese with Carrots and Peas + cucumber	
TUES	Breakfast	*Leftover* Peanut Apple Fritters + plain, full-fat cottage cheese	
	Lunch or Dinner	Edamame Tahini Dip + strips of whole-grain pita bread + tomato wedges	
WED	Breakfast	*Leftover* Nutty French Toast Casserole + ripe pear	
	Lunch or Dinner	Memere's Shepherd's Pie + steamed or roasted asparagus	
THURS	Breakfast	Peanut Butter Banana Mini Muffins + crème fraîche or plain, full-fat yogurt + ripe pear	
	Lunch or Dinner	Seafood Sliders with Lemon Aioli + mashed potatoes + cucumber	
FRI	Breakfast	Buttered whole wheat toast strips + applesauce mixed with 2 teaspoons tahini	
	Lunch or Dinner	*Leftover* Seafood Sliders with Lemon Aioli + corn on the cob + steamed or roasted broccoli	
SAT	Breakfast	*Leftover* Peanut Butter Banana Mini Muffins + plain, unsweetened soy yogurt + applesauce	
	Lunch or Dinner	Crab Linguine with Lemon and Basil + steamed green beans	

Week 5

Balanced, Baby-Friendly Meal Suggestions   **Allergens**

SUN	Breakfast	Toasted Coconut Pumpkin Pudding + buttered waffle strips + ripe pear	
	Lunch or Dinner	Huevos Rancheros Sheet Pan Eggs + mild salsa + soft corn tortillas + Baby-Friendly Cashew Dip	
MON	Breakfast	*Leftover* Huevos Rancheros Sheet Pan Eggs + mild salsa + soft corn tortilla	
	Lunch or Dinner	Easy Sheet Pan Salmon Dinner	
TUES	Breakfast	*Leftover* Toasted Coconut Pumpkin Pudding + oat O's cereal + ripe pear	
	Lunch or Dinner	*Leftover* Easy Sheet Pan Salmon Dinner	
WED	Breakfast	Baked PB Oatmeal Sticks + honeydew + plain, full-fat cottage cheese	
	Lunch or Dinner	Shrimp and Vegetable Fritters + corn on the cob + steamed green beans	
THURS	Breakfast	*Leftover* Baked PB Oatmeal Sticks + smashed blueberries + slice of fresh, full-fat mozzarella cheese	
	Lunch or Dinner	*Leftover* Shrimp and Vegetable Fritters + steamed broccoli + *leftover* Baby-Friendly Cashew Dip	
FRI	Breakfast	Walnut-Crusted Butternut French Toast + honeydew melon	
	Lunch or Dinner	Tahini Egg Salad + strips of whole wheat toast + steamed green beans	
SAT	Breakfast	*Leftover* Walnut-Crusted Butternut French Toast + smashed blueberries	
	Lunch or Dinner	*Leftover* Tahini Egg Salad + pita bread + cucumber	

Week 6

Balanced, Baby-Friendly Meal Suggestions

Allergens

		Balanced, Baby-Friendly Meal Suggestions	Allergens
SUN	Breakfast	Cinnamon Oat Breakfast Bars prepared with tofu + ripe mango + scrambled egg	
	Lunch or Dinner	Fall-Apart Slow Cooker Beef Stew + ripe tomato wedges	
MON	Breakfast	Cast-Iron Skillet Corn Bread + plain, full-fat yogurt + smashed blueberries	
	Lunch or Dinner	Turkey and Tempeh Slow Cooker Chili + *leftover* Cast-Iron Skillet Corn Bread + steamed green beans	
TUES	Breakfast	*Leftover* Cinnamon Oat Breakfast Bars prepared with tofu + plain, full-fat yogurt + ripe mango·	
	Lunch or Dinner	Many Nut Pesto Pasta + steamed cauliflower	
WED	Breakfast	Pumpkin Spice Cookies + quartered grapes + cheese shreds	
	Lunch or Dinner	Herbed Clam Chowder + steamed green beans	
THURS	Breakfast	Butternut Apple Muffin Cakes + mascarpone cheese + smashed blueberries	
	Lunch or Dinner	*Leftover* Herbed Clam Chowder + steamed cauliflower	
FRI	Breakfast	*Leftover* Butternut Apple Muffin Cakes + soft cooked apples + mascarpone cheese	
	Lunch or Dinner	Fishies Wearing Bowties	
SAT	Breakfast	*Leftover* Pumpkin Spice Cookies + quartered grapes + cheese shreds	
	Lunch or Dinner	*Leftover* Fishies Wearing Bowties	

Week 7

		Balanced, Baby-Friendly Meal Suggestions	Allergens
SUN	Breakfast	Peanut Butter Sweet Potato Casserole + cooked apples	
	Lunch or Dinner	Avgolemono + Zucchini Boats	
MON	Breakfast	Spinach Manchego Frittata + applesauce mixed with wheat germ	
	Lunch or Dinner	BLF Saag Paneer + strips of naan bread + sautéed, finely minced shrimp	
TUES	Breakfast	*Leftover* Peanut Butter Sweet Potato Casserole + cooked apples	
	Lunch or Dinner	Miso Mushroom Soup with Egg	
WED	Breakfast	Zucchini Walnut Bread (made without chocolate chips) + mascarpone cheese + smashed raspberries	
	Lunch or Dinner	Sheet Pan Za'atar Chicken Drumsticks + strips of naan bread + steamed broccoli	
THURS	Breakfast	Presto Pressed Pesto Grilled Cheese + smashed raspberries	
	Lunch or Dinner	*Leftover* Sheet Pan Za'atar Chicken Drumsticks + pita bread + steamed asparagus	
FRI	Breakfast	Oyster Noodle Casserole + steamed broccoli	
	Lunch or Dinner	Macadamia-Crusted Fish with Pineapple Ginger Glaze + steamed baby bok choy + rice	
SAT	Breakfast	Whole wheat toast strips topped with 2 teaspoons smooth peanut butter + thawed frozen strawberry	
	Lunch or Dinner	*Leftover* Macadamia-Crusted Fish with Pineapple Ginger Glaze + steamed baby bok choy + rice	

Week 8

Balanced, Baby-Friendly Meal Suggestions

Allergens

SUN	Breakfast	Veggie Strata + kiwi + Cherry Chocolate Ice Pops	
	Lunch or Dinner	Squid Stew + polenta + sautéed zucchini	
MON	Breakfast	Mascarpone Peanut Butter Melts + kiwi + oat O's cereal	
	Lunch or Dinner	Fish Fingers with Cashew Tartar Sauce + crinkle-cut baked potato "fries" + steamed broccoli	
TUES	Breakfast	Cheesy Crab Dip + sourdough bread + quartered grapes + sautéed peas	
	Lunch or Dinner	*Leftover* Fish Fingers + Cashew Tartar Sauce + steamed carrot sticks + mashed potatoes	
WED	Breakfast	Cherry Almond BLF Cookies + smashed blueberries + plain, full-fat yogurt	
	Lunch or Dinner	Spaghetti Squash Quinoa Bake + Pinkalicious Beet Hummus + pita bread	
THURS	Breakfast	Strawberry Mango Chia Seed Pudding + buttered waffle strips	
	Lunch or Dinner	Easy Slow Cooker Chicken Korma + basmati rice + sautéed zucchini + Peanut Butter Power Pops	
FRI	Breakfast	*Leftover* Cherry Chocolate Ice Pops + buttered waffle strips + scrambled egg	
	Lunch or Dinner	Greek Meatballs with Tomato Sauce and Orzo	
SAT	Breakfast	*Leftover* Peanut Butter Power Pops + oat O's cereal + smashed blueberries	
	Lunch or Dinner	Easy Maple Pecan Baby Back Ribs + rice + steamed broccoli	

15

Recipes for Baby and Family

It's time to get cooking! Here you will find delicious recipes that will help you expose your baby to top allergens and keep them in the rotation at any meal of the day. If you're already used to cooking at home, you might find that many of your go-to recipes already incorporate allergens, and those are great to keep in your repertoire, too (remember, with modifications, baby can eat almost all the same foods that you do!). These recipes each include at least one allergen and most contain multiple allergens for additional exposure.

As a home cook without formal culinary training, I develop recipes that involve simple prep and not too many steps. I try to use as few ingredients, as many common allergens, and as much inactive time as possible, because I know firsthand what it's like to try to cook while squeezing in a quick nursing session, chasing a toddler, managing calls for work, folding the laundry, and whatever else is high up on your to-do list.

I also aim to prioritize flavor and create recipes that the entire family can enjoy together, largely because the power of shared mealtimes and eating with your baby is real. At this stage, the most important role model in your baby's life is you!

Breakfast

In the following collection of family-friendly breakfast recipes, you'll find both sweet and savory options. Two of my girls generally gravitate toward sweet breakfast foods while the other strongly prefers a savory breakfast, so I wanted to include a range of choices. Some are easy to meal-prep on the weekend, some are make-ahead casseroles, some are quick to assemble, and others take a bit more time. My two favorites from this collection are the Almond Cardamom Sheet Pan Pancakes and the Walnut-Crusted Butternut French Toast. Enjoy!

On the Sweet Side . . .

Peanut Butter Banana Mini Muffins **131**

Zucchini Walnut Bread **132**

Mascarpone Peanut Butter Melts **133**

6-Allergen Blender Pancakes **134**

Almond Cardamom Sheet Pan Pancakes **135**

Apple Oat Baby Bars **136**

Nutty French Toast Casserole **137**

Peanut Butter and Jelly Muffins **138**

Cinnamon Oat Breakfast Bars **139**

Strawberry Mango Chia Seed Pudding **140**

Baked PB Oatmeal Sticks **141**

Butternut Apple Muffin Cakes **142**

Walnut-Crusted Butternut French Toast **144**

Tahini Date Shake **145**

On the Savory Side . . .

Veggie Strata **146**

Rainbow Egg Bites **147**

Spinach Manchego Frittata **148**

Huevos Rancheros Sheet Pan Eggs **149**

Savory Scones **150**

Shrimpy Grits **152**

Peanut Butter Banana Mini Muffins

PEANUTS · **EGGS** · **COW'S MILK** · FISH · TREE NUTS · **WHEAT** · SOY · SHELLFISH · SESAME
1 g   1 g   1 g   1 g

If you're wondering why this recipe makes a double batch, it's because whenever I make these satisfying, peanutty little muffins, they disappear as quickly as I can crank them out!

1. Preheat the oven to 375°F. Lightly oil two mini or standard muffin pans, spray with nonstick cooking spray, or line with paper or silicone liners.

2. In a large bowl, whisk together the flours, baking powder, baking soda, and salt.

3. In a medium bowl, whisk together the eggs, milk, peanut butter, banana, and vanilla.

4. Fold the wet ingredients into the dry and mix just until moistened. Do not overmix (a few lumps are OK). Gently fold in the oatmeal and chocolate chips (if using) until just combined.

5. Fill the prepared muffin cups about three-quarters of the way with batter.

6. Bake until the tops are lightly browned and a toothpick inserted into the center of a muffin comes out clean, about 15 minutes for mini muffins or 18 minutes for standard muffins.

7. Cool in the pans on a cooling rack for about 10 minutes before serving. For BLF, cut the muffins in half and consider adding a swipe of butter or mascarpone cheese for easier swallowing. Store leftovers in an airtight container at room temperature for 1–2 days, in the refrigerator for up to 5 days, or in the freezer for up to 3 months.

MAKE IT A MEAL Serve with smashed berries and cottage cheese.

YIELD Makes 48 mini muffins or 24 standard muffins (2 mini-muffins or 1 standard muffin per serving)
PREP TIME 15 minutes
COOK TIME 15–18 minutes

1 cup **all-purpose flour**

1 cup **whole-wheat flour**

2 teaspoons baking powder

1 teaspoon baking soda

½ teaspoon kosher salt

2 large **eggs**

1 cup **whole milk**

¾ cup smooth **peanut butter**

1½ cups mashed ripe bananas, mashed (about 3 bananas)

1 teaspoon vanilla extract

1 cup plain, cooked oatmeal (made with ½ cup quick-cooking oats plus 1 cup **whole milk**)

1 cup **semisweet chocolate chips** (optional; consider omitting for babies younger than 2 years)

Zucchini Walnut Bread

PEANUTS **EGGS** **COW'S MILK** FISH **TREE NUTS** **WHEAT** SOY SHELLFISH SESAME
        1 g   1 g*   1 g   1 g

YIELD Makes 18 slices
(1 slice per serving)
PREP TIME 12 minutes
COOK TIME 55 minutes

2 small zucchinis,
trimmed and grated

⅓ cup extra-virgin olive oil

1 cup pureed prunes baby food

⅔ cup ground **walnuts**

½ cup ground flaxseeds

1 cup **whole wheat flour**

1 cup **all-purpose flour**

1 tablespoon baking soda

2 teaspoons baking powder

2 teaspoons ground cinnamon

¾ teaspoon ground cloves

¼ teaspoon kosher salt

2 large **eggs**

¾ cup light brown sugar

1 teaspoon vanilla extract

1 cup mini **semisweet chocolate
chips** (optional; consider omitting
for babies younger than 2 years)

*If using chocolate chips

I tested this recipe more than five times using different types of flour. The combination of whole wheat and all-purpose works well, although if you are feeling adventurous, substituting 2 cups of spelt flour for the whole wheat and all-purpose flours produces a slightly softer and sweeter bread. *Note: To make this recipe, you will need a food processor or nut grinder.*

1. Preheat the oven to 350°F. Lightly oil an 8½ × 4½-inch loaf pan or spray with nonstick cooking spray.

2. In a medium bowl, combine the zucchinis, olive oil, prunes, walnuts, and flaxseeds. Mix with a silicone spatula until well combined. For BLF, be sure your walnuts are finely ground in a food processor or nut grinder, without any larger pieces.

3. In a large bowl, whisk together the flours, baking soda, baking powder, cinnamon, cloves, and salt.

4. In a small bowl, whisk together the eggs, sugar, and vanilla until smooth. Pour the egg mixture into the zucchini mixture and mix well.

5. Fold the wet mixture into the dry and stir just until moistened. Do not overmix. Fold in the chocolate chips (if using).

6. Pour the batter into the prepared loaf pan and bake until a toothpick inserted into the center comes out clean, about 55 minutes.

7. Cool on a cooling rack for about 10 minutes before removing the bread from the pan. Store leftovers in an airtight container in the refrigerator for up to 1 week or in the freezer for up to 3 months.

MAKE IT A MEAL Serve with smashed raspberries and a dollop of mascarpone cheese for a balanced baby meal.

Mascarpone Peanut Butter Melts

PEANUTS EGGS **COW'S MILK** FISH TREE NUTS WHEAT SOY SHELLFISH SESAME
1 g 1 g

These dime-sized little melts offer an easy way to provide your baby with flavor, teething relief, and an interesting texture that melts in the mouth, as well as early exposure to two top allergenic foods (peanuts and cow's milk) and lots of important nutrients babies need, including protein, fat, fiber, vitamins, and minerals.

. . . .

1. Line a small rimmed baking sheet or large plate with parchment paper (it must fit in your freezer).

2. In a small bowl, use a fork to mash the banana. Add the mascarpone cheese and spices and mix with a spoon until well combined. Add the peanut butter and stir until completely incorporated.

3. Using a ½-teaspoon measuring spoon, drop dime-sized spoonfuls of the mixture on the lined baking sheet and freeze for at least 2 hours.

4. Remove from the freezer and serve immediately. For BLF, this recipe works best for babies who are using a pincer grasp. Store in an airtight container in the freezer for up to 2 months.

MAKE IT A MEAL Serve with smashed blueberries and plain oat O's cereal.

YIELD Makes 50 melts
(10 melts per serving)
PREP TIME 10 minutes
INACTIVE PREP TIME 2 hours

½ large, ripe banana

½ cup **mascarpone cheese**

⅛ teaspoon ground allspice

⅛ teaspoon ground cloves

⅛ teaspoon ground cinnamon

1 tablespoon smooth **peanut butter**

6-Allergen Blender Pancakes

PEANUTS	**EGGS**	**COW'S MILK**	FISH	**TREE NUTS**	**WHEAT**	**SOY**	SHELLFISH	SESAME
2 g	6 g	1 g		7 g	4 g	1 g		

YIELD Makes 12 pancakes
(3 pancakes per serving)
PREP TIME 7 minutes
COOK TIME 10 minutes

1 cup **almond flour**

1 cup **all-purpose flour**

½ cup plus 2 tablespoons plain,
unsweetened **soy milk**

¼ cup plain, **full-fat Greek yogurt**

2 tablespoons smooth
peanut butter

4 large **eggs**

1 teaspoon vanilla extract

1 teaspoon freshly squeezed
lemon juice

1 teaspoon baking soda

¼ teaspoon kosher salt

2 tablespoons **ghee**
or **unsalted butter**

MAKE IT A MEAL Serve with smashed
blueberries for a balanced baby meal.

These pancakes provide an impressive amount of nutrition, and the batter comes together in under 5 minutes in a blender. Best of all, the mixture incorporates six different allergens. Double the batch and freeze the extras for easy baby meals in a pinch, and feel free to experiment with mix-ins (such as blueberries and raspberries) for added flavor, texture, and nutrients. *Note: To make this recipe, you will need a blender.*

1. Combine all the ingredients except the ghee in a blender and blend until smooth.

2. Melt the ghee in a large skillet over medium heat.

3. Pour the batter into the skillet in 4-inch pools, three or four at a time. Cook until bubbles form in the batter, about 2 minutes, then flip and cook until the pancakes are cooked through, about 2 minutes more.

4. For BLF, slice the pancakes into finger-length strips for babies using a palmar grasp and chickpea-sized bites for babies using a pincer grasp. Serve warm. Store any leftovers in an airtight container in the refrigerator for up to 3 days or in the freezer for up to 3 months (separate them with parchment paper to make it easy to remove one or two at a time).

RECIPE NOTE Optional flavor variations:

- Add 2 additional tablespoons of peanut butter to the batter for a more robust, peanutty flavor.

- Add a mashed ripe banana to the batter for added sweetness without added sugars.

Almond Cardamom Sheet Pan Pancakes

PEANUTS **EGGS** **COW'S MILK** FISH **TREE NUTS** **WHEAT** **SOY** SHELLFISH SESAME
2 g 2 g 4 g 2 g 1 g

All the fun and fluffy satisfaction of pancakes, but without the mess of cleaning the skillet and stovetop! These sheet pan pancakes have been a game-changer in my home. I love making a double batch on the weekends and pulling them out on busy weekday mornings. Before freezing, cut your pancakes into the finger-size shape that works well for babies using a palmar grasp and layer between sheets of parchment paper so it's easy to grab one or two for your baby whenever you need a quick meal or snack.

1. Preheat the oven to 425°F. Lightly oil a 13 × 18-inch rimmed baking sheet or spray with nonstick cooking spray.

2. In a large bowl, whisk together the flours, flaxseeds, baking powder, sugar, cinnamon, salt, and cardamom. Add the milks, eggs, and vanilla and stir to combine fully.

3. Pour the batter evenly into the prepared baking sheet. Arrange the raspberries and banana slices evenly over the top.

4. Bake for 15 minutes, or until lightly browned.

5. Brush the top with the melted butter and serve warm. For BLF, slice into finger-length strips and top with a dollop of yogurt or fruit puree for easier swallowing. Store any leftovers in an airtight container in the refrigerator for up to 5 days or in the freezer for up to 3 months.

MAKE IT A MEAL Serve with a dollop of plain, full-fat yogurt for a balanced baby meal.

YIELD Serves 8
PREP TIME 10 minutes
COOK TIME 15 minutes

1½ cups **all-purpose flour**

1¼ cups **almond flour**

¼ cup ground flaxseeds

2 tablespoons baking powder

2 tablespoons sugar

1 teaspoon ground cinnamon

½ teaspoon kosher salt

⅛ teaspoon ground cardamom

1½ cups **whole milk**

1 cup plain, unsweetened **soy milk**

3 large **eggs**

1 teaspoon vanilla extract

1 cup fresh or thawed frozen raspberries

1 ripe banana, sliced

2 tablespoons unsalted **butter**, melted

Plain, **full-fat yogurt** or fruit puree, for serving (optional)

Apple Oat Baby Bars

PEANUTS   EGGS   **COW'S MILK**   FISH   **TREE NUTS**   **WHEAT**   SOY   SHELLFISH   SESAME

                     1 g   2 g   1 g

YIELD Makes 12 bars
(1 bar per serving)
PREP TIME 10 minutes
COOK TIME 45 minutes

½ cup quick-cooking oats

½ cup old-fashioned rolled oats

½ cup **almond flour**

½ cup **all-purpose flour**

½ teaspoon baking powder

1½ teaspoons ground cinnamon

¼ teaspoon kosher salt

1¼ cups unsweetened applesauce

1 cup **whole milk**

2 tablespoons coconut oil
or melted **ghee**

1 teaspoon vanilla extract

For the toppings (optional)
3 tablespoons **almond butter**

3 tablespoons plain,
full-fat yogurt

½ teaspoon ground cinnamon

For babies and kids under age 4, raw chunks of apple are a choking hazard and need to be modified before serving. This tasty bar offers an alternative way to introduce the flavor of apple in a form that is easier for babies to manage. Packed with oats, milk, a hint of vanilla, and a dash of cinnamon, these bars are subtly sweet, nutrient-rich, and deliciously filling. Drizzle with almond butter and/or yogurt for a bigger nutrient boost and additional top allergen exposure.

1. Preheat the oven to 375°F. Line an 8 × 8-inch baking pan with parchment paper.

2. In a large bowl, whisk together the oats, flours, baking powder, cinnamon, and salt.

3. In a medium bowl, whisk together the applesauce, milk, coconut oil, and vanilla.

4. Gradually add the dry mixture to the wet and beat until combined.

5. Pour the mixture into the prepared baking pan.

6. Bake until the bars are light golden brown, 40–45 minutes.

7. Cool on a cooling rack for 20–30 minutes, then cut into 12 bars. Drizzle the top with almond butter or yogurt and sprinkle with cinnamon, if you like. Store the bars in an airtight container in the refrigerator for up to 5 days.

MAKE IT A MEAL Slice into bars about the length of your finger and serve with a dipping sauce of plain, full-fat yogurt mixed with almond butter along with a side of paper-thin slices of peeled cucumber.

Nutty French Toast Casserole

PEANUTS	EGGS	COW'S MILK	FISH	TREE NUTS	WHEAT	SOY	SHELLFISH	SESAME
2 g	5 g	1 g		1 g	3 g	1 g		

I love assembling this recipe on a quiet weekend evening and baking it first thing in the morning so that my girls wake up to the scent of cinnamon and roasted nuts. It's a great breakfast for days when there are lots of activities on the schedule and you're looking for something filling that provides long-lasting energy.

1. Lightly oil a 9 × 13-inch baking dish.

2. In a medium saucepan, combine the ghee, peanut butter, cashew butter, brown sugar, and 1 teaspoon cinnamon and cook over medium-low heat, stirring frequently, for 3–4 minutes, until the sugar has dissolved and the mixture is smooth. Pour the mixture into the prepared baking dish.

3. Scatter the bread cubes evenly over the top.

4. In a medium bowl, whisk together the eggs, milks, and vanilla. Pour the egg mixture evenly over the bread. Press the bread into the mixture so that all the pieces are moistened throughout. Sprinkle the remaining ½ teaspoon cinnamon over the top.

5. Cover and refrigerate for at least 1 hour, preferably overnight.

6. Preheat the oven to 350°F.

7. Uncover the casserole and bake for 50–55 minutes until lightly browned and pulling away from the sides of the baking dish. Cool on a cooling rack for about 10 minutes before serving. For BLF, slice into finger-length strips for babies using a palmar or pincer grasp and coach your baby to take small bites. Store leftovers in an airtight container in the refrigerator for up to 3 days.

MAKE IT A MEAL Serve with thin strips of ripe mango or pear.

YIELD Serves 8
PREP TIME 15 minutes
INACTIVE PREP TIME 1 hour
COOK TIME 55 minutes

½ cup **ghee**

¼ cup smooth **peanut butter**

¼ cup smooth **cashew butter**

½ cup brown sugar

1½ teaspoons ground cinnamon, divided

9-ounce loaf **sourdough bread**, cut into ½-inch cubes (about 4½ cups)

6 large **eggs**

1 cup **whole milk**

1 cup plain, unsweetened **soy milk**

1 teaspoon vanilla extract

Peanut Butter and Jelly Muffins

PEANUTS   **EGGS**   **COW'S MILK**   FISH   TREE NUTS   WHEAT   SOY   SHELLFISH   SESAME
2 g   1 g   1 g

YIELD Makes 12 muffins
(1 muffin per serving)
PREP TIME 10 minutes
COOK TIME 20 minutes

1 cup oat flour

1 teaspoon baking powder

1 teaspoon baking soda

1 large **egg**

2 large ripe bananas, mashed
(about 1 cup mashed banana)

½ cup smooth **peanut butter**

½ cup **sour cream**

1 teaspoon vanilla extract

½ cup raspberries

**Butter, ghee, mascarpone
cheese,** or **créme fraîche,**
for topping (optional)

MAKE IT A MEAL Serve with scrambled egg, additional smashed raspberries, and cheese shreds for a balanced baby meal.

These muffins make it easy and delicious to keep peanut consistently and frequently in your baby's diet. Experiment with adding different types of chopped fruit—smashed raspberries are my favorite, but blueberries and blackberries are tasty, nutritious options that work equally well.

1. Preheat the oven to 350°F. Lightly oil a standard muffin pan, spray with cooking spray, or line with paper or silicone liners.

2. In a large bowl, whisk together the flour, baking powder, and baking soda.

3. In a medium bowl, whisk the egg until smooth, then add the bananas, peanut butter, sour cream, and vanilla and whisk until well mixed.

4. Add the wet mixture to the dry and mix until just combined. Do not overmix. Fold in the raspberries.

5. Fill the prepared muffin cups about three-quarters of the way with batter.

6. Bake until the tops are lightly browned and a toothpick inserted into the center of a muffin comes out clean, 22–25 minutes.

7. Cool in the pan on a cooling rack for 10 minutes before serving. For BLF, cut the muffins in half and consider adding a thin layer of your favorite topping for easier swallowing. Store leftovers in an airtight container in the refrigerator for up to 5 days or in the freezer for up to 2 months. Thaw overnight in the fridge or for an hour at room temperature. Gently reheat in the oven or toaster oven on low heat.

Cinnamon Oat Breakfast Bars

PEANUTS **EGGS** COW'S MILK FISH **TREE NUTS** **WHEAT** **SOY** SHELLFISH SESAME
        1 g*   2 g   1 g   1 g*

These breakfast bars are a great option for weekend meal prep. I love prepping a batch on Sunday and having them on hand as a quick, portable breakfast for the busy weekdays ahead. If your baby or child struggles with constipation, the prune puree in these bars can help get things moving! The texture can sometimes be a bit sticky, so coach your baby to take small bites and, as always, supervise closely when serving. *Note: To make this recipe, you will need a blender or a food processor.*

1. Preheat the oven to 350°F. Line a rimmed baking sheet with parchment paper.

2. Put the prunes in a small bowl. Pour the boiling water over the prunes and let sit for 5 minutes.

3. While the prunes are hydrating, combine the flours, eggs, oil, flaxseeds, cinnamon, almond extract, and salt in a large bowl and mix until well combined. Fold in the oats.

4. Pour the prunes and soaking water into a blender or food processor and puree. Stir the pureed prunes into the batter and mix until well combined.

5. Scoop the mixture onto the prepared baking sheet. Spread it out evenly using a spatula until it's about ½ inch thick.

6. Bake until golden brown, about 15 minutes.

7. Cool for 10–15 minutes, then slice into 24 bars. Store in an airtight container in the refrigerator for up to 1 week.

MAKE IT A MEAL Serve with strips of fried egg and ripe cantaloupe for a balanced baby meal.

YIELD Makes 24 bars
(2 bars per serving)
PREP TIME 15 minutes
COOK TIME 15 minutes

2 cups pitted prunes

½ cup boiling water

1 cup **almond flour**

½ cup **all-purpose flour**

2 large **eggs**, beaten, or ½ cup **silken tofu**

⅓ cup avocado oil

⅓ cup ground flaxseeds

1 teaspoon ground cinnamon

½ teaspoon **almond extract**

¼ teaspoon kosher salt

½ cup quick-cooking oats

*Depending on whether you use eggs or tofu.

Strawberry Mango Chia Seed Pudding

PEANUTS	EGGS	COW'S MILK	FISH	TREE NUTS	WHEAT	SOY	SHELLFISH	SESAME
		1 g		1 g*		1 g		

YIELD Serves 6
(½ cup per serving)
PREP TIME 5 minutes

½ cup plain, unsweetened **soy milk**

½ cup canned full-fat coconut milk

½ cup plain, **whole kefir**

1 cup fresh or thawed frozen mango chunks

1 cup fresh or thawed frozen strawberries

1 tablespoon sugar

½ cup chia seeds

⅓ cup ground, toasted **macadamia nuts**, for topping (optional)

¼ cup toasted, shredded, unsweetened coconut, for topping (optional)

This pudding is high in protein, naturally sweet, and a great way to consistently include soy, tree nuts, and dairy in the diet. For optimal sweetness and texture, use very ripe mangoes. For a smooth, mousse-like texture, try blending the chia seeds along with the fruit mixture rather than stirring them in by hand. To make this recipe, you will need a high-speed blender.

1. Combine the milks, kefir, mango, strawberries, and sugar in a blender and puree, stopping to scrape down the sides as needed.

2. Transfer the mixture to a bowl and stir in the chia seeds. Cover and refrigerate for about 20 minutes, or until the pudding thickens.

3. Top with macadamia nuts and/or shredded coconut, if you like, and serve cold. Store leftovers in an airtight container in the refrigerator for up to 3 days.

MAKE IT A MEAL Serve with strips of French toast for a balanced baby breakfast.

*If using macadamia nuts

Baked PB Oatmeal Sticks

PEANUTS   **EGGS**   **COW'S MILK**   FISH   TREE NUTS   WHEAT   **SOY**   SHELLFISH   SESAME
2 g   2 g   1 g   1 g

When your baby is ready to self-feed, these bars offer a helpful way to serve oatmeal without the need for a spoon or bowl. Slice into finger-length sticks that your baby can easily grasp and nibble on. I've found these bars to be helpful for older kids as well on those wacky weekday mornings when the most we have time for is a grab-and-go breakfast option they can eat on their way to school.

1. Preheat the oven to 375°F. Lightly oil an 8 × 8-inch baking pan or spray with nonstick cooking spray.

2. In a large bowl, whisk together the oats, baking powder, cinnamon, and salt.

3. Cut one of the bananas into chickpea-sized bites and the other into thin rounds. Set the banana rounds aside.

4. Add the chopped bananas, milks, eggs, peanut butter, and vanilla to the dry ingredients. Mix with a silicone spatula until well combined.

5. Pour the mixture into the prepared baking pan and scatter the banana rounds evenly over the top of the mixture.

6. Bake until cooked through and lightly golden on top, 35–40 minutes.

7. Cool on a cooling rack for 10 minutes, then slice and serve. Store leftovers in an airtight container in the refrigerator for up to 4 days or in the freezer for up to 3 months.

RECIPE NOTE Gently reheat leftovers in an oven or toaster oven at 350°F for 5–10 minutes.

MAKE IT A MEAL Serve with a dollop of plain, full-fat cottage cheese and some smashed blackberries for a balanced baby breakfast.

YIELD Makes 8 bars
(1 bar per serving)
PREP TIME 10 minutes
COOK TIME 40 minutes

2 cups old-fashioned rolled oats

1 teaspoon baking powder

1 teaspoon ground cinnamon

½ teaspoon kosher salt

2 large bananas

1 cup **whole milk**

1 cup plain, unsweetened **soy milk**

2 large **eggs**

¼ cup smooth **peanut butter**

1 teaspoon vanilla extract

Butternut Apple Muffin Cakes

PEANUTS   **EGGS**   **COW'S MILK**   FISH   **TREE NUTS**   **WHEAT**   SOY   SHELLFISH   SESAME

         1 g   2 g   1 g   3 g

YIELD Makes 12 muffins
(1 muffin per serving)
PREP TIME 20 minutes
COOK TIME 20 minutes

A riff on classic morning glory muffins, this baby-friendly version gets a boost of fiber, vitamins, minerals, and antioxidants from butternut squash, walnuts, carrot, and apple. When my oldest turned 1, I topped these muffin cakes with homemade cream cheese frosting and served them at her first birthday party as individual nutrient-rich smash cakes that everyone could enjoy—babies and adults alike. *Note: To make this recipe, you will need a food processor and an electric mixer for the frosting.*

For the muffin cakes

1½ cups **whole wheat flour**

1 cup old-fashioned rolled oats

½ cup finely ground **walnuts, pecans,** or **hazelnuts**

⅓ cup white sugar

¼ cup shredded coconut (optional)

2 teaspoons pumpkin pie spice

1 teaspoon baking soda

½ teaspoon baking powder

2 large **eggs**

1 cup canned butternut squash puree

¾ cup peeled and finely grated apple (1 large or 2 small apples)

¾ cup peeled and finely grated carrot (1 large or 2 small carrots)

⅓ cup **whole milk**

¼ cup melted **ghee**

1 teaspoon vanilla extract

For the frosting

½ cup **heavy cream**

8 ounces **cream cheese**

2 tablespoons confectioners' sugar

½ teaspoon vanilla extract

1. Preheat the oven to 375°F. Lightly oil a standard muffin pan, spray with nonstick cooking spray, or line with paper or silicone liners.

2. In a medium bowl, whisk together the flour, oats, ground nuts, white sugar, coconut (if using), pumpkin pie spice, baking soda, and baking powder. For BLF, be sure your nuts are finely ground in a food processor or nut grinder, without any larger pieces.

3. In a large bowl, whisk together the eggs, butternut squash, apple, carrot, milk, ghee, and vanilla.

4. Add the dry ingredients to the wet and use a silicone spatula to combine.

5. Fill the prepared muffin cups about three-quarters of the way with batter.

6. Bake until a toothpick inserted into a muffin cake comes out clean, about 20 minutes.

7. Cool completely in the pan on a cooling rack before frosting.

8. To make the frosting, whip the cream with an electric mixer on medium-high speed until it is billowy and forms soft peaks.

9. Add the cream cheese, confectioners' sugar, and vanilla and beat until smooth.

10. Once the muffin cakes are cool, frost and serve. For BLF, cut the muffins in half and coach your baby to take small bites. Store unfrosted muffin cakes in an airtight container in the refrigerator for up to 5 days or in the freezer for up to 3 months. Extra frosting will keep in an airtight container in the refrigerator for up to 2 weeks and in the freezer for up to 3 months.

RECIPE NOTES

- If you prefer to make your own butternut squash puree, peel, seed, and cube a medium butternut squash, toss with 1 tablespoon olive oil in a large baking pan, and bake for 25–35 minutes at 400°F. Cool, then puree in a food processor or blender with about ½ cup water, adding more if needed to achieve the desired consistency.

- The medium or fine side of a box grater works well to finely grate the apples and carrots.

- For nut-free muffin cakes, omit the walnuts.

- To save time, use unsweetened applesauce instead of grated fresh apples and finely chop the carrots in a food processor.

MAKE IT A MEAL Offer with a strip of scrambled egg and a thawed frozen strawberry.

Walnut-Crusted Butternut French Toast

PEANUTS   **EGGS**   **COW'S MILK**   FISH   **TREE NUTS**   **WHEAT**   SOY   SHELLFISH   SESAME
　　　　　　3 g　　　　1 g　　　　　　　　　3 g　　　　4 g

SERVINGS Serves 4
(1 slice per serving)
PREP TIME 10 minutes
COOK TIME 10 minutes

2 large **eggs**

¼ cup **whole milk**

¼ cup canned butternut squash puree

½ teaspoon vanilla extract

1 teaspoon pumpkin pie spice, divided

1 cup ground **walnuts, pecans, or almonds**

4 slices **whole wheat sourdough bread**

1 tablespoon **ghee**

MAKE IT A MEAL Serve with quartered grapes and a dollop of plain, full-fat yogurt for a balanced baby breakfast. You can boost the nutritional content of this meal even further by adding nutrient-dense (and tasty!) toppings, such as a drizzle of fruit puree or nut or seed butter.

The aromas of pumpkin pie spice and toasty walnuts never fail to draw my girls into the kitchen whenever I cook this nutrient-rich classic boosted with vitamin-rich butternut squash puree and a brain-building crust of ground walnuts. Butternut squash is rich in vitamin C and a good source of beta carotene, the plant form of vitamin A, which supports overall growth as well as eye and bone health. *Note: To make this recipe, you will need a food processor.*

1. In a large, shallow bowl, whisk together the eggs, milk, butternut squash, vanilla, and ½ teaspoon pumpkin pie spice.

2. In a separate shallow bowl, mix the ground nuts and remaining ½ teaspoon pumpkin pie spice. For BLF, be sure your nuts are finely ground in a food processor or nut grinder, without any larger pieces.

3. Dredge each slice of bread in the egg mixture, fully coating both sides. Then press each side of the bread into the nut mixture until coated.

4. Melt the ghee in a large skillet (preferably cast iron, to help boost your baby's iron intake) over medium heat. Place the bread in the skillet in a single layer (work in batches if you need to) and cook until golden brown, 3–4 minutes per side.

5. For babies and toddlers, cut into strips or small bites. Store leftovers in an airtight container in the refrigerator for up to 3 days.

RECIPE NOTE To make this recipe nut-free, replace the walnuts with 1 cup quick-cooking oats or a mixture of hemp and ground flaxseeds.

Tahini Date Shake

PEANUTS   EGGS   COW'S MILK   FISH   TREE NUTS   WHEAT   **SOY**   SHELLFISH   **SESAME**

                                                          4 g   5 g

The natural sweetness of bananas and dates will make you feel like you're drinking a milkshake when you taste this creamy, Middle East–inspired drink. But thanks to the filling doses of protein and fat from the soy milk and tahini, it's wholesome and satisfying enough to work well as a breakfast or afternoon snack. *Note: To make this recipe, you will need a blender.*

....

1. If you do not have a high-speed blender, soak the dates in the milk for 15 minutes beforehand to soften them and make them easier to blend.

2. Combine the dates, milk, frozen bananas, tahini, vanilla, and cinnamon in a high-speed or regular blender and blend until smooth. Taste and add more vanilla or cinnamon if desired.

3. Garnish with a sprinkle of cinnamon and sesame seeds and serve. This smoothie does not keep well in the refrigerator and is best enjoyed right away as a beverage. If you have leftovers, you can pour them into ice pop molds and freeze for up to 3 months.

MAKE IT A MEAL Serve with plain oat O's cereal and orange slices for a balanced baby meal.

YIELD Serves 2 (1 cup per serving)
PREP TIME 5–20 minutes

4 Medjool dates, pitted

1 cup plain, unsweetened **soy milk**

2 sliced, frozen bananas

¼ cup **tahini (sesame paste)**

½ teaspoon vanilla extract, plus more to taste

½ teaspoon ground cinnamon, plus more for optional garnish

Sesame seeds, for garnish (optional)

Veggie Strata

PEANUTS **EGGS** **COW'S MILK** FISH TREE NUTS **WHEAT** **SOY** SHELLFISH SESAME
6 g 7 g 3 g 2 g

YIELD Serves 12
PREP TIME 25 minutes
INACTIVE PREP TIME 1 hour
COOK TIME 1 hour

12 large **eggs**

3 cups plain, unsweetened **soy milk**

1 teaspoon dried thyme

½ teaspoon garlic powder

½ teaspoon kosher salt

½ teaspoon freshly ground black pepper

1½ cups shredded **sharp cheddar cheese** (about 9 ounces)

1½ cups shredded **smoked Gouda cheese** (about 9 ounces)

1 cup finely chopped mushrooms

1 cup finely chopped scallions (green parts only)

1 cup finely chopped baby spinach

½ cup finely chopped roasted red pepper

1 (12-ounce) loaf **sourdough bread,** cut into ½-inch cubes (about 8 cups)

This strata is a great make-ahead breakfast option when you have overnight guests or are feeding a large group. Prepare and refrigerate it the night before and pop it in the oven first thing in the morning. If you have a food processor, save time by using it to finely chop your veggies.

1. Lightly oil a 9 × 13-inch baking pan or 3-quart casserole dish or spray with nonstick cooking spray.

2. In a large bowl, whisk together the eggs, milk, thyme, garlic powder, salt, and pepper. Add the cheeses, mushrooms, scallions, spinach, and red pepper and stir to combine.

3. Scatter the bread evenly across the bottom of the prepared baking pan, then pour the egg mixture over the top. Gently fold the ingredients together until all of the bread has been moistened. Cover with aluminum foil and refrigerate for at least 1 hour or preferably overnight.

4. Preheat the oven to 375°F.

5. Bake the strata (still covered with foil) for 30 minutes, then remove the foil, rotate the pan for even cooking, and bake until the top is lightly browned and the eggs are set throughout, about 30 minutes more.

6. Cool for 5 minutes, then slice and serve. For BLF, slice into strips for babies using a palmar grasp and coach your baby to take small bites. For babies using a pincer grasp, you can still serve strips, or cut into bite-sized pieces for self-feeding. Store leftovers in an airtight container in the refrigerator for up to 5 days or in the freezer for up to 3 months.

MAKE IT A MEAL Serve with sticks of cantaloupe or honeydew melon.

Rainbow Egg Bites

PEANUTS | **EGGS** | **COW'S MILK** | FISH | TREE NUTS | **WHEAT** | **SOY** | SHELLFISH | SESAME
8 g | 1 g | | | <1 g | 1 g

Packed with protein, choline, vitamin D, and plenty of vegetables, these egg bites build four top allergens into one easy dish. For the full rainbow effect, use a combination of red, orange, and green bell peppers. You can always change up the mix-ins to match your preferences or use up whatever veggies you happen to have in your refrigerator.

1. Preheat the oven to 350°F. Lightly oil a standard muffin pan, spray with nonstick cooking spray, or line with paper or silicone liners. Sprinkle a bit of flour evenly into each muffin cup.

2. In a large bowl, whisk together the eggs and tofu just until smooth. Do not overbeat or the egg bites will deflate. Add the flour, baking soda, salt, pepper, garlic powder, Italian seasoning, and smoked paprika. Gently whisk until combined. Stir in the diced peppers, onion, and cheese.

3. Fill the prepared muffin cups about three-quarters of the way with batter.

4. Place a large rimmed baking sheet on the oven rack, then place the muffin pan on the baking sheet. Pour enough water into the baking sheet so that the muffin pan sits in ½ inch or so of water without overflowing.

5. Bake until the eggs are set and cooked through, about 30 minutes.

6. Cool in the pan on a cooling rack for about 10 minutes before serving. For BLF, cut the egg bites in half for babies using a palmar grasp and cut into chickpea-sized bites for babies using a pincer grasp. Store in an airtight container in the refrigerator for up to 2 days or in the freezer for up to 1 month.

MAKE IT A MEAL Serve with hash browns and strips of cantaloupe.

YIELD Makes 12 bites
(2 bites per serving)
PREP TIME 15 minutes
COOK TIME 30 minutes

2 tablespoons **all-purpose flour**, plus more for sprinkling

8 large **eggs**

½ cup **silken tofu**

1 teaspoon baking soda

½ teaspoon kosher salt

¼ teaspoon freshly ground black pepper

¼ teaspoon garlic powder

¼ teaspoon Italian seasoning

⅛ teaspoon smoked paprika

¾ cup diced bell peppers (any color or a mix)

⅓ cup diced red onion

½ cup grated **Parmesan cheese**

RECIPE NOTE Make a double batch on the weekend and freeze for busy weekday mornings. Leftovers can be gently reheated in the microwave or oven.

BREAKFAST

Spinach Manchego Frittata

PEANUTS **EGGS** **COW'S MILK** FISH TREE NUTS WHEAT SOY SHELLFISH SESAME
         9 g   2 g

YIELD Serves 6
PREP TIME 10 minutes
COOK TIME 25 minutes

9 large **eggs**

3 tablespoons whole **milk**

½ cup grated **Manchego cheese** (about 4 ounces), plus 2 tablespoons for topping

1 teaspoon dried parsley or 1 tablespoon minced fresh flat-leaf parsley

½ teaspoon kosher salt

⅛ teaspoon freshly ground black pepper

2 tablespoons extra-virgin olive oil

1 medium onion, diced

1 garlic clove, minced

10 ounces baby spinach

MAKE IT A MEAL Serve with strips of buttered toast and wedges of orange for a balanced baby meal.

RECIPE NOTE The recipe also works well with grated cheddar, Parmesan, or Colby Jack cheese.

I'm a sucker for easy, tasty recipes that come together quickly, and I love having this recipe on hand for busy evenings when I don't have much time to cook. Save more time by skipping the fresh spinach and instead using frozen spinach that has been thawed and squeezed to remove excess moisture.

1. In a medium bowl, whisk together the eggs, milk, cheese, parsley, salt, and pepper; set aside.

2. In a 10-inch cast-iron skillet, heat the olive oil over medium heat. Add the onion and cook, stirring continuously, until softened and translucent, about 5 minutes. Add the garlic and cook until fragrant, about 1 minute. Add the spinach a little at a time and stir until it all cooks down and fits in the skillet, about 4 minutes.

3. Pour the egg mixture into the skillet and tilt it until the eggs are evenly distributed under and around the vegetables throughout the pan. Sprinkle a little more cheese evenly across the top. Turn the heat down to low, cover, and cook until the frittata is set around the edges but still jiggly in the middle, about 15 minutes.

4. While the frittata cooks, position an oven rack in the highest position and preheat the oven to broil.

5. Transfer the skillet to the oven and broil until the top of the frittata is lightly browned, about 1 minute.

6. Cool in the skillet for about 5 minutes, then cut into 6 wedges and serve. For BLF, slice the frittata into finger-length strips for babies using a palmar grasp or chickpea-sized bites for babies using a pincer grasp. Store leftovers in an airtight container in the refrigerator for up to 3 days.

Huevos Rancheros Sheet Pan Eggs

PEANUTS   **EGGS**   **COW'S MILK**   FISH   TREE NUTS   WHEAT   **SOY**   SHELLFISH   SESAME
           14 g   2 g   1 g

This twist on classic huevos rancheros is convenient for feeding large families and makes it easy to whip up a quick, balanced meal. Eggs provide zinc, which supports the developing immune system, and choline, which is important for brain development. The addition of black beans provides plant-based protein, fiber, and iron, which benefits from increased absorption thanks to vitamin C–rich tomatoes.

1. Preheat the oven to 350°F. Lightly oil the bottom and sides of a 13 × 18-inch rimmed baking sheet or spray with nonstick cooking spray.

2. Heat the olive oil in a medium skillet over medium heat. Add the tomato and onion and cook, stirring continuously, until soft, about 3 minutes. Remove the pan from the heat.

3. Whisk the eggs, milk, lime juice, garlic powder, onion powder, oregano, cumin, paprika, and pepper in a large bowl until smooth. Add the sautéed tomato and onion and the cheese and gently stir.

4. Pour the mixture into the prepared baking sheet. Sprinkle the black beans and scallions evenly over the top.

5. Bake for 20 minutes, or until the center of the egg mixture is set.

6. Garnish with the cilantro and serve warm. For BLF, use the flat side of a fork to smash any black beans in the slices for your baby. Cut into finger-length strips for babies using a palmar grasp or small bites for babies using a pincer grasp, or mash into a shallow bowl and allow your baby to scoop with hands. Store leftovers in an airtight container in the refrigerator for up to 3 days.

MAKE IT A MEAL Serve with a side of steamed green beans and baked potato fries for a balanced meal.

YIELD Serves 8
PREP TIME 15 minutes
COOK TIME 20 minutes

1 teaspoon extra-virgin olive oil

¾ cup diced tomato

⅓ cup finely diced red onion

18 large **eggs**

½ cup plain, unsweetened **soy milk**

1 tablespoon freshly squeezed lime juice

½ teaspoon garlic powder

½ teaspoon onion powder

½ teaspoon dried oregano

½ teaspoon ground cumin

½ teaspoon paprika

¼ teaspoon freshly ground black pepper

½ cup shredded **cheddar cheese**

½ cup canned low-sodium black beans

2 tablespoons finely chopped scallions (green parts only)

¼ cup finely chopped cilantro

149

Savory Scones

PEANUTS   EGGS   **COW'S MILK**   FISH   TREE NUTS   **WHEAT**   **SOY**   SHELLFISH   SESAME
                         2 g   2 g   <1 g

YIELD Makes 8 scones
(1 scone per serving)
PREP TIME 15 minutes
COOK TIME 35 minutes

My middle daughter has always loved savory breakfasts, and these scones are one of her favorites. For best results, be sure your butter, yogurt, and soy milk are as cold as possible to ensure the scones rise during the baking process.

1⅓ cups **all-purpose flour**, plus more for dusting

2½ teaspoons baking powder

1 teaspoon kosher salt

1 cup grated **Parmesan cheese**

5 tablespoons unsalted **butter**, well chilled and cubed, plus more for serving

¼ cup finely chopped fresh chives

1 tablespoon finely chopped fresh basil

¼ teaspoon freshly ground black pepper

¼ cup plain, **full-fat Greek yogurt**, well chilled

¼ cup plain, unsweetened **soy milk**, well chilled

1. Preheat the oven to 375°F. Line a rimmed baking sheet with parchment paper.

2. In a food processor, gently pulse the flour, baking powder, salt, and cheese a few times, just until mixed (or hand mix with a silicone spatula in a large bowl).

3. Add the cold butter and gently pulse (or hand mix) until the pieces of butter are about the size of corn kernels.

4. If using a food processor, transfer the mixture to a large bowl. Add the chives, basil, and pepper and gently stir to combine.

5. In a small bowl, mix the cold yogurt and milk, then add to the flour mixture and mix with a fork until most of the dry ingredients are moistened (a few dry spots are OK).

6. Using your hands, knead the dough five or six times inside the bowl until the dough just barely comes together, taking care not to oversoften the butter or overwork the dough, as this will prevent the scones from rising.

7. Sprinkle a bit of flour on the parchment-lined baking sheet. Form the dough into a 1-inch-thick circle on the parchment. Slice the circle into four equal quarters like a pizza, then slice each quarter in half, creating eight even wedges. Spread out the wedges on the parchment.

8. Bake until puffy and lightly golden, about 35 minutes.

9. Transfer the scones to a cooling rack and cool for 10 minutes before serving. For BLF, slice into finger-length strips and top with a little butter for easier swallowing. These scones are best enjoyed fresh out of the oven, but leftovers can be stored in an airtight container at room temperature for up to 2 days.

MAKE IT A MEAL Serve with scrambled eggs and strips of soft, ripe cantaloupe for a balanced baby meal.

Shrimpy Grits

PEANUTS   EGGS   **COW'S MILK**   FISH   TREE NUTS   WHEAT   **SOY**   **SHELLFISH**   SESAME
9 g   2 g   23 g

YIELD Serves 4 (1 cup per serving)
PREP TIME 12 minutes
COOK TIME 15 minutes

2 cups low-sodium chicken broth

1 cup **whole milk**

1 cup plain, unsweetened **soy milk**

1 tablespoon tomato paste

1 tablespoon **ghee**

½ teaspoon kosher salt

¼ teaspoon freshly ground
black pepper

¾ cup old-fashioned grits

1 cup shredded **cheddar cheese**

1 pound large raw **shrimp**
(16–20 per pound), peeled and
deveined

1 tablespoon Italian seasoning

1 teaspoon paprika

6 slices bacon

3 garlic cloves, minced

2 tablespoons finely chopped
fresh chives

This traditional breakfast dish has its origins in South Carolina. The soft, flexible texture of the cheesy grits holds together well and can work as a finger food for babies who are inclined to self-feed. Mix the shredded shrimp into your baby's portion of grits so it's easier for them to scoop everything up with their hands.

1. In a large saucepan, combine the broth, milks, tomato paste, ghee, salt, and pepper and bring to a boil over medium-high heat. Turn the heat down to low, add the grits, cover, and simmer, stirring occasionally, until thickened, 10–15 minutes. Fold in the cheese and stir to combine.

2. While the grits cook, toss the shrimp in a medium bowl with the Italian seasoning and paprika until coated; set aside.

3. Fry the bacon in a large skillet over medium heat until browned and crispy, 5–6 minutes. Transfer the bacon to a paper towel–lined plate, then drain off most of the bacon drippings from the skillet, leaving about 1 tablespoon in the skillet.

4. Add the shrimp and garlic to the skillet and cook over medium heat until the shrimp is pink and cooked through, about 4 minutes. Remove the pan from the heat.

5. Crumble the bacon into bits.

6. Serve the grits topped with the shrimp, bacon bits, and chives. For BLF, finely mince the shrimp and bacon and mix them into the grits, then serve on a preloaded spoon or allow your baby to scoop with their hands from a shallow bowl. Store leftovers in an airtight container in the refrigerator for up to 2 days.

MAKE IT A MEAL Serve with sticks or wedges of watermelon.

I categorized the lighter, less time-consuming recipes in this book as lunches, but truth be told, all of the lunch and dinner recipes are interchangeable and can be served at whatever time of the day suits you best. Keep an eye out for the Shrimp and Vegetable Fritters and the Shells and Cheese with Carrots and Peas— my girls can't get enough of them.

Seafood and Poultry

Sardine Avotoasts 154

Super Salmon Salad with Pickled Red Onion 155

Cheesy Crab Dip 156

Shrimp and Vegetable Fritters 157

Seafood Sliders with Lemon Aioli 158

Shrimp and Broccoli Croquettes 160

Tarragon Chicken Salad 162

Plant-Based

Sesame Eggplant Dip 163

Edamame Tahini Dip 164

English Muffin Baby Pizzas 165

Baby-Friendly Cashew Dip 166

Peanut Apple Fritters 167

Sweet Potato Almond Butter Mash 168

Shells and Cheese with Carrots and Peas 169

Cottage Cheese Mash 170

Pinkalicious Beet Hummus 171

Tahini Egg Salad 172

Presto Pressed Pesto Grilled Cheese 173

Lunch

Sardine Avotoasts

PEANUTS **EGGS** COW'S MILK **FISH** TREE NUTS **WHEAT** SOY SHELLFISH SESAME
       3 g   7 g   4 g

YIELD Makes 4 toasts
(1 toast per serving)
PREP TIME 10 minutes
COOK TIME 15 minutes

2 large **eggs**

1 (4-ounce) can boneless, skinless **sardines** in olive oil

2 teaspoons **mayonnaise**

2 teaspoons finely chopped scallions (green parts only)

1 teaspoon drained capers, rinsed

1 teaspoon chopped fresh dill

Grated zest of 1 lemon, plus 1 tablespoon freshly squeezed lemon juice

½ teaspoon Dijon mustard

4 slices whole-grain **sourdough bread**

½ avocado, peeled and pitted

This balanced meal is a nutrient powerhouse for babies and comes together quickly and easily. It provides exposure to three top allergens along with several key nutrients that help support growing brains and bodies, including omega-3 fatty acids, iron, and choline.

1. Put the eggs in a small saucepan and cover with water. Bring to a boil, then turn the heat down to a simmer and cook for 14 minutes, until hard-boiled. Transfer the eggs to a strainer and cool for a few minutes under cold running water.

2. While the eggs are cooking, in a medium bowl, combine the sardines, mayonnaise, scallions, capers, dill, lemon zest and juice, and mustard and mix well, breaking up the sardines into small flakes.

3. Toast the bread until it is lightly browned but still has some give.

4. Peel the eggs and thinly slice.

5. Mash a quarter of the avocado onto each toast and top with slices of hard-boiled egg and sardine salad. For BLF, slice the toasts into strips and hand to baby at chest level for self-feeding, coaching your baby to take small bites. You can also deconstruct the recipe and serve the eggs sliced into wedges, the avocado on toast cut into strips, and the sardine mixture in a shallow bowl for scooping with hands or on a preloaded spoon. This recipe is best eaten right away and does not store well.

MAKE IT A MEAL Serve with steamed broccoli florets for a balanced baby meal.

Super Salmon Salad with Pickled Red Onion

PEANUTS   **EGGS**   **COW'S MILK**   **FISH**   TREE NUTS   WHEAT   SOY   SHELLFISH   SESAME
          <1 g   1 g   18 g

This salmon salad is a versatile, simple way to enjoy a protein-packed meal over a bed of greens, in a sandwich, or, if serving to your baby, on a strip of toast. The fat in the Greek yogurt and mayonnaise makes this salad easier for babies to swallow, and the pickled onions are a great potential source of probiotics. When pickling your onions, choose diluted and filtered apple cider vinegar without honey.

1. Put the onion in a small bowl, pour in the vinegar, cover, and refrigerate for at least 1 hour (or overnight for more flavor).

2. Finely dice the pickled red onion and transfer to a medium bowl. Add the remaining ingredients and mix well with a fork.

3. Serve this salmon salad on toast, crackers, or greens. For BLF, serve on a strip of toast, on a preloaded spoon, or in a shallow bowl for scooping with hands. Store leftovers in an airtight container in the refrigerator for up to 3 days.

RECIPE NOTE This type of pickled onion is appropriate for temporary refrigeration only—not canning—and will last in an airtight container in the refrigerator for up to 2 weeks.

MAKE IT A MEAL Serve with wedges of tomato for a balanced baby meal.

YIELD Serves 2
(¾ cup per serving)
PREP TIME 10 minutes
INACTIVE PREP TIME 1 hours

½ cup apple cider vinegar

½ red onion, peeled and thinly sliced

1 (6-ounce) can **salmon**, drained

1 tablespoon plain, **full-fat Greek yogurt**

1 tablespoon **mayonnaise**

¼ cup finely grated carrot

1 tablespoon freshly squeezed lemon juice

½ teaspoon dried dill

½ teaspoon garlic powder

½ teaspoon ground mustard

¼ teaspoon kosher salt (optional)

Cheesy Crab Dip

PEANUTS   **EGGS**   **COW'S MILK**   FISH   TREE NUTS   **WHEAT**   SOY   **SHELLFISH**   SESAME
              <1 g   4 g   4 g   15 g

YIELD Serves 6
(⅓ cup per serving)
PREP TIME 8 minutes
COOK TIME 20 minutes

1 pound **lump crabmeat**

2 tablespoons freshly squeezed lemon juice

4 ounces **cream cheese**

½ cup shredded **sharp cheddar cheese**

½ cup **sour cream**

¼ cup **mayonnaise**

½ teaspoon onion powder

¼ teaspoon garlic powder

½ teaspoon kosher salt

¼ teaspoon freshly ground black pepper

1 (16-ounce) round loaf **sourdough bread**

1 tablespoon finely chopped fresh chives (optional)

This dip works well as a family-friendly appetizer or lunch option when you're feeding a group. Save the piece that you slice off the rounded top of the sourdough loaf; it works well for babies to use as a "teether" or "dipper" to scoop up the dip and/or poke around inside the mouth—especially helpful if you have a baby with an extra-sensitive gag reflex.

1. Preheat the oven to 350°F.

2. In a medium bowl, toss the crabmeat with the lemon juice. Add the cheeses, sour cream, mayonnaise, onion powder, garlic powder, salt, and pepper and stir with a silicone spatula until combined.

3. Transfer to a 1-quart casserole dish and bake for 25 minutes.

4. While the dip bakes, cut a thin slice off the top of the sourdough loaf and scoop out the bread with your hands so that it creates a "bowl." Arrange the pieces of bread from inside the loaf on a serving plate around the "bowl" to use for dipping.

5. When the dip is baked, spoon it into the bread bowl.

6. Garnish the dip with the chives and serve warm. For BLF, check that the lumps of crab are finely shredded in portions served to baby. Allow baby to scoop the dip with the heel of the sourdough loaf or with their hands, or serve on a preloaded spoon. This dip does not store well and is best eaten on the day it is prepared.

MAKE IT A MEAL Serve with Roasted Zucchini Sticks (page 218) and wedges of watermelon for a balanced baby meal.

Shrimp and Vegetable Fritters

PEANUTS	**EGGS**	**COW'S MILK**	FISH	TREE NUTS	**WHEAT**	SOY	**SHELLFISH**	SESAME
	3 g	1 g			3 g		23 g	

Cooking minced shrimp into fritters is a great way to offer shellfish to babies. These fritters taste amazing with Cashew Tartar Sauce (page 180) and are a great way to keep four top allergens regularly in the diet.

1. In a large skillet, melt the ghee over medium heat. Add the shrimp and cook, stirring continuously, until fully cooked and no longer translucent, about 4 minutes. Transfer to a cutting board and let cool, then finely chop. Wipe out the skillet and reserve.

2. In a medium bowl, whisk together the flour, baking powder, salt, and pepper. Add the milk and eggs and whisk to combine. Add the shrimp, bell pepper, onion, and parsley and mix well so that ingredients are blended evenly throughout.

3. Pour about ¼ inch oil into the skillet and heat over medium-high heat to 375°F using an instant-read thermometer.

4. Using an ice cream scoop or ⅓-cup measuring cup, drop three or four spoonfuls of batter into the hot oil, flattening each with a spatula. Fry until lightly golden brown, about 3 minutes per side. Use a slotted spoon to transfer the fritters to a paper towel–lined plate to drain and repeat to fry the remaining fritters.

5. Serve warm. For BLF, slice fritters into strips for babies using a palmar grasp and coach baby to take small bites. For babies using a pincer grasp, you can serve strips or chop into bite-sized pieces. Store leftovers in an airtight container in the refrigerator for up to 2 days.

MAKE IT A MEAL Serve with corn on the cob, sliced cucumbers, and Cashew Tartar Sauce (page 180) as a topping or dip.

YIELD Serves 4
(2–3 fritters per serving)
PREP TIME 15 minutes
COOK TIME 25 minutes

1 teaspoon **ghee**

1 pound large raw **shrimp**
(16–20 per pound),
peeled and deveined

1 cup **whole wheat flour**

1 teaspoon baking powder

1 teaspoon kosher salt

¼ teaspoon freshly ground
black pepper

¼ cup whole **milk**

2 large **eggs**

½ cup minced red bell pepper

2 tablespoons minced
yellow onion

¼ cup finely chopped
fresh flat-leaf parsley

Canola or vegetable oil, for frying

LUNCH

Seafood Sliders with Lemon Aioli

PEANUTS   **EGGS**   COW'S MILK   **FISH**   **TREE NUTS**   **WHEAT**   SOY   **SHELLFISH**   SESAME
        3 g   17 g   1 g   1 g   9 g

YIELD Makes 5 sliders
(1 slider per serving)
PREP TIME 15 minutes
COOK TIME 22 minutes

These sliders are a fun departure from your typical burger night and a great way to boost the brain-building omega-3 fatty acids in your baby's diet. As an alternative to burger buns, which can form a gummy ball in a baby's mouth and increase choking risk, I love serving them between Arnold's Whole Wheat Sandwich Thins.

For the sliders
4 tablespoons extra-virgin olive oil, divided

2 shallots, peeled and minced

8 ounces large raw **shrimp** (16–20 per pound), peeled and deveined

1 (14.5-ounce) can boneless, skinless **salmon**, drained

2 large **eggs**

¼ cup **panko breadcrumbs**

¼ cup **almond flour**

2 tablespoons freshly squeezed lemon juice

2 teaspoons Dijon mustard

1 teaspoon onion powder, divided

1 teaspoon garlic powder, divided

1 teaspoon kosher salt, divided

½ teaspoon freshly ground black pepper

For the aioli
½ cup **mayonnaise**

1 teaspoon finely grated lemon zest

2 tablespoons freshly squeezed lemon juice

2½ tablespoons finely chopped fresh dill

1 tablespoon Dijon mustard

⅛ teaspoon kosher salt

¼ teaspoon freshly ground black pepper

1. In a large skillet, heat 1 tablespoon oil over medium heat. Add the shallots and cook, stirring continuously, for 5 minutes. Add the shrimp and cook, stirring continuously, until the shrimp is pink and cooked through, about 4 minutes. Transfer the shrimp and shallots to a cutting board and let cool, then finely chop the shrimp. Reserve the skillet.

2. Transfer the shrimp and shallots to a medium bowl and add the salmon, eggs, breadcrumbs, flour, lemon juice, Dijon mustard, onion and garlic powders, salt, and pepper. Mix well, then cover and refrigerate for 20 minutes.

3. Meanwhile, in a small bowl, combine all of the aioli ingredients and mix well. Cover and refrigerate.

4. Form the chilled seafood mixture into five equal-sized patties.

5. Heat the remaining 3 tablespoons olive oil in the skillet over medium heat. Add the sliders and cook until golden brown and no longer flowing with juices, about 6 minutes per side. Serve warm with aioli. For BLF, cut cooked sliders into strips for babies using a palmar grasp or into small bites for babies using a pincer grasp. Serving with aioli as a dip or topping will help make the slider easier for babies to "chew" and swallow. Store leftovers in an airtight container in the refrigerator for up to 2 days.

MAKE IT A MEAL Serve with baked sweet potato fries and steamed broccoli for a balanced meal.

Shrimp and Broccoli Croquettes

PEANUTS | **EGGS** | **COW'S MILK** | FISH | TREE NUTS | **WHEAT** | SOY | **SHELLFISH** | SESAME
2 g | 3 g | | | 2 g | | 11 g

YIELD Makes 12 croquettes
(3 croquettes per serving)
PREP TIME 15 minutes
COOK TIME 30 minutes
INACTIVE PREP TIME 30 minutes

Croquettes are the perfect size and soft texture for little hands and mouths. With the inclusion of potato, broccoli, shrimp, cheese, and plenty of seasonings, these croquettes offer balanced nutrition, lots of flavor, and exposure to four top allergens all in one mighty little ball.

2 large russet potatoes, peeled and roughly chopped

2 tablespoons unsalted **butter**, at room temperature

2 tablespoons **sour cream**

1 cup plus 1 tablespoon vegetable or canola oil, divided

1 pound large raw **shrimp** (16–20 per pound), peeled and deveined

1 teaspoon onion powder, divided

1 teaspoon garlic powder, divided

½ cup shredded **mozzarella** cheese

½ cup finely chopped fresh or thawed frozen broccoli

¼ teaspoon ground cumin

¼ teaspoon ground coriander

1 large **egg**

½ cup **all-purpose flour**

1. Bring a large pot of water to boil. Add the potatoes and cook until fork-tender, about 15 minutes. Drain and transfer to a large bowl. Add the butter and sour cream and mash with a fork or potato masher until creamy and smooth. Cover and refrigerate for 20–30 minutes.

2. Meanwhile, heat 1 tablespoon oil in a large skillet over medium heat. Add the shrimp, season with ½ teaspoon each onion and garlic powders, and cook, stirring continuously, until the shrimp is pink and cooked through, about 4 minutes. Transfer to a cutting board and let cool, then finely chop. Wipe out the skillet and reserve.

3. Add the shrimp, cheese, broccoli, cumin, coriander, and remaining ½ teaspoon each of the onion and garlic powders to the chilled potatoes. Mix until well incorporated.

4. Beat the egg in a small, shallow bowl and put the flour in a separate shallow bowl.

5. Using an ice cream scoop or ¼-cup measuring cup, scoop the croquette mixture into your hands. Roll into a ball and coat with flour, then coat with egg, then coat again with flour and set aside. Repeat until all of the mixture has been shaped.

6. Heat the remaining 1 cup oil in the skillet over high heat. Add four croquettes to the hot oil and fry until golden brown on all sides, about 5 minutes. Use a slotted spoon to transfer the croquettes to a paper towel–lined plate and repeat to cook the remaining two batches. Serve warm. For BLF, serve as a finger food for self-feeding and coach your baby to take small bites. Store leftovers in an airtight container in the refrigerator for up to 2 days.

RECIPE NOTE Customize your croquettes with different vegetables to build more variety into your baby's diet. Peas or shredded carrot work well.

MAKE IT A MEAL Serve with ripe tomato wedges and thinly sliced cucumber for a balanced baby meal.

Tarragon Chicken Salad

PEANUTS   **EGGS**   **COW'S MILK**   FISH   **TREE NUTS**   WHEAT   SOY   SHELLFISH   SESAME
             <1 g   1 g   1 g

YIELD Serves 5
(½ cup per serving)
PREP TIME 12 minutes
COOK TIME 15 minutes
INACTIVE PREP TIME 30 minutes

1 pound boneless, skinless chicken breasts

1 teaspoon dried thyme

1 teaspoon kosher salt, divided

½ cup **mayonnaise**

½ cup **sour cream**

¾ cup quartered grapes

½ cup minced red onion

¼ cup finely ground **walnuts**

1 tablespoon finely chopped fresh tarragon

1 tablespoon finely chopped fresh flat-leaf parsley

¼ teaspoon freshly ground black pepper

MAKE IT A MEAL Serve with strips of buttered whole-grain toast and paper-thin slices of cucumber for a balanced baby meal.

Chicken salad is a palate-pleasing way to introduce your baby to a little dairy, egg, and nuts, but many varieties contain pieces of toasted nuts, which are a choking hazard for infants. This recipe uses finely ground walnuts instead. If you're short on time, skip step 1 and use 2 cups shredded meat from a store-bought rotisserie chicken. Look for a low-sodium rotisserie chicken; some grocery chains (including Kroger and Wegmans) sell rotisserie chickens with under 100 mg sodium per 3-ounce serving. *Note: To make this recipe, you will need a food processor or nut grinder.*

1. Put the chicken breasts in a large saucepan and add enough cold water to cover by about 1 inch. Add the thyme and ½ teaspoon salt and bring to a gentle simmer over medium heat. Turn the heat down to low, cover, and cook for 15 minutes. When the chicken has reached an internal temperature of 165°F (you can check by inserting an instant-read thermometer into the thickest part of the breast), use tongs to transfer to a medium bowl and cool for 5–10 minutes.

2. Shred the chicken with two forks or a handheld mixer. Cover and refrigerate until chilled, about 30 minutes.

3. Add the mayonnaise, sour cream, grapes, onion, ground walnuts, tarragon, parsley, remaining ½ teaspoon salt, and pepper and mix to combine. For BLF, be sure your walnuts are finely ground in a food processor or nut grinder, without any larger pieces.

4. Serve cold. For BLF, serve in a shallow bowl with a strip of buttered toast and allow baby to scoop with their hands, or serve on a preloaded spoon. Store leftovers in an airtight container in the refrigerator for up to 5 days.

Sesame Eggplant Dip

PEANUTS   EGGS   COW'S MILK   FISH   TREE NUTS   WHEAT   SOY   SHELLFISH   **SESAME**
2 g

Spread this tasty dip on sandwiches or serve with wedges of soft pita bread for dipping. If you have toddlers or small children who aren't big fans of veggies, try serving them with a dip. There is something magical about the capacity of dips to increase a child's acceptance of other foods served at the same time. Perhaps because in a world where much is decided for them, kids appreciate getting to choose whether and how much to dip. *Note: To make this recipe, you will need a blender or food processor.*

1. Preheat the oven to 425°F. Lightly oil a 9 × 13-inch baking pan or spray with nonstick cooking spray.

2. Poke two or three holes in the eggplant with a fork or knife. Put the eggplant in the prepared baking pan and roast until the eggplant is tender and the skin has loosened, about 35 minutes.

3. While the eggplant bakes, heat the olive oil in a medium skillet over medium heat. Add the onion and garlic and cook, stirring continuously, until fragrant and tender, about 3 minutes. Remove the pan from the heat.

4. When the eggplant is cool enough to handle, slice off the stem end and discard. Cut the eggplant into a few big chunks and put it in a blender. Add the onion, garlic, tahini, lemon juice, za'atar, salt, and pepper and blend until smooth.

5. Taste and adjust the seasonings as desired. Garnish with the parsley and serve warm. For BLF, serve in a shallow bowl for scooping with hands, spread on strips of pita bread or toast, or serve on a preloaded spoon for self-feeding. Store leftovers in an airtight container in the refrigerator for up to 1 week.

YIELD Serves 4
(½ cup per serving)
PREP TIME 10 minutes
COOK TIME 35 minutes

1 (1½-pound) eggplant

1½ tablespoons extra-virgin olive oil

1 small onion, chopped

1 garlic clove, chopped

3 tablespoons **tahini (sesame paste)**

2½ tablespoons freshly squeezed lemon juice (or the juice from 1 lemon)

1 tablespoon za'atar seasoning

¾ teaspoon kosher salt

¼ teaspoon freshly ground black pepper

1 tablespoon minced fresh flat-leaf parsley

MAKE IT A MEAL Serve with strips of naan or pita bread for dipping, thin slices of cucumber, and orange wedges for a balanced baby meal.

LUNCH

Edamame Tahini Dip

PEANUTS   EGGS   COW'S MILK   FISH   TREE NUTS   WHEAT   **SOY**   SHELLFISH   **SESAME**
                                                              3 g   1 g

YIELD Serves 8
(¼ cup per serving)
PREP TIME 5 minutes
COOK TIME 5 minutes

1½ cups shelled **edamame**

¼ cup **tahini (sesame paste)**

½ cup water

½ teaspoon grated lemon zest,
plus juice of 1 lemon

1 garlic clove, peeled and halved

½ teaspoon kosher salt (optional)

½ teaspoon ground cumin

¼ cup extra-virgin olive oil

Move over, chickpeas! Edamame makes a fantastic base for dips and spreads and includes the added benefit of being a complete source of plant-based protein while also providing an allergen exposure. *Note: To make this recipe, you will need a high-speed blender or food processor.*

1. Put the edamame in a medium saucepan, cover with water, and bring to a boil. Cook for 5 minutes, then drain.

2. Transfer the edamame to a high-speed blender or food processor, add the tahini, water, lemon zest and juice, garlic, salt (if using), and cumin and blend until smooth. With the motor still running, slowly drizzle in the olive oil until evenly mixed.

3. For BLF, offer on a preloaded spoon, spread on strips of naan bread, or serve in a shallow bowl for dipping or scooping with hands. Store leftovers in an airtight container in the refrigerator for up to 5 days or in the freezer for up to 3 months.

MAKE IT A MEAL Serve with strips of naan bread and wedges of soft, ripe tomato for a balanced baby meal.

English Muffin Baby Pizzas

PEANUTS   EGGS   **COW'S MILK**   FISH   TREE NUTS   **WHEAT**   SOY   SHELLFISH   SESAME
                    3 g   3 g

Have you noticed that certain kids are absolutely delighted by miniature versions of things? My middle daughter has always loved making tiny replicas of her favorite items out of clay or playdough ("teeny-weenies," she used to call them). Maybe that's partly why she has also loved these mini pizzas since her babyhood. On nights when my patience and bandwidth are low for meal prep, these pizzas are a godsend!

1. Preheat the oven or toaster oven to 325°F.

2. If including broccoli or another vegetable topping, steam until fork-tender. Chop into chickpea-sized bites and set aside.

3. Split each English muffin in half and toast in the oven or toaster oven until lightly browned, about 5 minutes.

4. Spread 2 tablespoons tomato sauce on each English muffin half. Sprinkle the Italian seasoning, garlic powder, vegetable (if using), and cheese evenly over each muffin.

5. Toast until the cheese is melted, about 1 minute.

6. Cool for about 1 minute before serving. For BLF, slice into finger-sized strips or small bites.

MAKE IT A MEAL Serve with paper-thin slices of cucumber and wedges of ripe avocado for a balanced baby meal.

YIELD Makes 4 mini pizzas
(1 mini pizza per serving)
PREP TIME 5 minutes
COOK TIME 6 minutes

¼ cup broccoli florets or another vegetable of your choice (optional)

2 **English muffins**
(Ezekiel Sprouted Whole Grain English Muffins are my favorite)

½ cup low-sodium, no-added-sugar tomato sauce

½ teaspoon Italian seasoning

¼ teaspoon garlic powder

½ cup shredded **mozzarella cheese** (about 2 ounces)

Baby-Friendly Cashew Dip

PEANUTS   EGGS   COW'S MILK   FISH   **TREE NUTS**   WHEAT   SOY   SHELLFISH   SESAME
5 g

YIELD Serves 9
(¼ cup per serving)
PREP TIME 5 minutes
TOTAL TIME 10 minutes

2 cups raw **cashews**

2 cups boiling water

⅓ cup fresh dill

⅓ cup fresh flat-leaf parsley

⅓ cup fresh chives

2 tablespoons white wine vinegar

1 teaspoon kosher salt

This easy, quick dip works well for babies, but it's equally appetizing for kids and adults. I brought it to an adults-only dinner party the other night, and it was a hit! I love how dips like this help encourage more vegetable acceptance in people of all ages and also work well as a salad dressing, pasta sauce, cooked veggie topping, or sandwich spread. For older kids and adults, serve with raw vegetables or whole-grain crackers for dipping. *Note: To make this recipe, you will need a high-speed blender or food processor.*

1. Put the cashews in a medium bowl and pour in the boiling water. Cover and set aside for 10 minutes.

2. Set a strainer over a large bowl and drain the cashews, reserving the soaking water. Transfer the cashews to a high-speed blender or food processor. Add the herbs, vinegar, salt, and 1 cup of the soaking water and blend until creamy and smooth. Add more soaking water if needed, until the dip reaches a consistency you like.

3. For BLF, serve to babies on a preloaded spoon, on a strip of toast, or in a shallow bowl for scooping with hands. For younger babies without teeth, offer a hard stick of raw vegetable to use as a dipper. The dipper isn't meant to be eaten, but rather as a way to get the dip from bowl to mouth while using the dipper to poke around inside the mouth and help increase familiarity with the structures inside—great for babies with an overactive gag reflex! Store leftovers in an airtight container in the refrigerator for up to 7 days or in the freezer for up to 6 months.

MAKE IT A MEAL Offer as a part of a balanced meal with strips of toast or naan bread and florets of steamed cauliflower and broccoli for your baby to use as dippers.

Peanut Apple Fritters

PEANUTS 3 g **EGGS** 3 g **COW'S MILK** <1 g FISH TREE NUTS WHEAT SOY SHELLFISH SESAME

Soft in texture and juicy but with no added sugar or salt, these fritters offer an easy and nutrient-dense way to consistently serve peanuts to babies in an infant-safe form.

1. Put the diced apples in a medium bowl and toss with the lemon juice to prevent browning.

2. In a large bowl, whisk together the flours and baking powder. Add the eggs and milk and whisk until combined. Fold in the diced apples.

3. Pour ¼ inch oil into a large cast-iron skillet and heat over medium-high heat to 375°F using an instant-read thermometer.

4. Using a ¼-cup measuring cup, drop three or four spoonfuls of batter into the hot oil and fry until golden brown, 2–2½ minutes per side. Test doneness by inserting a small knife into the center of a fritter. If it does not come out clean, fry a little longer. Use a slotted spoon to transfer the fritters to a paper towel–lined plate to drain and repeat to fry the remaining fritters.

5. Serve warm. For BLF, cut fritters into strips for babies using a palmar grasp, or small chickpea-sized bites for babies using a pincer grasp. Store leftovers in an airtight container in the refrigerator for up to 5 days or in the freezer for up to 2 months.

MAKE IT A MEAL Serve with smashed blueberries for a balanced baby breakfast or lunch.

YIELD Makes 10 fritters (2 fritters per serving)
PREP TIME 10 minutes
COOK TIME 10 minutes

2 large apples (Granny Smith, Pink Lady, or Honeycrisp work well), peeled, cored, and diced

2 teaspoons freshly squeezed lemon juice

½ cup **peanut flour**

½ cup oat flour

2 teaspoons baking powder

2 large **eggs**, at room temperature

¼ cup **whole milk**

Vegetable oil, for frying

LUNCH

167

Sweet Potato Almond Butter Mash

PEANUTS   EGGS   COW'S MILK   FISH   **TREE NUTS**   WHEAT   SOY   SHELLFISH   SESAME

3 g

YIELD Serves 5
(½ cup per serving)
PREP TIME 10 minutes
COOK TIME 1 hour

2 medium sweet potatoes (about 1½ pounds total)

¼ cup smooth **almond butter**

There is something irresistible about the combination of rich, gooey almond butter and satisfying sweet potato that can't be beaten. Oddly, my girls have referred to this dish as "mash" since they were babies and still regularly ask me to add it to the meal rotation.

1. Preheat the oven to 400°F. Line a rimmed baking sheet with parchment paper.

2. Pierce the sweet potatoes a few times on all sides with a fork. Place on the prepared baking sheet and bake until the flesh is very tender, about 1 hour. Let cool for about 15 minutes.

3. When cool enough to handle, cut the sweet potatoes in half and scoop the flesh into a medium bowl, discarding the peels. Mash the sweet potatoes with the almond butter until well combined.

4. Serve warm. For BLF, offer in a shallow bowl and allow baby to scoop with their hands or offer on a preloaded spoon. Store leftovers in an airtight container in the refrigerator for up to 5 days or in the freezer for up to 3 months.

MAKE IT A MEAL Offer with Spaghetti Squash Quinoa Bake (page 220) for a balanced meal.

Shells and Cheese with Carrots and Peas

PEANUTS   EGGS   **COW'S MILK**   FISH   TREE NUTS   **WHEAT**   **SOY**   SHELLFISH   SESAME
                   8 g   7 g   5 g

The secret ingredient in this healthier twist on a family favorite is the mascarpone cheese, which lends a rich, creamy texture to the cheese sauce. If you can't find small pasta shells, look for rigatoni, penne, or fusilli, which are all easier for babies to self-feed thanks to their texture and larger size.

. . . .

1. Bring a large pot of water to boil, add the pasta, and cook according to the package directions. Add the peas and carrots during the last 5 minutes of cooking. Drain the pasta and vegetables.

2. In a large pot, melt the ghee over medium heat. Add the garlic and cook, stirring continuously, until fragrant, 1–2 minutes. Sprinkle in the arrowroot and mustard and whisk until the mixture browns slightly and smells toasty, 2–3 minutes. Pour in the warm milk, whisking until the mixture starts to simmer and thicken, about 2 minutes. Turn the heat down to low, stir in the cheddar, mascarpone, paprika, and thyme, and season with the salt and pepper (if using).

3. Add the cooked pasta and vegetables and stir to combine. Don't worry if the mixture looks too wet, as the pasta will continue to absorb more of the liquid from the sauce as it cools.

4. Remove the pot from the heat, cover, and let stand for 5 minutes before serving. Store leftovers in an airtight container in the refrigerator for up to 5 days or in the freezer for up to 3 months.

MAKE IT A MEAL Serve with steamed broccoli for a balanced baby meal.

YIELD Serves 4
(2 cups per serving)
PREP TIME 10 minutes
COOK TIME 15 minutes

8 ounces (2 cups) **pasta shells**

1 cup frozen peas and cubed carrots

2 tablespoons **ghee**

2 garlic cloves, minced

3 tablespoons arrowroot powder or cornstarch

½ teaspoon ground mustard

2½ cups plain, unsweetened **soy milk**, warmed to about 105°F

1 cup shredded **cheddar cheese** (about 8 ounces)

2 ounces **mascarpone cheese** or **sour cream**

¾ teaspoon paprika

¾ teaspoon dried thyme

½ teaspoon fine sea salt, plus more to taste (optional)

¼ teaspoon freshly ground black pepper (optional)

LUNCH

Cottage Cheese Mash

PEANUTS	EGGS	COW'S MILK	FISH	TREE NUTS	WHEAT	SOY	SHELLFISH	SESAME
		2 g			2 g			

YIELD Serves 2
(¼ cup per serving)
PREP TIME 2 minutes

2 tablespoons **full-fat cottage cheese**

2 tablespoons unsweetened applesauce

2 tablespoons **wheat germ**

My oldest daughter ate this powered-up puree often as a baby and continued to ask for the same combination of foods long into her preschool years. The lumpy, mixed texture helps advance a baby's feeding skills while offering a blend of proteins, carbohydrates, and fats all in one tasty dish.

1. Gently mix all of the ingredients together in a small bowl.

2. For BLF, offer on a preloaded spoon or in a shallow bowl for scooping with hands. Leftovers tend to get overly mushy quickly, so this recipe is best assembled right before it is served.

MAKE IT A MEAL Serve with a side of freeze-dried strawberries and some plain oat O's cereal for a balanced baby meal that offers a range of textures and nutrients.

Pinkalicious Beet Hummus

PEANUTS   EGGS   COW'S MILK   FISH   TREE NUTS   WHEAT   SOY   SHELLFISH   **SESAME**
1 g

This vibrant, nutritious hummus provides plenty of plant-based protein, as well as fiber to help optimize digestion. Try it on strips of fresh pita bread, as a sandwich filler, or as a dip for your favorite veggies. The chickpeas are also a great source of key nutrients for babies, including iron and zinc. If you use marinated instead of steamed or roasted beets, consider using the juice of only half a lemon so your hummus isn't too acidic. Love Beets is a brand of refrigerated cooked beets that are marinated in vinegar only, with minimal sodium and no added sugar. *Note: To make this recipe, you will need a high-speed blender or food processor.*

1. Combine the beet, chickpeas (but not their liquid), tahini, lemon zest and juice, garlic, salt, and pepper in a high-speed blender or food processor and blend until smooth. With the motor running, drizzle in the olive oil.

2. Taste and adjust the seasonings as needed. If the hummus is too thick, add a bit of the chickpea liquid. For BLF, serve on a preloaded spoon, offer in a shallow bowl for scooping with hands, or spread on strips of toast, pita, or naan bread. Store leftovers in an airtight container in the refrigerator for up to 1 week.

RECIPE NOTE Some hummus recipes call for removing the skins of the chickpeas in order to produce a smoother hummus, but I usually skip this step—removing the skins takes time and also reduces the amount of fiber in the hummus. If you want a smoother, creamier hummus, blend for a full 1 or 2 minutes. You can also try adding 2 or 3 ice cubes to the food processor while blending for a lighter, fluffier texture.

MAKE IT A MEAL Serve with Spaghetti Squash Quinoa Bake (page 220) and strips of pita bread for a balanced meal.

YIELD Serves 8
(¼ cup per serving)
PREP TIME 5 minutes

1 small steamed or roasted beet or 3–4 vinegar-marinated baby beets

1 (15-ounce) can chickpeas, drained with liquid reserved

2 tablespoons **tahini (sesame paste)**

Grated zest and juice of 1 large lemon

1 garlic clove, peeled and halved

½ teaspoon kosher salt

¼ teaspoon freshly ground black pepper

1 tablespoon extra-virgin olive oil

LUNCH

Tahini Egg Salad

PEANUTS · **EGGS** · COW'S MILK · FISH · TREE NUTS · WHEAT · SOY · SHELLFISH · **SESAME**
9 g   3 g

YIELD Serves 4
(½ cup per serving)
PREP TIME 10 minutes
COOK TIME 15 minutes

6 large **eggs**

¼ cup **tahini (sesame paste)**

¼ cup freshly squeezed
lemon juice

2 tablespoons water

2 garlic cloves, minced

¼ cup minced fresh
flat-leaf parsley

¼ teaspoon kosher salt

¼ teaspoon freshly ground
black pepper

½ teaspoon paprika,
plus more for sprinkling

Egg salad is typically made with mayonnaise, but this version (inspired by Habeeb Salloum's recipe for mutabbalat taheena in *Classic Vegetarian Cooking from the Middle East & North Africa*) uses a mixture of tahini and lemon juice as an alternative creamy base. It works equally well as a sandwich filling, salad topper, or dip.

1. Put the eggs in a medium saucepan and cover with water. Bring to a boil, then turn the heat down to a simmer and cook for 14 minutes, until hard-boiled. Transfer the eggs to a strainer and cool for a few minutes under cold running water.

2. In a medium bowl, whisk together the tahini, lemon juice, and water until well combined. Peel the eggs and mash them into the tahini mixture. Add the garlic, parsley, salt, pepper, and paprika and stir gently until well mixed. Sprinkle additional paprika on top.

3. For BLF, serve in a shallow bowl for scooping with hands or preload a spoon and hand to baby for self-feeding. Alternatively, you can load egg salad onto strips of toast. Store leftovers in an airtight container in the refrigerator for up to 4 days.

MAKE IT A MEAL Serve with strips of toast, wedges of kiwi, and paper-thin slices of cucumber for a balanced baby meal.

Presto Pressed Pesto Grilled Cheese

PEANUTS   **EGGS**   **COW'S MILK**   FISH   **TREE NUTS**   **WHEAT**   SOY   SHELLFISH   SESAME
            <1 g   16 g   1 g   8 g

The addition of my Many Nut Pesto (page 214) is easy and quick, but it definitely takes the flavor and allergen exposure of classic grilled cheese and tomato up a notch! If you don't have it on hand, you can substitute store-bought pesto (or another homemade version), and the sandwiches will still provide allergen exposures to wheat, milk, egg, and nuts. Bookmark this recipe for when you need a satisfying lunch recipe that is ready in under 15 minutes!

1. Spread 1 teaspoon mayonnaise evenly on one side of each slice of bread.

2. Place 2 slices of bread mayonnaise-side down in a large skillet. Divide the cheese and tomato slices evenly between both slices.

3. Coat the non-mayonnaise side of each of the remaining 2 slices of bread evenly with 1 tablespoon pesto and place pesto-side down on top of the cheese and tomato layers.

4. Cover the sandwiches with a sheet of aluminum foil and place a heavy pot or pan (cast iron works well) on top of the foil to press the sandwiches. Cook over medium-low heat until lightly golden, about 5 minutes, then flip the sandwiches, cover again with foil, press, and cook for 5 minutes on the other side.

5. Serve warm. For BLF, slice into finger-length strips for babies using a palmar grasp and coach your baby to take small bites. For babies using a pincer grasp, you can continue to offer strips or chop into bite-sized pieces. Kitchen shears work well for this!

MAKE IT A MEAL Serve with smashed cannellini beans and quartered grapes for a balanced baby meal.

YIELD Serves 2
PREP TIME 5 minutes
COOK TIME 10 minutes

4 teaspoons **mayonnaise**

4 slices **whole wheat bread**

6 slices **Muenster cheese**

1 medium tomato, thinly sliced

2 tablespoons **Many Nut Pesto** (page 214)

> As soon as my baby started eating solids, kitchen shears became my fave and most important kitchen tool. I never really used them before, and now I can't live without them!"
>
> HOLLY, MOM OF
> 17-MONTH-OLD GRETA

LUNCH

173

Dinner + Sides

In this section, you'll find dinner options categorized into three groups of recipes: seafood, poultry and meat, and plant-based/vegetarian. You'll also find several nods to my Greek heritage and background. All of the recipes are easy to make—even the ones that don't look simple! So please don't be intimidated by the longer lists of ingredients or cook times. And if you see opportunities I don't mention to take shortcuts and lighten the load in the meal prep department, please know that I support and encourage every single one of them!

Seafood

Easy Sheet Pan Salmon Dinner **176**

Easy Foil-Grilled Haddock **178**

Fish Fingers **179**

Cashew Tartar Sauce **180**

Macadamia-Crusted Fish
with Pineapple Ginger Glaze **181**

Cod Tacos with Lime Sauce **182**

Fishies Wearing Bow Ties **184**

Avocado Crab Quesadillas **186**

Oyster Noodle Casserole **187**

Sheet Pan Shrimp and Tofu Fajitas **188**

Crab Linguine with Lemon and Basil **190**

Squid Stew **191**

Herbed Clam Chowder **192**

Poultry and Meat

Avgolemono
(Greek Egg and Lemon Soup) **194**

Easy Slow Cooker Chicken Korma **195**

Sheet Pan Za'atar Chicken Drumsticks **196**

Turkey and Tempeh Slow Cooker Chili **198**

Greek Meatballs with
Tomato Sauce and Orzo **200**

Memere's Shepherd's Pie **202**

Fall-Apart Slow Cooker Beef Stew **204**

Easy Maple Pecan Baby Back Ribs **206**

Skillet Macaroni with Veggies and Beef **208**

Plant-Based and Vegetarian

Cast-Iron Skillet Corn Bread **209**

Coconut Curry Lentil Stew **210**

Lasagna Roll-Ups **212**

Many Nut Pesto Pasta **214**

Peanut Butter Sweet Potato
Casserole **215**

Miso Mushroom Soup with Egg **216**

Roasted Zucchini Sticks **218**

Zucchini Boats **219**

Spaghetti Squash Quinoa Bake **220**

African Peanut Stew **222**

BLF Saag Paneer **224**

Lemon Tahini Lentil Stew **225**

Easy Sheet Pan Salmon Dinner

PEANUTS   EGGS   **COW'S MILK**   **FISH**   TREE NUTS   **WHEAT**   SOY   SHELLFISH   SESAME

                                                                   <1 g   23 g   1 g

YIELD Serves 4
PREP TIME 20 minutes
COOK TIME 35 minutes

This simple, balanced dinner comes together quickly and works well on busy weekday evenings. Asparagus is nutrient-rich and contains prebiotics that feed friendly bacteria in the gut and help contribute to a healthy microbiome. It's a wonderful early food for babies during BLF because it's shaped perfectly for little hands and offers a tender tip that is fun for babies to nibble. But be forewarned! Babies and kids tend to enjoy only the tops because the bottom halves of asparagus stalks can be a bit too stringy and fibrous for them to manage. If your kids are anything like mine, they'll be enjoying the tops and handing you the bottoms for the next several years.

1½ pounds Yukon Gold potatoes, peeled and sliced into steak fries

6 tablespoons extra-virgin olive oil, divided

4 garlic cloves, minced, divided

1 teaspoon kosher salt, divided

½ teaspoon freshly ground black pepper, divided

2 tablespoons freshly squeezed lemon juice

2 tablespoons minced fresh dill

1 tablespoon melted **ghee** or **unsalted butter**

⅓ cup **panko breadcrumbs**

1 pound skin-on **salmon fillets**

1 bunch asparagus, trimmed

1. Position oven racks in the top and bottom thirds of the oven. Preheat the oven to 400°F. Line two rimmed baking sheets with parchment paper.

2. On one of the prepared baking sheets, toss the potatoes with 2 tablespoons olive oil, half of the garlic, ½ teaspoon salt, and ¼ teaspoon pepper. Spread out the potatoes in a single layer and roast on the lower oven rack for 15 minutes.

3. Meanwhile, mix the remaining 4 tablespoons olive oil, the lemon juice, dill, remaining garlic, remaining ½ teaspoon salt, and remaining ¼ teaspoon pepper in a small bowl. In a separate small bowl, mix the melted ghee and breadcrumbs.

4. Arrange the salmon on the other prepared baking sheet and cover with half of the dill sauce. Sprinkle the tops with the buttered breadcrumbs. Scatter the asparagus in a single layer around the salmon and drizzle the remaining dill sauce over the asparagus, tossing lightly to coat.

5. After the fries have roasted for 15 minutes, flip them and rotate the baking sheet for even cooking. Place the salmon and asparagus baking sheet pan on the upper oven rack. Roast until the fries and asparagus are lightly browned and tender and the fish has a minimum internal temperature of 145°F and flakes easily with a fork, about 20 minutes.

6. Serve warm. For BLF, check that the fish is fully cooked and remove any bones. Offer in a shallow bowl for scooping with hands or on a preloaded spoon or fork. Store leftovers in an airtight container in the refrigerator and enjoy the salmon within 2 days and the fries and asparagus within 5 days.

Easy Foil-Grilled Haddock

PEANUTS   EGGS   COW'S MILK   **FISH**   TREE NUTS   WHEAT   SOY   SHELLFISH   SESAME
27 g

YIELD Serves 4
ACTIVE PREP TIME 10 minutes
INACTIVE PREP TIME 30 minutes
COOK TIME 10 minutes

2 tablespoons extra-virgin olive oil

2 tablespoons freshly squeezed lemon juice

2 garlic cloves, minced

1 teaspoon garlic powder

1 teaspoon ground turmeric

½ teaspoon kosher salt

¼ teaspoon freshly ground black pepper

4 (5- to 6-ounce) skinless **haddock fillets**

Post-meal cleanup doesn't get any easier than this! Both the grill and the sealed aluminum packets help contain meal prep mess and minimize the use of dishes and pans. If you are feeling adventurous, experiment with garnishing your grilled fish with different finely chopped fresh herbs.

1. In a small bowl, whisk together the olive oil, lemon juice, garlic, garlic powder, turmeric, salt, and pepper.

2. Lay out four sheets of aluminum foil, each large enough to create a sealed packet for one fish fillet. Place the fillets on the foil, pour one-quarter of the marinade over each, and fold and crimp to seal each packet. Refrigerate for 30 minutes.

3. Preheat a grill to medium-high heat and brush the grates with a bit of canola oil.

4. Lay the sealed foil packets on the grill grates, close the lid, and grill until the fish has a minimum internal temperature of 145°F and flakes easily with a fork, about 10 minutes.

5. Serve immediately. For BLF, check that the fish is fully cooked and remove any bones. Offer in a shallow bowl for scooping with hands or on a preloaded spoon or fork. Store leftovers in an airtight container in the refrigerator for up to 2 days.

MAKE IT A MEAL Serve with Many Nut Pesto Pasta (page 214) and tender-cooked asparagus for a balanced meal.

Fish Fingers

PEANUTS **EGGS** **COW'S MILK** **FISH** TREE NUTS **WHEAT** SOY SHELLFISH SESAME
      2 g   1 g   20 g   1 g

Cod is a great choice for babies and kids. Low in mercury and high in omega-3s, it's a flaky white fish with a mild flavor that plays well with all sorts of seasonings and ingredients. This healthier version of fried fish is a great way to familiarize your baby early on with the flavor and texture of brain-building seafood while providing exposure to four top allergens, all in one dish.

1. Preheat the oven to 375°F. Line a rimmed baking sheet with parchment paper.

2. Put the flour in a shallow bowl. Whisk together the egg and milk in a second shallow bowl. Whisk together the breadcrumbs, cheese, paprika, and garlic powder in a third shallow bowl.

3. Pat the fish dry with paper towels. Coat each piece of fish first in the flour, then the egg, then the breadcrumb mixture. Arrange the coated fish fingers in a single layer on the prepared baking sheet.

4. Bake until the fish flakes easily with a fork, about 15 minutes.

5. Cool on the baking sheet on a cooling rack for about 5 minutes before serving. For BLF, check that the fish is fully cooked and remove any bones. Offer in a shallow bowl for scooping with hands or on a preloaded spoon or fork. Store leftovers in an airtight container in the refrigerator and enjoy within 2 days.

MAKE IT A MEAL For a balanced meal, serve with Cashew Tartar Sauce (page 180) for dipping, along with some oven-baked fries and steamed broccoli.

YIELD Serves 4
(3 fish fingers per serving)
PREP TIME 20 minutes
COOK TIME 15 minutes

½ cup **all-purpose flour**

1 large **egg**, beaten

2 tablespoons **milk**

¾ cup panko **breadcrumbs**

2 tablespoons grated **Parmesan cheese**

1 teaspoon paprika

1 teaspoon garlic powder

1 pound **cod**, cut into 1-inch strips

Cashew Tartar Sauce

PEANUTS   EGGS   COW'S MILK   FISH   **TREE NUTS**   WHEAT   SOY   SHELLFISH   SESAME
2 g

YIELD Makes 1½ cups
(2 tablespoons per serving)
PREP TIME 10 minutes
INACTIVE PREP TIME 30 minutes

1 cup raw **cashews**

½ cup water

2 tablespoons fresh lemon juice

1 tablespoon apple cider vinegar

1 teaspoon ground mustard

1 teaspoon garlic powder

¼ cup finely chopped pickles

¼ cup minced yellow onion

½ teaspoon kosher salt

¼ teaspoon freshly ground
black pepper

This nutrient-dense twist on traditional tartar sauce offers an opportunity to keep tree nuts in the diet consistently once they have been introduced. Teach your baby to use Cashew Tartar Sauce as a dip—it tastes great on Shrimp and Vegetable Fritters (page 157) and complements the Seafood Sliders (page 158) as an alternative to the lemon aioli. *Note: To make this recipe, you will need a high-speed blender or food processor.*

1. Put the cashews and water in a high-speed blender and set aside to soak for 30 minutes.

2. Add the lemon juice, vinegar, mustard, and garlic powder to the blender and blend until smooth.

3. Transfer the cashew mixture to a medium bowl. Add the pickles and onion and season with the salt and pepper. Stir to combine, cover, and refrigerate for 30–60 minutes before serving. Store in an airtight container in the refrigerator for up to 1 week.

MAKE IT A MEAL Serve with Shrimp and Vegetable Fritters (page 157), corn on the cob, and paper-thin cucumber slices for a balanced baby meal.

Macadamia-Crusted Fish with Pineapple Ginger Glaze

PEANUTS   **EGGS**   **COW'S MILK**   **FISH**   **TREE NUTS**   **WHEAT**   **SOY**   SHELLFISH   SESAME
            2 g   <1 g   23 g   1 g   1 g   1 g

Low-mercury, high omega-3 fish like rainbow trout are ideal for babies. Rainbow trout can be white, pink, or orange and has a flaky, soft texture and mild flavor that pairs well with nuts; haddock or cod would also work. *Note: To make this recipe, you will need a food processor.*

1. Preheat the oven to 400°F. Lightly oil a 9 × 13-inch baking pan or spray with nonstick cooking spray.

2. In a large saucepan, heat the pineapple juice, garlic, and ginger over medium-high heat, stirring occasionally, until the liquid is reduced by two-thirds, about 15 minutes. Stir in the soy sauce and continue to cook until the mixture is reduced again by half, about 6 minutes, then remove from the heat, strain, and set aside. You should have about ¼ cup glaze.

3. While the glaze reduces, put the flour in a shallow bowl. Whisk together the milk and egg in a second shallow bowl. Sprinkle the ground macadamia nuts in a third shallow bowl. For BLF, be sure your nuts are finely ground in a food processor or nut grinder, without any larger pieces.

4. Dredge the fillets first in the flour, then in the egg mixture, and then in the nuts.

5. Place the coated fillets on the prepared baking sheet and bake until the fish flakes easily when nudged with a fork, 15–20 minutes.

6. Serve warm with a drizzle of pineapple ginger glaze. For BLF, check that the fish is fully cooked and remove any bones. Offer in a shallow bowl for scooping with hands. Store leftovers in an airtight container in the refrigerator for up to 2 days.

YIELD Serves 4
PREP TIME 15 minutes
COOK TIME 30 minutes

For the glaze
2 cups pineapple juice

3 garlic cloves, minced

1 teaspoon minced fresh ginger or ginger paste

2½ tablespoons low-sodium **soy sauce**

For the fish
¼ cup **all-purpose flour**

1 tablespoon **milk**

1 large **egg**

½ cup finely ground **macadamia nuts**

4 (4-ounce) skinless **rainbow trout, haddock,** or **cod fillets**

MAKE IT A MEAL Serve over rice with steamed baby bok choy for a balanced meal.

Cod Tacos with Lime Sauce

PEANUTS   **EGGS**   **COW'S MILK**   **FISH**   TREE NUTS   WHEAT   SOY   SHELLFISH   SESAME

           <1 g   <1 g   30 g

YIELD Makes 8 tacos
(2 tacos per serving)
PREP TIME 15 minutes
COOK TIME 15 minutes

This meal has been my oldest daughter's favorite dinner since she was a toddler. When deconstructed, fish tacos work well for babies. But if you have older children and picky eaters, meals like these that offer choices and allow kids to assemble their own plates help give kids a greater sense of ownership and control over their food, which can help decrease food refusal. I've seen it work in my home time and time again!

For the tacos

1 teaspoon ground cumin

1 teaspoon ground coriander

½ teaspoon paprika

½ teaspoon garlic powder

½ teaspoon kosher salt

¼ teaspoon freshly ground black pepper

1½ pounds **cod, pollock,** or **haddock fillets**

8 (6-inch) corn tortillas

1 avocado, peeled, pitted, and cubed

1 tomato, chopped

1 cup thinly sliced red cabbage

For the lime sauce

3 tablespoons **mayonnaise**

3 tablespoons **sour cream**

1 garlic clove, minced

1 scallion (green part only), finely chopped

2 tablespoons finely chopped fresh cilantro

Grated zest and juice of 1 medium lime

1. Preheat the oven to 425°F. Line a rimmed baking sheet with parchment paper.

2. In a small bowl, mix the cumin, coriander, paprika, garlic powder, salt, and pepper. Sprinkle each fish fillet evenly with the spice mixture and place on the prepared baking sheet. Bake until the fish flakes easily with a fork, about 15 minutes.

3. While the fish bakes, in a small bowl, mix all of the lime sauce ingredients together and set aside.

4. When the fish is done, gently heat the tortillas one by one in a dry skillet over medium-high heat for 30 seconds.

5. Distribute the fish evenly into the tortillas and top with the avocado, tomato, cabbage, and lime sauce as desired. For BLF, check that there are no bones in the cod portions you will be serving to your baby and serve the tacos deconstructed: Skip the cabbage and offer strips of tortilla and flaked fish topped with lime sauce and some chopped tomato and avocado. This recipe does not keep well and is best enjoyed right away.

MAKE IT A MEAL The different components of this dish already create a balanced meal, but when I have the time, I love serving these tacos along with a side of black beans and a green salad.

Fishies Wearing Bow Ties

PEANUTS   EGGS   COW'S MILK   **FISH**   TREE NUTS   **WHEAT**   **SOY**   SHELLFISH   **SESAME**
5 g   16 g   11 g   5 g   3 g

YIELD Serves 4
PREP TIME 30 minutes
COOK TIME 15 minutes

This recipe has a lot of ingredients, but it's actually quite simple and mostly a matter of assembling. Depending on how many of the little eaters at my table like adding more sauce to their bowl, I often have some of the savory, nutty sauce left over, which tastes amazing on noodles or pasta over the next few days. Pro tip: Pour your prepared sauce into a squeezy condiment bottle (the kind you find in diners). It's easy to store in the refrigerator, shakes well, and makes it easy for kids to add their own squeeze of sauce without drowning the bowl. *Note: To make this recipe, you will need a blender.*

For the sauce
3 garlic cloves, peeled and halved

⅓ cup smooth **peanut butter**

2 tablespoons **tahini**

2 tablespoons low-sodium **soy sauce**

2 tablespoons rice vinegar

2 tablespoons vegetable oil

2 tablespoons **toasted sesame oil**

2 teaspoons minced fresh ginger or ginger paste

½ teaspoon sriracha (optional)

For the pasta and fish
12 ounces **bow tie pasta**

4 (4-ounce) skin-on **black sea bass fillets**

1 tablespoon **toasted sesame oil**

For the toppings
3 cups broccoli florets (1 medium broccoli head)

½ cup **edamame**

½ medium cucumber, peeled, halved lengthwise, and sliced crosswise into paper-thin half-rounds

1 carrot, peeled and finely grated

2 scallions (green parts only), finely chopped

¼ cup finely chopped fresh cilantro

¼ cup **sesame seeds**, toasted

1. In a blender, puree all of the sauce ingredients, stopping to scrape down the sides as needed. Set aside.

2. Bring a large pot of water to a boil, add the pasta, and cook until very tender, 1–2 minutes longer than recommended on the package directions. Before draining, remove 1 cup of the cooking water and blend it into the sauce until smooth. Drain the pasta and set aside.

3. While the pasta cooks, pour an inch of water into a medium saucepan fitted with a steamer basket and bring to a boil over medium-high heat. Add the broccoli and edamame, cover, and steam until fork-tender, 5–6 minutes. Drain and set aside.

4. Pat the fish fillets dry with paper towels. Heat the sesame oil in a large, nonstick skillet over medium-high heat. Add the fish skin-side down and cook, pressing down lightly with a spatula until the skin is crispy, about 2 minutes. Flip and cook without moving until the fish flakes easily, about 2 minutes. Remove the pan from the heat and set aside.

5. In a large bowl, toss the pasta with 1 cup of the sauce until coated.

6. Serve the fish over a bed of pasta, drizzle with the remaining sauce, and set out the toppings for people to add as desired. For BLF, slip the edamame from their skins and smash before serving. Store leftovers in airtight containers in the refrigerator and enjoy the fish within 2 days, the pasta and vegetables within 5 days, and the sauce within 1 week.

MAKE IT A MEAL This customizable meal is balanced on its own and a great option for babies as well for older children who tend toward more selective eating, as it allows them more control over their plate.

RECIPE NOTES
- To toast the sesame seeds, line a toaster oven tray with aluminum foil, spread the sesame seeds on the foil, and gently toast until lightly browned and fragrant, 2–3 minutes. Or spread in a medium skillet and toast over medium-low heat until lightly brown, 2–3 minutes.

- Cooking the fish with the skin on increases the flavor and helps prevent the fillets from falling apart. Once you flip the fish in the pan, be sure not to move it around or it may flake apart.

Avocado Crab Quesadillas

PEANUTS   EGGS   **COW'S MILK**   FISH   TREE NUTS   WHEAT   SOY   **SHELLFISH**   SESAME
                   5 g   7 g

YIELD Makes 6 quesadillas
(1 quesadilla per serving)
PREP TIME 20 minutes
COOK TIME 20 minutes

2 tablespoons extra-virgin
olive oil, divided

¾ cup diced onion

1 teaspoon ground cumin

¾ cup diced tomato

1 medium avocado,
peeled, pitted, and diced

2 tablespoons freshly squeezed
lime juice

Kosher salt and freshly ground
black pepper to taste (optional)

6 (8-inch) corn tortillas

1 cup shredded **Monterey Jack
cheese**

8 ounces **lump crabmeat**

⅓ cup **sour cream**

¼ cup finely chopped
fresh cilantro

Quesadillas are always a big hit with my kids. If your babies are
anything like mine, they will soon be regularly begging for you to make
this recipe. Pro tip: Use kitchen shears to cut quesadillas into strips or
small chickpea-sized bites—so easy and quick!

1. In a small skillet, heat 1 tablespoon oil over medium-low heat. Add
   the onion and sauté until translucent, about 8 minutes. Transfer
   the onion to a medium bowl, add the cumin, and stir to combine.

2. Add the tomato and avocado to the bowl with the onion. Sprinkle
   with the lime juice and season with salt and pepper (if using).

3. Lay the tortillas on a work surface. Evenly spread about
   3 tablespoons avocado mixture, 3 tablespoons cheese, and
   1 heaping tablespoon crabmeat across half of each tortilla, then
   fold in half.

4. In a large skillet, heat the remaining 1 tablespoon oil over medium
   heat. Working in batches as necessary, cook the quesadillas until
   the cheese is melted and the tortillas are lightly browned, about
   3 minutes per side. Transfer the quesadillas to plates.

5. Gently open each quesadilla and add 1 tablespoon sour cream
   and a sprinkle of cilantro, then reclose. Serve immediately, as the
   quesadillas do not keep well. For BLF, cut the quesadilla into finger-
   length strips or chickpea-sized bites using kitchen shears and
   offer in a shallow bowl for easier self-feeding. Check that all lumps
   of crabmeat in the quesadillas served to your baby have been
   shredded so there are no larger bites.

MAKE IT A MEAL Serve with smashed black beans and steamed
zucchini for a balanced meal.

Oyster Noodle Casserole

PEANUTS   **EGGS**   **COW'S MILK**   FISH   TREE NUTS   **WHEAT**   SOY   **SHELLFISH**   SESAME
           2 g   4 g   2 g   2 g

Raw and smoked fish and shellfish carry a higher risk of foodborne illness and are not safe for babies, but infants can eat cooked oysters if they are finely minced. Oysters contain greater quantities of zinc than any other food and can help boost a baby's intake of this essential nutrient for growth and immune health. Oysters can also break the bank when purchased fresh, but you can find them pre-shucked in a jar or can, which helps save both money and prep time. Look for low-salt or no-added-salt brands and thoroughly rinse before using.

1. Preheat the oven to 400°F. Lightly oil a 9 × 13-inch baking pan or spray with nonstick cooking spray.

2. Bring a large pot of water to a boil, add the egg noodles, and cook until almost tender, 1 minute earlier than recommended on the package directions. Drain and set aside.

3. While the noodles cook, melt the ghee in a medium saucepan over medium heat. Add the broccoli and cook, stirring frequently, for 4 minutes. Remove the pan from the heat.

4. In a medium bowl, whisk together the half-and-half, soup, and flour, making sure to disperse any pockets of flour.

5. Add the oysters, peas, broccoli, and noodles, season with the pepper, and stir to combine.

6. Spread the mixture evenly in the prepared baking pan and sprinkle the cheese evenly over the top.

7. Bake for 20 minutes. Cool on a cooling rack for 10 minutes before serving. Store leftovers in an airtight container in the refrigerator for up to 3 days.

YIELD Serves 6
PREP TIME 10 minutes
COOK TIME 20 minutes

8 ounces dry **egg noodles**

¼ cup **ghee**

3 cups broccoli florets (1 medium broccoli head), finely minced

1½ cups **half-and-half**

1 (10½-ounce) can low-sodium **cream of celery soup**

2 tablespoons **all-purpose flour**

6 ounces canned or jarred shucked **oysters**, rinsed, drained, and minced

⅓ cup frozen peas

¼ teaspoon freshly ground black pepper

⅓ cup grated sharp **cheddar cheese**

MAKE IT A MEAL This casserole is a balanced meal on its own, but I love to serve it with a side of tomato, onion, lettuce, and cucumber salad.

Sheet Pan Shrimp and Tofu Fajitas

PEANUTS   EGGS   **COW'S MILK**   FISH   **TREE NUTS**   WHEAT   **SOY**   **SHELLFISH**   SESAME
                          3 g*   4 g   7 g   15 g

YIELD Serves 6
PREP TIME 15 minutes
COOK TIME 20 minutes

This easy sheet pan recipe produces a balanced meal that provides plenty of dietary variety and many of the nutrients babies need to thrive and grow, including omega-3 fatty acids and iron.

For the fajitas
1 (14-ounce) package extra-firm **tofu**

1 red bell pepper, sliced into long, thin strips

1 small onion, sliced into long, thin strips

1 portobello mushroom cap, sliced into long, thin strips

¼ cup avocado or extra-virgin olive oil

Grated zest and juice of 2 medium limes

2 teaspoons garlic powder

2 teaspoons ground cumin

1 teaspoon dried oregano

1 teaspoon kosher salt

½ teaspoon freshly ground black pepper

½ teaspoon chili powder, or more to taste

¼ teaspoon cayenne pepper (optional)

1 pound large raw **shrimp** (16–20 per pound), peeled and deveined

8–10 **almond flour tortillas** or corn tortillas

For the toppings (optional)
½ cup shredded **Monterey Jack** or **cheddar cheese** (about 2 ounces)

½ cup **sour cream**

¼ cup finely chopped fresh cilantro

Lime wedges, for garnish

*If using cheese and sour cream

1. Position oven racks in the top and bottom thirds of the oven. Preheat the oven to 425°F. Line two rimmed baking sheets with aluminum foil.

2. Wrap the tofu in a clean tea towel or paper towels, place on a large plate, and place a heavy pan or canned goods on top. Let sit to press out excess moisture for 10 minutes. Unwrap and slice into strips about the size of an adult finger.

3. Put the tofu strips on one prepared baking sheet and the bell pepper, onion, and mushrooms on the other.

4. In a small bowl, mix the oil, lime zest and juice, garlic powder, cumin, oregano, salt, black pepper, chili powder, and cayenne pepper (if using). Drizzle about three-quarters of the spice mixture evenly over the contents of both baking sheets and toss gently to coat, then spread out the tofu strips and vegetables in a single layer on their respective sheets.

5. Place the tofu on the upper oven rack and the vegetables on the lower rack. Roast for 15 minutes, stirring the vegetables and flipping the tofu once halfway through cooking.

6. While the tofu and vegetables roast, add the shrimp to the bowl with the remaining spice mixture and toss to coat. Set aside.

7. At the 15-minute mark, push the vegetables and tofu to the side of each baking sheet and add the shrimp in a single layer, half on each sheet. Continue to roast until the shrimp are cooked through, about 5 minutes.

8. Gently heat the tortillas one by one in a dry skillet over medium-high heat for 30 seconds, then remove to a plate and cover with a clean kitchen towel once warmed.

9. Serve the tofu, shrimp, and vegetables over warm tortillas with toppings as desired. For BLF, this meal works well when served deconstructed: Slice the tortillas into strips, cut the cherry tomatoes into halves or quarters, finely mince or shred the shrimp, and top with sour cream and shredded cheese. Store leftovers in an airtight container in the refrigerator for up to 2 days.

MAKE IT A MEAL This dish is a balanced meal on its own, but the girls and I love eating the fajitas with a side of black beans and chopped avocado for additional variety and nutrients.

Crab Linguine with Lemon and Basil

PEANUTS   **EGGS**   COW'S MILK   FISH   TREE NUTS   **WHEAT**   SOY   **SHELLFISH**   SESAME
5 g   6 g   11 g

YIELD Serves 4
PREP TIME 10 minutes
COOK TIME 15 minutes

⅓ cup extra-virgin olive oil

2 garlic cloves, roughly chopped

1 pound fresh **linguine**

Grated zest and juice of 1½ lemons

8 ounces cooked white **crabmeat**, finely chopped

1 large handful fresh basil leaves, torn into small pieces

½ teaspoon kosher salt (optional)

¼ teaspoon freshly ground black pepper

Red pepper flakes, for garnish (optional)

In my home, the birthday girl always gets to choose what's on the menu on her special day. This meal has been my youngest daughter's birthday dinner pick for the last 5 years, ever since she tried it for the first time. There is something deeply satisfying about the flavors of lemon and basil enveloping linguine and briny, sweet crab. I like to finish my serving with an extra sprinkle of kosher salt to enhance the flavors even more. Do note that unlike most dry pastas, the majority of fresh pastas are made with eggs and will provide an egg exposure.

1. Heat the olive oil in a small skillet over low heat. Add the garlic and sauté for 1–2 minutes, until fragrant. Remove the pan from the heat.

2. Bring a large pot of water to a boil, add the linguine, and cook until very tender, 1–2 minutes longer than recommended on the package directions. Drain, then return the linguine to the pot. Add the lemon juice, crabmeat, and garlic oil and cook over low heat, tossing gently to combine, until the crab is warmed through, about 2 minutes.

3. Add the basil and lemon zest and toss. Season with salt (if using), black pepper, and red pepper flakes (if using), and serve warm. For BLF, cut the linguine into finger-length pieces and make sure that the crab is finely shredded (no lumps). This meal does not keep well and is best eaten the day it's made.

MAKE IT A MEAL Serve with soft-steamed asparagus and a green salad for a balanced meal.

Squid Stew

PEANUTS   EGGS   COW'S MILK   FISH   TREE NUTS   WHEAT   SOY   **SHELLFISH**   SESAME
11 g

Squid is one of the best types of seafood for babies because it is nutrient-rich, naturally low in sodium, a great source of protein, and very high in brain-building omega-3 fatty acids. The more you help your baby get familiar with the flavor and texture of squid now, the more likely they'll be to eat it down the road.

....

1. Rinse the thawed squid, then slice the tentacles in half and the tubes into ½-inch rings.

2. Heat the olive oil in a large saucepan over medium heat. Add the onion and garlic and cook, stirring continuously, until softened, about 8 minutes. Add the tomato paste and stir continuously for 2 minutes. Add the squid, tomatoes with their juices, thyme, salt, and pepper and stir to combine. Turn the heat down to low, cover, and simmer for 35 minutes.

3. Remove the pan from the heat and stir in the harissa and lemon zest.

4. Top the stew with the parsley, capers, and kalamata olives if you like and serve warm. For BLF, finely chop the squid tentacles and tubes to reduce choking risk. Hold off on garnishing your baby's portion with capers and olives as both contain higher than optimal amounts of sodium. This recipe is best eaten the day it is made, but leftovers will keep in an airtight container in the refrigerator for up to 2 days.

RECIPE NOTE Thaw the squid in the refrigerator overnight or keep the squid in the freezer bag and defrost it in a bowl of cold water for about 30 minutes.

MAKE IT A MEAL Serve over farro, polenta, or couscous with a side of steamed cauliflower.

YIELD Serves 6 (1 cup per serving)
PREP TIME 20 minutes
COOK TIME 45 minutes

2 pounds frozen **squid tubes and tentacles**, thawed

2 tablespoons extra-virgin olive oil

1 small yellow onion, diced

4 garlic cloves, minced

1 (6-ounce) can tomato paste

1 (14-ounce) can diced tomatoes

1 teaspoon dried thyme

½ teaspoon kosher salt

¼ teaspoon freshly ground black pepper

1½ teaspoons mild harissa paste

2 teaspoons grated lemon zest

1 tablespoon minced fresh flat-leaf parsley (optional)

2 tablespoons drained capers (optional)

½ cup pitted and chopped kalamata olives (optional)

Herbed Clam Chowder

PEANUTS   **EGGS**   **COW'S MILK**   FISH   TREE NUTS   **WHEAT**   **SOY**   **SHELLFISH**   SESAME
         1 g   2 g   1 g   2 g   6 g

YIELD Serves 6
(1 cup per serving)
PREP TIME 20 minutes
COOK TIME 50 minutes

If you can swing it, don't skip the herbs on top of this tasty chowder! Fresh tarragon and chives complement the flavors of the clams and bacon and will help expand your baby's palate in interesting ways. This chowder is higher in sodium than is ideal, given how hard it is to find a low-sodium clam juice. On a day when you serve it, be mindful about the rest of the foods offered to your baby and avoid higher-sodium options.

. . . .

2 (6½-ounce) cans minced **clams**

2–3 cups **clam juice**

4 slices lower-sodium bacon

1 medium onion, diced

2 tablespoons **all-purpose flour**

2 pounds russet, Yukon Gold, or red potatoes, peeled and cut into ½-inch cubes

5 thyme sprigs, tied together with kitchen string, or 1 teaspoon dried thyme

½ teaspoon kosher salt

¼ teaspoon freshly ground black pepper

2 large **egg yolks**

1½ cups **whole milk**, divided

1½ cups plain, unsweetened **soy milk**

1 tablespoon finely chopped fresh tarragon (optional)

1 tablespoon finely chopped fresh chives (optional)

1. Drain the canned clams over a large liquid measuring cup. Add enough bottled clam juice to measure 3 cups total. Set aside the clam juice and clams.

2. In a large stockpot, cook the bacon over medium heat until crispy, 5–6 minutes. Transfer the bacon to a paper towel–lined plate.

3. Add the onion to the bacon grease in the pot and sauté until translucent, about 7 minutes. Add the flour and stir to form a light golden roux, 2–3 minutes. Do not let it turn dark. Whisk in the clam juice, turn the heat up to medium-high, and bring to a boil. Turn the heat back down to medium and cook for 5 minutes, stirring occasionally. The mixture should take on a creamy consistency.

4. Turn the heat down to low, add the potatoes and thyme (tying one end of the kitchen string to the handle of the pot), and season with the salt and pepper. Simmer until the potatoes are fork-tender, 12–15 minutes.

5. While the potatoes simmer, break the bacon into bits and set aside.

6. In a medium bowl, whisk together the egg yolks and 1 cup whole milk. While whisking, add 2–3 tablespoons hot chowder liquid, 1 tablespoon at a time, to gently temper the eggs.

7. Once the potatoes are cooked, stir the warm egg mixture into the pot. Add the soy milk and remaining ½ cup whole milk. Bring to a simmer, then cook over low heat for 1 minute. Add the clams and cook for 1 more minute.

8. Remove the pot from the heat. Pull the kitchen string and thyme stems from the soup and discard. Garnish the chowder with the tarragon (if using), chives (if using), and bacon bits and serve warm. For BLF, check that the clams are finely minced and the potatoes are fork-tender and not too hot. Serve on a preloaded spoon or in a bowl with strips of garlic bread for dipping into the soup. Store leftovers in an airtight container in the refrigerator for up to 3 days or in the freezer for up to 3 months.

MAKE IT A MEAL For a balanced meal, serve with strips of garlic bread and a green salad.

Avgolemono
(Greek Egg and Lemon Soup)

PEANUTS   **EGGS**   COW'S MILK   FISH   TREE NUTS   **WHEAT**   SOY   SHELLFISH   SESAME
          3 g   2 g

YIELD Serves 6
(1½ cups per serving)
PREP TIME 20 minutes
COOK TIME 45 minutes

8 cups low-sodium chicken broth

2 bone-in chicken breasts, skin removed

3 medium carrots, peeled and diced

2 large celery ribs, diced

¾ cup **orzo**

3 large **eggs**, separated

½ teaspoon kosher salt

3 tablespoons freshly squeezed lemon juice

¼ teaspoon freshly ground black pepper

½ cup finely chopped fresh flat-leaf parsley

MAKE IT A MEAL Serve with soft-steamed broccoli florets and a green salad.

A nod to my Greek heritage, this recipe has been passed down in my family for generations. It takes its name from the egg and lemon sauce that provides the distinctive rich, citrusy flavor. My mother has always added chicken, making it the kind of heartier meal I want when I need comfort food or to be reminded of home.

1. In a large pot, bring the chicken broth to a boil over high heat. Turn the heat down to low, add the chicken, and simmer for 30 minutes, or until a thermometer inserted into the center of each chicken breast reads 165°F. Using tongs, transfer the chicken to a plate to cool.

2. Add the carrots, celery, and orzo to the pot, partially cover, and simmer until the vegetables are tender, about 15 minutes. Remove ½ cup broth from the pot and set aside. Leave the pot on the stove and turn off the heat.

3. Remove the chicken meat from the bones and finely chop.

4. In a medium bowl, beat the egg whites until frothy using a wire whisk or handheld mixer, about 4 minutes. Add the yolks and salt and beat until blended, about 2 minutes. Gradually add the lemon juice, beating until just combined.

5. Slowly stir the ½ cup reserved hot broth into the egg mixture (adding the hot liquid slowly helps prevent curdling). Gradually add the egg and broth mixture to the pot, whisking the entire time.

6. Add the chopped chicken and season with the pepper. Serve warm, garnished with the parsley. Store leftovers in the refrigerator for up to 5 days or in the freezer for up to 3 months.

Easy Slow Cooker Chicken Korma

PEANUTS   EGGS   **COW'S MILK**   FISH   **TREE NUTS**   WHEAT   **SOY**   SHELLFISH   SESAME
4 g   4 g   1 g

When it comes to a mouthwatering blend of spices and seasonings, this popular Indian comfort food hits the spot. Chicken korma is a dish with Mughlai origins, although there are many different takes on the recipe that are associated with different South Asian regions.
I like to add a bit more salt to my own portion when serving. *Note: To make this recipe, you will need a 4-quart (or larger) slow cooker and a high-speed blender or food processor.*

....

1. Put the cashews in a small bowl, cover with hot water, and let soak for 30 minutes.

2. Drain the cashews and transfer to a high-speed blender. Add the broth, yogurt, soy milk, tomato paste, ginger, garam masala, cumin, paprika, turmeric, salt, cardamom, and cinnamon and blend until smooth.

3. Pour the blended mixture into a 4-quart (or larger) slow cooker, add the chicken, onion, and garlic, and stir to combine. Cover and cook on low for 4 hours, or until the chicken is fall-apart tender.

4. Serve warm, garnished with red pepper flakes and cilantro, if you like. For BLF, shred the chicken with a fork and mix the shreds into the sauce for easier swallowing. Serve in a shallow bowl for scooping with hands or offer on a preloaded spoon. Store leftovers in an airtight container in the refrigerator for up to 5 days or in the freezer for up to 3 months.

MAKE IT A MEAL Serve over steamed basmati rice with strips of naan bread and steamed broccoli.

YIELD Serves 6
PREP TIME 25 minutes
INACTIVE PREP TIME 30 minutes
COOK TIME 4 hours

1 cup raw **cashews**

1 cup low-sodium chicken broth

1 cup plain, **full-fat Greek yogurt**

1 cup plain, unsweetened **soy milk**

3 tablespoons tomato paste

2 teaspoons chopped fresh ginger

2 teaspoons garam masala

1 teaspoon ground cumin

1 teaspoon paprika

1 teaspoon ground turmeric

1 teaspoon kosher salt

½ teaspoon ground cardamom

½ teaspoon ground cinnamon

1½ pounds boneless, skinless chicken thighs, cut into 1-inch pieces

1 medium yellow onion, diced

6 garlic cloves, minced

Red pepper flakes, for garnish (optional)

¼ cup finely chopped fresh cilantro (optional)

DINNER + SIDES

195

Sheet Pan Za'atar Chicken Drumsticks

PEANUTS   EGGS   **COW'S MILK**   FISH   TREE NUTS   WHEAT   SOY   SHELLFISH   **SESAME**
                        5 g   2 g

YIELD Serves 4
PREP TIME 20 minutes
COOK TIME 1 hour

Chicken drumsticks come with their own natural handle, which is convenient for self-feeding and seemingly designed for little hands—there may be nothing cuter on earth than a baby munching on one! Don't skip the za'atar seasoning, a Middle Eastern blend of spices that adds tons of toasty and savory flavors. It's delicious on all sorts of dishes, including poultry, meats, legumes, and vegetables. If you can find labneh (Lebanese strained yogurt), swap it for Greek yogurt in the sauce.

For the chicken

3 tablespoons extra-virgin olive oil, divided

2 tablespoons **tahini (sesame paste)**

2 garlic cloves, minced

2 tablespoons za'atar seasoning

1½ teaspoons kosher salt, divided

8 bone-in, skin-on chicken drumsticks or thighs (about 3 pounds total)

3 large shallots, peeled and quartered

1 red bell pepper, sliced into strips

1 cup cherry tomatoes

For the sauce

1 cup plain, **full-fat Greek yogurt** or **labneh**

2 tablespoons extra-virgin olive oil

1 tablespoon za'atar seasoning

1 garlic clove, minced

¼ teaspoon kosher salt

For serving

1 tablespoon **sesame seeds**, toasted (optional)

Lemon wedges, for garnish (optional)

1. Preheat the oven to 400°F. Lightly oil a rimmed baking sheet.

2. In a large bowl, mix 2 tablespoons olive oil, the tahini, garlic, za'atar, and 1 teaspoon salt. Add the chicken and toss to coat on all sides. Transfer the chicken to the prepared baking sheet. Spoon any remaining marinade over the top.

3. Bake for 30 minutes, rotating the baking sheet halfway through.

4. While the chicken roasts, combine the shallots, bell pepper, and tomatoes in a large bowl. Add the remaining 1 tablespoon olive oil and remaining ½ teaspoon salt and toss to coat; set aside.

5. In a small bowl, combine all of the sauce ingredients and mix well. Cover and refrigerate.

6. After 30 minutes, remove the chicken from the oven and carefully flip it over. Arrange the vegetables evenly around the chicken and bake, rotating the baking sheet halfway through, until the internal temperature reaches 165°F, about 30 minutes.

7. Garnish the chicken and vegetables with a dollop of sauce and a sprinkle of toasted sesame seeds (if using). Serve warm with lemon wedges (if using) and pita bread. For BLF, remove the skin, gristle, and any protruding bones from the chicken. You can also remove the tender meat from the bones and serve it in finger-length strips or chickpea-sized pieces, depending on how your baby is currently grasping food for self-feeding. Teach your baby to dip the chicken into the sauce for added flavor, nutrients, and allergen exposure. Store leftover chicken and vegetables in an airtight container in the refrigerator for up to 5 days or in the freezer for up to 3 months. Store leftover sauce in a separate airtight container in the refrigerator for up to 1 week.

MAKE IT A MEAL For a balanced meal, serve with pita bread, warmed and sliced into wedges, and a side of steamed broccoli.

RECIPE NOTES

• If you have time when making the sauce, heat the oil in a small skillet over medium heat, add the za'atar, mix quickly, and remove from the heat. In a small bowl, mix the yogurt, garlic, and salt. Once the spiced oil has cooled, pour it over the top of the yogurt mixture.

• To toast the sesame seeds, line a toaster oven tray with aluminum foil, spread the sesame seeds on the foil, and gently toast until lightly browned and fragrant, 2–3 minutes. Or spread in a medium skillet and toast over medium-low heat until lightly browned, 2–3 minutes.

Turkey and Tempeh Slow Cooker Chili

PEANUTS   EGGS   **COW'S MILK**   FISH   TREE NUTS   WHEAT   **SOY**   SHELLFISH   SESAME

COW'S MILK 2 g   **SOY** 5 g

YIELD Serves 10
(1½ cups per serving)
PREP TIME 30 minutes
COOK TIME 2½ hours

This chili has a good amount of texture and is better suited to babies who are 9 months and up. For littles under 12 months, omit the corn kernels, which can increase choking risk in younger babies who don't yet have molars or a lot of experience chewing firmer foods. *Note: To make this recipe, you will need an 8-quart slow cooker.*

- 2 tablespoons extra-virgin olive oil
- 1 pound 85–94% lean ground turkey
- 1 (8-ounce) package **tempeh**, grated
- 1 large red onion, diced
- 2 medium green bell peppers, diced
- 8 ounces mushrooms, diced
- 3 garlic cloves, minced
- 2 (28-ounce) cans diced tomatoes
- 1 (15-ounce) can low-sodium black beans, rinsed and drained
- 1 (15-ounce) can low-sodium kidney beans, rinsed and drained
- 8 ounces fresh or frozen corn kernels
- 2 cups low-sodium vegetable or chicken broth
- 2 (6-ounce) cans low-sodium tomato paste
- 1 teaspoon chili powder
- 1 teaspoon kosher salt
- ½ teaspoon freshly ground black pepper
- ½ teaspoon ground cumin
- ½ teaspoon garlic powder
- ½ cup **sour cream**
- ½ cup **shredded cheddar** or **Colby Jack cheese**

1. Heat the olive oil in a large skillet over medium heat. Add the turkey and grated tempeh and cook, breaking up the turkey into crumbles and stirring occasionally, until browned, about 15 minutes. Transfer to an 8-quart slow cooker.

2. Add the onion, bell peppers, and mushrooms to the same skillet and cook, stirring continuously, until softened, about 8 minutes. Add the garlic and cook until fragrant, about 2 minutes. Transfer to the slow cooker.

3. Add the tomatoes with their juices, beans, corn, broth, tomato paste, chili powder, salt, pepper, cumin, and garlic powder to the slow cooker and stir to combine. Cover and cook on low for 2 hours, or until heated evenly throughout.

4. Serve warm, topped with sour cream and shredded cheese. For BLF, mash the beans and make sure to break up any larger chunks of turkey. Store leftovers in an airtight container in the refrigerator for up to 5 days or in the freezer for up to 3 months.

MAKE IT A MEAL Serve with Cast-Iron Skillet Corn Bread (page 209) and steamed green beans for a balanced meal.

Greek Meatballs with Tomato Sauce and Orzo

PEANUTS **EGGS** COW'S MILK FISH TREE NUTS **WHEAT** SOY SHELLFISH SESAME
         2 g   7 g

YIELD Serves 6
(3–4 meatballs per serving)
PREP TIME 25 minutes
COOK TIME 2½ hours

Gently cooking meats (like these meatballs) for a long time over low heat helps produce soft, tender textures that are easier for babies to manage. My Greek grandmother taught me to cover the meatball mixture and refrigerate it for at least 1 hour before cooking to let the flavors marry. I don't always have time for this step, but when I do, it's worth it!

For the meatballs

2 tablespoons extra-virgin olive oil

1½ pounds 80% lean ground beef

½ cup **panko breadcrumbs**

1 large **egg**

1 medium onion, finely chopped

2 tablespoons finely chopped fresh mint

2 tablespoons finely chopped fresh flat-leaf parsley

1 teaspoon dried oregano

1 teaspoon dried sage

1 teaspoon kosher salt

1 teaspoon freshly ground black pepper

For the sauce and orzo

2 tablespoons extra-virgin olive oil

2 (6-ounce) cans tomato paste

1 (14½-ounce) can fire-roasted diced tomatoes

2 cups water

2 garlic cloves, minced

2 tablespoons minced fresh flat-leaf parsley

1 tablespoon dried oregano

1 teaspoon kosher salt

1 teaspoon freshly ground black pepper

8 ounces green beans

1 cup **orzo**

1. Preheat the oven to 350°F. Line a rimmed baking sheet with parchment paper.

2. Combine all of the meatball ingredients in a large bowl and mix well. Shape into 2-inch meatballs and place about 1 inch apart on the prepared baking sheet. You should get about 20.

3. Bake, turning halfway through, until lightly browned, about 20 minutes.

4. Heat the olive oil in a large saucepan over medium heat. Add the tomato paste, tomatoes with their juices, water, garlic, parsley, oregano, salt, and pepper and bring to a simmer. Add the cooked meatballs, turn the heat down to low, cover, and simmer for 1½ hours.

5. Add the green beans and cook for another 30 minutes.

6. During the last few minutes of cooking, bring a medium pot of water to a boil, add the orzo, and cook according to the package directions. Drain.

7. Serve the warm meatballs and sauce over the orzo. For BLF, for babies using a palmar grasp, serve whole meatballs (slightly cooled) and coach your baby to take small bites. For babies using a pincer grasp, cut meatballs into chickpea-sized bites. Store leftovers in an airtight container in the refrigerator for up to 5 days or in the freezer for up to 3 months.

MAKE IT A MEAL This recipe is already well balanced and complete, but I love serving it along with a green salad.

Memere's Shepherd's Pie

PEANUTS   EGGS   **COW'S MILK**   **FISH**   TREE NUTS   **WHEAT**   **SOY**   SHELLFISH   SESAME
                       1 g   <1 g   <1 g   6 g

YIELD Serves 8
PREP TIME 20 minutes
COOK TIME 1 hour

For as long as I have had children, this has been the number one recipe my kids ask my mother to make whenever she comes to visit. The iron-rich dish is ideal for babies when you consider the nutrient profile, the soft mix of textures that are easy to manage in the mouth, the savory blend of flavors, and the way it incorporates foods from multiple food groups. I hope you love it as much as we do! You can shave about 10 minutes off your prep time by chopping the vegetables and herbs in a food processor. If you are allergic to fish, note that Worcestershire sauce does typically contain anchovies.

For the topping
2 pounds russet potatoes, peeled and cubed (about 5 cups)

8 tablespoons (1 stick) unsalted **butter**, at room temperature

½ cup **half-and-half**

2 tablespoons **sour cream**

½ teaspoon garlic powder

¼ teaspoon kosher salt

¼ teaspoon freshly ground black pepper

¼ cup grated **Parmesan cheese**

For the filling
2 tablespoons extra-virgin olive oil

1 cup diced onion

1 pound 85% lean ground beef

1 (8-ounce) package **tempeh**, grated

3 medium carrots, peeled and grated (about 1 cup)

2 tablespoons finely chopped fresh flat-leaf parsley

½ teaspoon minced fresh rosemary

1 teaspoon kosher salt

½ teaspoon freshly ground black pepper

2 tablespoons **Worcestershire sauce**

3 garlic cloves, minced

3 tablespoons **all-purpose flour**

1 cup low-sodium beef broth

¼ cup low-sodium tomato paste

1. Preheat the oven to 400°F. Lightly oil a 9-inch pie plate or spray with nonstick cooking spray.

2. Bring a large pot of water to a gentle boil, add the potatoes, and cook until tender, about 15 minutes.

3. While the potatoes cook, make the filling. Heat the olive oil in a large skillet over medium heat. Add the onion and cook until soft, about 5 minutes. Add the beef, tempeh, carrots, parsley, rosemary, salt, and pepper, and cook, breaking up the beef into crumbles and stirring occasionally, until the meat is browned, 6–8 minutes. Add the Worcestershire sauce, garlic, flour, broth, and tomato paste. Stir well and bring to a simmer. Turn the heat down to low and cook for 5 minutes, then remove the pan from the heat.

4. When the potatoes are cooked, drain, return to the pot, and add the butter, half-and-half, sour cream, garlic powder, salt, and pepper. Using an immersion blender or potato masher, blend or mash until smooth. Add the Parmesan and stir to combine.

5. Transfer the meat mixture to the prepared pie plate, then spoon the potato mixture over the meat and smooth the top.

6. Place the pie plate on a rimmed baking sheet to catch spills and bake until the potato topping is set and lightly browned, about 30 minutes.

7. Serve warm. For BLF, serve in a shallow bowl and allow your baby to scoop with hands, or offer on a preloaded spoon. Store leftovers in an airtight container in the refrigerator for up to 5 days or in the freezer for up to 3 months.

MAKE IT A MEAL Serve with steamed broccoli for a balanced meal.

Fall-Apart Slow Cooker Beef Stew

PEANUTS · **EGGS** · COW'S MILK · FISH · TREE NUTS · **WHEAT** · SOY · SHELLFISH · SESAME
2 g · 2 g

YIELD Serves 6
(1½ cups per serving)
PREP TIME 25 minutes
INACTIVE COOK TIME 7 hours

Brimming with key nutrients for babies and richly flavored with fresh herbs, this stew is deeply nourishing for little bodies. We find it especially comforting during the colder months of the year. Depending on how quickly you can prep vegetables, you can shave about 10 minutes off the active prep time for this recipe if you chop the onion, carrots, and celery in a food processor. *Note: To make this recipe, you will need a 6-quart (or larger) slow cooker.*

2 tablespoons extra-virgin olive oil

2 pounds boneless beef chuck roast, cut into 1-inch pieces

½ teaspoon kosher salt

¼ teaspoon freshly ground black pepper

1 medium yellow onion, diced

4 cups low-sodium beef broth, divided

3 garlic cloves, chopped

2 celery ribs, chopped

4 large carrots, peeled and diced

1 rosemary sprig

2 teaspoons chopped fresh thyme leaves

2 teaspoons chopped fresh flat-leaf parsley leaves

½ teaspoon dried marjoram

½ teaspoon dried basil

10 ounces **egg noodles**

1. Heat the oil in a large skillet over high heat. Pat the beef dry with paper towels and season with the salt and pepper. Add the beef to the skillet and briefly sear until brown, leaving the meat undisturbed for 1–2 minutes per side. The meat will stick to the pan at first and then loosen and lift away from the surface of the pan once it is seared. Transfer the beef to a 6-quart (or larger) slow cooker.

2. Add the onion to the drippings left in the skillet and cook over medium-high heat until lightly browned, about 10 minutes. Transfer to the slow cooker.

3. Pour 1 cup beef broth into the skillet and scrape the bottom with a whisk, mixing until all of the cooked bits have come unstuck, then add the broth and drippings to the slow cooker.

4. Add the remaining 3 cups broth, the garlic, celery, carrots, rosemary, thyme, parsley, marjoram, and basil to the slow cooker, cover, and cook on low until the meat is fall-apart tender, 6–7 hours.

5. During the last few minutes of cooking, bring a large pot of water to a boil, add the egg noodles, and cook according to the package directions. Drain and stir into the stew. Serve warm. For BLF, serve in a small shallow bowl and allow baby to self-feed by scooping up with hands or with a preloaded spoon. Be sure to squish-test before serving and ensure that all pieces are tender. If you notice that your baby is struggling with the texture, you can always cut the meat into even smaller bites or puree a portion of the stew in a blender and serve on a preloaded spoon. Store leftovers in an airtight container in the refrigerator for up to 5 days or in the freezer for up to 3 months.

MAKE IT A MEAL Serve with a side of steamed green beans for a balanced meal.

Easy Maple Pecan Baby Back Ribs

PEANUTS EGGS COW'S MILK FISH **TREE NUTS** **WHEAT** SOY SHELLFISH SESAME
                                      2 g   1 g

YIELD Serves 4
PREP TIME 20 minutes
INACTIVE COOK TIME 6 hours

Pork is an excellent source of zinc, a key nutrient during infancy. The flavors of the meat and spices are enhanced in this crowd-pleaser by a touch of maple syrup. If you want to keep the added sugar content low in the rest of the ingredients, look for an unsweetened barbecue sauce. The one by Primal Kitchen is particularly good! *Note: To make this recipe, you will need a food processor and a 6-quart (or larger) slow cooker.*

¼ cup water

2–3 pounds baby back pork ribs

½ cup maple syrup, divided

1 tablespoon smoked paprika

½ teaspoon onion powder

½ teaspoon garlic powder

1½ teaspoons kosher salt

½ teaspoon freshly ground black pepper

½ cup ground **pecans**

3 tablespoons **all-purpose flour**

¾ cup barbecue sauce

1. To remove and discard the silvery membrane from the back of the ribs, make a small cut in the skin on the edge of the rack, then pull it away in one piece by grasping it with a paper towel for better traction. Cut the ribs into three or four sections.

2. Pour the water into a 6-quart (or larger) slow cooker.

3. In a small bowl, mix ¼ cup maple syrup, the smoked paprika, onion powder, garlic powder, salt, and pepper. Rub evenly on all sides of the ribs and place in the slow cooker. Cover and cook on low for 8 hours, medium for 6 hours, or high for 4 hours.

4. In a shallow bowl, combine the ground pecans and flour. For BLF, be sure your pecans are finely ground in a food processor or nut grinder, without any larger pieces. Mix the remaining ¼ cup maple syrup with the barbecue sauce in a separate bowl.

5. When the ribs are cooked, position an oven rack in the highest position and preheat the oven to broil. Lightly oil a rimmed baking sheet.

6. Press the meaty side of the ribs into the pecan-flour mixture and transfer to the prepared baking sheet in a single layer with the nut side up. Spoon the barbecue sauce mixture evenly over the ribs and broil until the sauce begins to caramelize lightly, about 2 minutes.

7. Serve warm. For BLF, offer your baby a whole rib for self-feeding, bone and all. Slow cooking the meat makes it tender and easy to "chew" with gums, and gnawing on the bone helps strengthen muscles needed for chewing and speaking. Alternatively, you can cut the meat off the bone into chickpea-sized bites and offer it on a preloaded fork or in a shallow bowl for self-feeding. Store leftovers (if you have any!) in an airtight container in the refrigerator for up to 4 days.

RECIPE NOTE For a deeper, toastier flavor, toast the pecans before grinding by lining a toaster oven tray with aluminum foil, spreading a heaping ½ cup pecan halves on the foil, and gently toasting until lightly browned and fragrant, 2–3 minutes.

MAKE IT A MEAL Serve with corn on the cob and steamed green beans for a balanced baby meal.

Skillet Macaroni with Veggies and Beef

PEANUTS	EGGS	**COW'S MILK**	**FISH**	TREE NUTS	**WHEAT**	SOY	SHELLFISH	SESAME
		14 g	<1 g		3 g			

YIELD Serves 8
PREP TIME 20 minutes
COOK TIME 40 minutes

1 pound 90% lean ground beef

2 teaspoons **ghee** or extra-virgin olive oil

1 medium green bell pepper, diced

1 medium yellow onion, diced

8 ounces mushrooms, diced

2 celery stalks, diced

1 carrot, diced

2 garlic cloves, minced

1½ cups water

1 (28-ounce) can diced tomatoes

1 tablespoon **Worcestershire** sauce

1 teaspoon dried oregano

½ teaspoon dried basil

½ teaspoon kosher salt

¼ teaspoon ground black pepper

8 ounces **macaroni**

1½ cups (6 ounces) grated **sharp cheddar cheese**

When I was growing up, my grandmother would often make a version of this cozy comfort food and I couldn't get enough of it. As a mom, I love that it offers all the components of a balanced meal in one skillet. You can always customize the recipe with other chopped veggies or a different type of cheese if you prefer. If you are allergic to fish, note that Worcestershire sauce does typically contain anchovies.

1. In a large skillet, cook the beef over medium-high heat, breaking it apart into crumbles and stirring occasionally, until browned, about 10 minutes. Drain the beef and set aside.

2. In the same skillet, melt the ghee over medium-high heat. Add the bell pepper, onion, mushrooms, celery, carrot, and garlic and cook, stirring continuously, until tender, about 15 minutes.

3. Return the beef to the skillet and add the water, tomatoes with their juices, Worcestershire, oregano, basil, salt, and pepper. Turn the heat up to high and bring the mixture to a simmer, stirring occasionally. Add the macaroni, cover, and cook until the macaroni is tender and has absorbed the liquid, about 10 minutes.

4. Turn off the heat, scatter the cheese evenly over the top, and cover for 1 minute to allow the cheese to melt. Serve warm. For BLF, serve in a small shallow bowl and allow baby to self-feed by scooping up with hands or using a preloaded spoon. Store leftovers in an airtight container in the refrigerator for up to 5 days or in the freezer for up to 3 months.

SAFE & SIMPLE FOOD ALLERGY PREVENTION

Cast-Iron Skillet Corn Bread

PEANUTS · **EGGS** · **COW'S MILK** · FISH · **TREE NUTS** · **WHEAT** · **SOY** · SHELLFISH · SESAME
　　　　　2 g　　　3 g　　　　　　　3 g　　　1 g　　1 g

People sometimes have strong opinions about whether corn bread should be sweet or savory. For babies, I prefer savory versions to help keep added sugar intake low, and this corn bread recipe is especially helpful at packing in good amounts of five top allergens. If you have leftovers (I usually do as the yield is generous), try gently reheating in a toaster and serving with butter and jam for breakfast.

. . . .

1. Place a 9-inch cast-iron skillet in the oven, then preheat to 425°F.

2. In a large bowl, whisk together the cornmeal, flours, baking powder, baking soda, and salt. Whisk in the milks and eggs, then 6 tablespoons melted butter. Do not overmix. Gently fold in the cheese.

3. Turn the oven temperature down to 375°F and carefully remove the skillet. Use the remaining 2 tablespoons butter to grease the inside of the skillet, then pour in the batter.

4. Bake until a toothpick inserted into the center comes out clean, 25–28 minutes. Serve warm or at room temperature. For BLF, serve finger-length strips of corn bread for babies using a palmar or pincer grasp and coach your baby to take small bites. Store leftovers in an airtight container in the refrigerator for up to 1 week or in the freezer for up to 3 months.

MAKE IT A MEAL Serve with Turkey and Tempeh Slow Cooker Chili (page 198) and a side of steamed green beans.

YIELD Serves 10
PREP TIME 10 minutes
COOK TIME 25 minutes

1¼ cups stone-ground yellow cornmeal

1 cup **all-purpose flour**

1 cup **almond flour**

1 tablespoon baking powder

½ teaspoon baking soda

½ teaspoon kosher salt

1 cup **buttermilk**

1½ cups plain, unsweetened **soy milk**

3 large **eggs**

8 tablespoons (1 stick) unsalted **butter,** melted, divided

1 cup shredded **Colby Jack cheese**

Coconut Curry Lentil Stew

PEANUTS   EGGS   **COW'S MILK**   FISH   **TREE NUTS**   WHEAT   **SOY**   SHELLFISH   SESAME

                   <1 g   1 g   4 g

YIELD Serves 8
(1¾ cups per serving)
PREP TIME 20 minutes
COOK TIME 45 minutes

I've been serving different versions of this stew to my daughters since they were babies. Slightly spicy but also subtly sweet, the stew is a complete, balanced meal on its own with plenty of carbohydrates from the starchy vegetables, but you can always serve it over basmati rice or another grain if you prefer. *Note: To make this recipe, you will need a blender.*

½ cup **raw cashews**

2 teaspoons **ghee** or avocado oil

2 large shallots, peeled and diced

1 large carrot, peeled and diced

2 garlic cloves, minced

2 teaspoons minced fresh ginger

1 (28-ounce) can diced tomatoes

4 cups low-sodium vegetable broth

2 (14-ounce) cans full-fat coconut milk

¾ cup dried red lentils, rinsed and picked through

1 large sweet potato, peeled and diced

1 large parsnip, peeled and diced

1 tablespoon curry powder

1 tablespoon ground turmeric

1 teaspoon kosher salt

1 teaspoon ground cumin

½ teaspoon ground coriander

½ teaspoon ground cinnamon

¼ teaspoon freshly ground black pepper

1 (14-ounce) package **extra-firm tofu**, cut into ½-inch cubes

2 large handfuls baby spinach

2 tablespoons minced fresh cilantro

1. Put the cashews in a small bowl, cover with hot water, and let soak for 30 minutes.

2. Meanwhile, in a large stockpot, melt the ghee over medium-high heat. Add the shallots and carrot and cook, stirring continuously, until the vegetables begin to soften, about 8 minutes. Turn the heat down to medium, add the garlic and ginger, and cook until fragrant, 2–3 minutes.

3. Add the tomatoes with their juices, the broth, coconut milk, lentils, sweet potato, parsnip, curry powder, turmeric, salt, cumin, coriander, cinnamon, and pepper. Bring to a boil, turn the heat down to medium-low, and simmer for 20 minutes.

4. Add the tofu and continue to simmer until the lentils, sweet potato, and parsnip are tender, about 10 minutes.

5. Drain the cashews and transfer to a blender. Remove 1 cup of the hot broth and add to the blender with the cashews. Remove the center cap from the blender lid and hold a towel over the hole to allow steam to escape. Blend until smooth.

6. Add the blended mixture to the soup, along with the spinach. Stir to combine. Garnish with the cilantro and serve warm. Store leftovers in an airtight container in the refrigerator for up to 5 days or in the freezer for up to 3 months.

MAKE IT A MEAL Serve with steamed asparagus for a balanced baby meal.

Lasagna Roll-Ups

PEANUTS **EGGS** **COW'S MILK** FISH **TREE NUTS** WHEAT SOY SHELLFISH SESAME
        2 g   8 g   4 g

YIELD Makes 8 roll-ups
(1 roll-up per serving)
PREP TIME 30 minutes
COOK TIME 35 minutes

These lasagna roll-ups are very filling because they are rolled in lasagna sheets made with almonds, which are higher in protein and fiber than regular wheat-based pasta. Because they are so delicious, the girls and I are often tempted to each take two rolls . . . but we often don't end up finishing both because just one is such a satisfying serving, even for an adult.

1 (32-ounce jar) low-sodium, no-sugar-added marinara sauce, divided

1¾ cups **full-fat ricotta cheese**

2 large **eggs**

1 (10-ounce) package frozen spinach, thawed and squeezed dry

2 garlic cloves, minced

1 teaspoon dried oregano

½ teaspoon kosher salt

¼ teaspoon freshly ground black pepper

⅛ teaspoon ground nutmeg

1 cup (4 ounces) shredded **mozzarella cheese**, divided

½ cup grated **Parmesan cheese**, divided

8 no-cook **almond flour lasagna sheets** (I love Capello's brand)

1. Preheat the oven to 350°F.

2. Spread 2 cups marinara sauce in the bottom of a 9 × 13-inch baking pan.

3. In a medium bowl, mix the ricotta cheese, eggs, spinach, garlic, oregano, salt, pepper, nutmeg, and half each of the mozzarella and Parmesan cheeses. Stir until well combined.

4. Spread ⅓ cup cheese mixture over the length of each lasagna noodle. Carefully roll up and place seam-side down on top of the sauce in the baking pan.

5. Spoon the remaining marinara sauce over the rolls and sprinkle with the remaining cheeses.

6. Cover loosely with aluminum foil and bake until the filling is cooked through and the cheese is melted, about 35 minutes. Serve warm. For BLF, if you have a baby who tends to overstuff their mouth, consider cutting these lasagna rolls into small bites before serving. Coach your baby to take only one bite at a time and chew carefully before swallowing. The almond flour lasagna sheets are very soft and easy to mash down and move around inside the mouth, but some babies may be tempted to try and shove in the whole roll. Store leftovers in an airtight container in the refrigerator for up to 5 days.

RECIPE NOTE If you can't find no-cook almond flour lasagna noodles or prefer not to use them, you can substitute regular wheat-based lasagna noodles and cook them before filling and rolling. They tend to be narrower than the almond flour version, so instead of filling 8 roll-ups with ⅓ cup filling, aim for 10–11 roll-ups with about ¼ cup filling instead.

MAKE IT A MEAL Serve with Roasted Zucchini Sticks (page 218) for a balanced baby meal.

Many Nut Pesto Pasta

PEANUTS   EGGS   **COW'S MILK**   FISH   **TREE NUTS**   **WHEAT**   SOY   SHELLFISH   SESAME
                           3 g   4 g   7 g

YIELD Serves 4
(⅓ cup per serving)
PREP TIME 15 minutes

¼ cup shelled, roasted, unsalted **pistachios**

¼ cup raw **walnuts**

¼ cup **pine nuts**

5–6 garlic cloves, minced

4 cups fresh basil leaves

Juice of 1 lemon

½ teaspoon kosher salt

¼ teaspoon freshly ground black pepper

⅔ cup extra-virgin olive oil

½ cup grated **Parmesan** cheese

8 ounces **rigatoni**

2 cups cherry or grape tomatoes, quartered

If you can't find rigatoni, look for other large pasta shapes that have texture and are easier for babies to grip, such as fusilli, penne, and shells. If you have leftover pesto, freeze it in silicone ice cube trays for up to 6 months. This way when you want to use pesto in a recipe like the Presto Pressed Pesto Grilled Cheese sandwiches on page 173, it's easy to defrost only as many cubes as you need. *Note: To make this recipe, you will need a high-speed blender or food processor.*

1. In a high-speed blender, pulse the pistachios, walnuts, pine nuts, garlic, basil, lemon juice, salt, and pepper, stopping to scrape down the sides as needed, until finely chopped.

2. With the motor running, slowly drizzle in the olive oil and process until everything is finely chopped and well incorporated. Fold in the cheese and stir by hand to combine.

3. Bring a medium pot of water to a boil, add the rigatoni, and cook until very tender, 1–2 minutes longer than recommended on the package directions. Before draining, remove ½ cup of the cooking water.

4. Toss the pasta and tomatoes with ⅔ cup pesto and 2 tablespoons of the reserved pasta cooking water. A tablespoon at a time, add more water and/or pesto if needed, until the pasta reaches your desired level of creaminess. Serve warm. Store leftover pesto pasta in an airtight container in the refrigerator for up to 5 days or in the freezer for up to 3 months. Store leftover pesto in an airtight container in the refrigerator for up to 1 week.

MAKE IT A MEAL This meal provides a good balance of nutrients on its own, but for some added iron, protein, and fiber, consider including a side of smashed cannellini beans.

Peanut Butter Sweet Potato Casserole

PEANUTS **EGGS** **COW'S MILK** FISH TREE NUTS **WHEAT** SOY SHELLFISH SESAME
3 g   1 g   1 g   1 g

Peanut butter and sweet potatoes blend beautifully in this cozy dish, which incorporates multiple top allergens and works well at any meal of the day. *Note: To make this recipe, you will need a food processor.*

1. Preheat the oven to 425°F. Line a rimmed baking sheet with parchment paper and lightly oil an 8 × 8-inch baking pan or spray with nonstick cooking spray.

2. Pierce the sweet potatoes a few times on all sides with a fork. Place on the prepared baking sheet and roast until tender and cooked through, about 55 minutes. Set aside to cool, and turn the oven temperature down to 350°F.

3. Once the potatoes are cool enough to handle, cut them in half, scoop the flesh into a medium bowl, and mash (discard the skins). Add the eggs, milk, peanut butter, and vanilla and mix until smooth. Spread evenly in the prepared baking pan.

4. Sprinkle the ground peanuts and breadcrumbs evenly over the top and bake until the center is set, about 35 minutes. Serve warm. For BLF, offer in a shallow bowl for scooping with hands or on a preloaded spoon. Store leftovers in an airtight container in the refrigerator for up to 5 days or in the freezer for up to 3 months.

MAKE IT A MEAL Serve with roasted chicken and a side of steamed green beans for a balanced baby dinner (or perhaps some cooked cinnamon apples if serving for breakfast or lunch).

YIELD Serves 12
(½ cup per serving)
PREP TIME 10 minutes
COOK TIME 1½ hours

2 pounds sweet potatoes

2 large **eggs**

¾ cup whole **milk**

½ cup smooth **peanut butter**

1 teaspoon vanilla extract

½ cup ground roasted, unsalted **peanuts**

½ cup **panko breadcrumbs**

Miso Mushroom Soup with Egg

PEANUTS **EGGS** COW'S MILK FISH TREE NUTS **WHEAT** **SOY** SHELLFISH **SESAME**
  6 g   8 g   11 g   <1 g

YIELD Serves 4
(2½ cups per serving)
PREP TIME 30 minutes
COOK TIME 30 minutes

During the colder months, I often make a double batch of this recipe and freeze single servings (without the eggs) for nights when only one or two of my girls are home and we don't feel like cooking. It keeps exceptionally well and makes a warming, balanced, one-bowl meal that is perfect for movie night.

4 large **eggs**

9 ounces **udon noodles**

1 (14-ounce) package extra-firm **tofu**

3 tablespoons avocado oil, divided

2 teaspoons **toasted sesame oil**

2 garlic cloves, minced

1 teaspoon grated fresh ginger

8 cups low-sodium vegetable or mushroom broth

2 tablespoons low-sodium **soy sauce**

1 pound baby bok choy, trimmed and finely chopped

4 ounces shiitake mushrooms, stemmed and diced

1 tablespoon white **miso paste**

1 tablespoon **sesame seeds** (optional)

2 scallions (green parts only), finely chopped (optional)

1. Put the eggs in a medium saucepan, cover with water, and bring to a boil. Turn the heat down to low and simmer for about 14 minutes, until hard-boiled. Transfer the eggs to a strainer and cool for a few minutes under cold running water.

2. While the eggs are cooking, bring a large pot of water to a boil, add the udon noodles, and cook according to the package directions. Drain and set aside.

3. Wrap the tofu in a clean tea towel or paper towels, place on a large plate, and place a heavy pan or canned goods on top. Let sit to press out excess moisture for 10 minutes. Unwrap and cut into ½-inch cubes; set aside.

4. In a large saucepan, heat 1 tablespoon avocado oil over medium heat. Add the sesame oil, garlic, and ginger and cook, stirring continuously, until fragrant, about 1 minute. Add the broth and soy sauce, turn the heat up to medium-high, and bring to a boil. Turn the heat down to low, cover, and simmer for 10 minutes.

5. While the broth simmers, heat the 2 remaining tablespoons of avocado oil in a large skillet over medium heat. Add the bok choy and mushrooms and cook, stirring occasionally, until the vegetables are soft and lightly browned, about 10 minutes. Add the vegetables and cubed tofu to the broth.

6. Turn off the heat under the broth. Ladle about ½ cup broth into a small bowl, add the miso paste, and whisk to combine. Pour the mixture back into the broth.

7. Peel and slice the eggs (halves for adults, quarters or small bites for babies).

8. Serve bowls of broth topped with noodles and egg, and garnished with sesame seeds and scallions, if you like. For BLF, offer a deconstructed version of this soup with wedges of egg, a shallow bowl of mushrooms and bok choy for scooping with hands, soft cubes of tofu, and a shallow bowl of broth with noodles cut into 2-inch long strands to make it easier for your baby to "chew." (Divided plates work great for this dish!) Store leftover soup in an airtight container in the refrigerator for up to 5 days or in the freezer for up to 3 months.

Roasted Zucchini Sticks

PEANUTS · **EGGS** 2 g · **COW'S MILK** 1 g · FISH · TREE NUTS · **WHEAT** 1 g · SOY · SHELLFISH · SESAME

YIELD Serves 4
PREP TIME 15 minutes
COOK TIME 30 minutes

1 large **egg**

2 tablespoons **whole milk**

¼ cup **breadcrumbs**

2 tablespoons grated **Parmesan cheese**

1 teaspoon pizza seasoning, dried oregano, Italian seasoning, or ground cumin

2 medium zucchinis, cut into finger-length, ½-inch-thick sticks

These roasted zucchini sticks are an ideal food for young eaters. Fall-apart tender on the inside and slightly crunchy on the outside, they are easy to mash down with gums and offer plenty of flavor along with exposure to three top allergens. As your baby grows, feel free to slice the zucchini into rounds rather than sticks. We eat these often in my home and my girls affectionately refer to them as "zucchini chips" while gobbling them up.

1. Preheat the oven to 400°F. Line a rimmed baking sheet with parchment paper.

2. In a shallow bowl, whisk the egg and milk until smooth.

3. Combine the breadcrumbs, cheese, and seasoning in a separate shallow bowl.

4. Dip the zucchini sticks first in the egg mixture, then coat with the breadcrumb mixture. Arrange in a single layer on the prepared baking sheet.

5. Roast until the zucchini sticks are fork-tender and lightly browned, about 30 minutes.

6. Cool on the baking sheet on a cooling rack for about 5 minutes before serving. These are best eaten the day they are cooked, as leftovers can get mushy quickly when refrigerated.

MAKE IT A MEAL Serve with Easy Foil-Grilled Haddock (page 178) and baked potato for a balanced baby meal.

Zucchini Boats

PEANUTS   **EGGS**   **COW'S MILK**   FISH   TREE NUTS   **WHEAT**   SOY   SHELLFISH   SESAME
       2 g   6 g   1 g

These boats taste like a lighter version of spanakopita (Greek spinach pie), and the filling is adapted from a family recipe. Given how high feta and cottage cheeses are in sodium, the recipe is better suited to babies ages 1 and up, although a taste here and there for younger babies is fine.

1. Preheat the oven to 350°F and lightly oil a 9×13-inch baking pan.

2. Halve the zucchinis lengthwise and scoop out the middles with a spoon until they look like boats. Discard or repurpose the scooped-out portions.

3. In a medium skillet, heat 1 tablespoon olive oil over medium-high heat. Add the onion and cook until tender and translucent, about 2 minutes. Add the spinach and cook until heated through, about 5 minutes.

4. Transfer the mixture to a large bowl and add the dill, cottage cheese, feta, eggs, remaining 1 tablespoon olive oil, salt, and pepper and stir until combined.

5. Fill the center of each zucchini boat with the spinach mixture, top with a sprinkle of breadcrumbs and a drizzle of melted ghee, and place in the prepared baking pan.

6. Bake for 45 minutes. Serve warm. For BLF, cut boats into bite-sized pieces before serving. Store leftovers in an airtight container in the refrigerator for up to 5 days.

MAKE IT A MEAL Serve with baked potato fries, strips of roasted red bell pepper, and strips of grilled steak for a balanced baby meal.

YIELD Serves 6
(1 zucchini boat per serving)
PREP TIME 20 minutes
COOK TIME 1 hour

3 medium zucchinis

2 tablespoons extra-virgin olive oil, divided

1 cup diced white onion

5 ounces frozen spinach, thawed and squeezed dry

½ cup finely chopped fresh dill

½ cup **full-fat cottage cheese**

1 cup crumbled **feta cheese**

2 large **eggs**

½ teaspoon kosher salt

¼ teaspoon freshly ground black pepper

½ cup **panko breadcrumbs**

1 tablespoon **ghee**, melted

DINNER + SIDES

219

Spaghetti Squash Quinoa Bake

PEANUTS   EGGS   **COW'S MILK**   FISH   TREE NUTS   WHEAT   **SOY**   SHELLFISH   SESAME

                         3 g   1 g

YIELD Serves 6
(1½ cups per serving)
PREP TIME 15 minutes
COOK TIME 50 minutes

This balanced dish includes several key nutrients for babies, including iron for growth and brain development, zinc for immune health, omega-3 fatty acids for heart health, and calcium for strong bones. If you have toddlers, they may get a kick out of the fact that the spaghetti squash skins are a natural serving dish for the casserole created by Mother Nature herself.

1 spaghetti squash

⅓ cup quinoa

2 teaspoons **ghee**

5 ounces baby spinach

1 (14-ounce) can quartered artichoke hearts, drained and chopped

1 cup **cream cheese**

½ cup **silken tofu**

1 teaspoon dried basil

½ teaspoon dried thyme

½ teaspoon kosher salt

¼ teaspoon ground black pepper

½ cup grated **Parmesan cheese**, divided

2 tablespoons finely chopped fresh chives (optional)

1. Position oven racks in the top and bottom thirds of the oven. Preheat the oven to 400°F. Line a rimmed baking sheet with parchment paper.

2. Cut the squash in half lengthwise. Place it cut-side down on the prepared baking sheet and bake on the lower rack until tender, about 45 minutes.

3. While the squash bakes, cook the quinoa according to the package directions, then transfer to a large bowl.

4. In a large skillet, melt the ghee over medium-high heat. Add the spinach and cook, stirring continuously until wilted, about 4 minutes. Add the spinach to the quinoa.

5. When the squash is done, remove it from the oven and preheat the broiler.

6. When the squash is cool enough to handle, use a large spoon to scoop out the squash from the skin and add it to the quinoa. Do not discard the squash skins.

7. Add the artichoke hearts, cream cheese, tofu, basil, thyme, salt, pepper, and ¼ cup Parmesan cheese. Stir to combine. Scoop the mixture evenly into both squash skins and sprinkle the remaining ¼ cup cheese and the chives (if using) over the tops.

8. Broil until the cheese is melted and lightly browned, about 3 minutes. Garnish with the chives if you like. For BLF, serve in a shallow bowl for scooping with hands or on a preloaded spoon. Store leftovers in an airtight container in the refrigerator for up to 5 days or in the freezer for up to 3 months.

MAKE IT A MEAL Serve with Pinkalicious Beet Hummus (page 171) and strips of pita bread for a balanced meal.

African Peanut Stew

PEANUTS **EGGS** **COW'S MILK** FISH TREE NUTS WHEAT SOY SHELLFISH SESAME
5 g 4 g <1 g

YIELD Serves 6
(1½ cups per serving)
PREP TIME 30 minutes
COOK TIME 6 hours

If you are a weekend meal prepper, you'll love this hearty, nutritious recipe that combines iron-rich (chickpeas, peanut butter), vitamin C–rich (kale), and energy-rich (sweet potatoes) ingredients all in one pot. As a mom, I find that balanced, make-ahead options like this that keep well in the refrigerator or freezer save me a ton of time in the long run. Double the batch and freeze the extra for chilly winter evenings when you don't feel like cooking. *Note: To make this recipe, you will need a 6-quart (or larger) slow cooker and a blender or food processor.*

For the stew
1 teaspoon **ghee** or **unsalted butter**

1 yellow onion, diced

1 (28-ounce) can low-sodium diced tomatoes

½ cup smooth **peanut butter**

3 garlic cloves, peeled and halved

2 teaspoons ground cumin

1 teaspoon kosher salt (optional)

½ teaspoon ground cinnamon

¼ teaspoon smoked paprika

3 pounds sweet potatoes (about 6 medium), peeled and cut into 1-inch pieces

1 (15-ounce) can low-sodium chickpeas, rinsed and drained

1 cup low-sodium vegetable broth

8 cups finely chopped stemmed kale

For the toppings
4 large **eggs**

1 cup fresh cilantro leaves, finely chopped

2 tablespoons ground **peanuts**

1. Melt the ghee in a medium skillet over medium heat. Add the onion and cook until soft, 5–6 minutes. Transfer to a 6-quart slow cooker.

2. In a blender or food processor, puree the tomatoes with their juices, the peanut butter, garlic, cumin, salt (if using), cinnamon, and paprika. Transfer the blended mixture to the slow cooker.

3. Add the sweet potatoes, chickpeas, and broth and stir to combine. Cover and cook on low for 6 hours, or until the potatoes are soft. Stir in the kale during the last 30 minutes.

4. When the stew is almost done, put the eggs in a small saucepan, cover with water, and bring to a boil. Turn the heat down to low and simmer for about 14 minutes, until hard-boiled. Transfer the eggs to a strainer and cool for a few minutes under cold running water, then peel and chop.

5. Top the stew with the eggs, cilantro, and peanuts and serve warm. For BLF, smash the chickpeas with the back of a fork before serving to your baby and serve on a preloaded spoon or in a shallow bowl and allow your baby to scoop with their hands. Store leftovers in an airtight container in the refrigerator for up to 5 days or in the freezer for up to 3 months.

BLF Saag Paneer

PEANUTS   EGGS   **COW'S MILK**   FISH   TREE NUTS   WHEAT   SOY   SHELLFISH   SESAME
14 g

YIELD Serves 4
(1 cup per serving)
PREP TIME 15 minutes
COOK TIME 35 minutes

10 ounces fresh or frozen spinach or stemmed kale

2 tablespoons **ghee**, divided

12 ounces **paneer**, cut into ½-inch cubes

1 teaspoon cumin seeds

1 small yellow onion, diced

4 garlic cloves, minced

1 (1-inch) piece ginger, peeled and minced

½ serrano or other mild chile, seeded and finely chopped

1 teaspoon garam masala

½ teaspoon kosher salt

¼ cup **heavy cream**

2 tablespoons water

Paneer is an Indian cheese made from curdled milk that is ideal for baby-led feeding because of its soft texture and low sodium content. Babies will benefit from the complex flavors and nutrient-rich sauce in this family favorite! *Note: To make this recipe, you will need a blender or a food processor.*

1. Pour 1 inch of water into a medium saucepan fitted with a steamer basket and bring to a boil. Add the spinach, cover, and steam for 3 minutes. Transfer the spinach to a blender or food processor and blend until smooth, then set aside.

2. In a large skillet, melt 1 tablespoon ghee over medium heat. Working in batches, add the paneer and fry until lightly browned, about 8 minutes. Transfer to a plate and set aside.

3. Melt the remaining 1 tablespoon ghee in the same skillet over medium heat. Add the cumin seeds and cook for 2 minutes. Add the onion and cook, stirring continuously, until softened, about 8 minutes. Add the garlic, ginger, serrano, garam masala, salt, and pureed spinach and stir until combined and softly bubbling, about 2 minutes.

4. Stir in the cream and water. Add the cheese, turn the heat down to low, cover, and simmer for 15 minutes.

5. Serve warm. Store in an airtight container in the refrigerator for up to 5 days or in the freezer for up to 3 months.

MAKE IT A MEAL Serve with naan bread for dipping and slices of fresh tomato for a balanced baby meal.

Lemon Tahini Lentil Stew

PEANUTS   EGGS   COW'S MILK   FISH   TREE NUTS   WHEAT   SOY   SHELLFISH   **SESAME**
2 g

The texture of this stew is very thick and ideal for babies who like to use their hands to explore food and self-feed. Tahini works well as a way to thicken the broth and tastes amazing, but if you don't have access to tahini or want to try an alternative option, the stew tastes slightly sweeter and just as creamy with an equal amount of raw cashews blended into the broth. *Note: To make this recipe, you will need a blender.*

1. Combine the carrots, celery, broth, lentils, coriander, and cumin in a large stockpot and bring to a boil over high heat. Turn the heat down to medium-low, cover, and simmer until the lentils and vegetables are softened, about 15 minutes.

2. Transfer 1 cup of the hot broth to a blender and add the tahini. Remove the center cap from the blender lid and hold a towel over the hole to allow steam to escape. Blend until smooth.

3. Add the blended mixture to the soup, along with the spinach, and stir to combine. Heat over medium heat until the spinach is just wilted, about 3 minutes.

4. Remove from the heat, add the lemon juice, salt, and pepper, and stir to combine. Garnish with the parsley and serve warm. For BLF, this stew works well served on a preloaded spoon. You can also serve it in a shallow bowl and allow your baby to scoop with their hands. Store leftovers in an airtight container in the refrigerator for up to 5 days or in the freezer for up to 3 months.

MAKE IT A MEAL This meal provides a good balance of nutrients on its own, but it tastes great with a side of garlic bread and a green salad.

YIELD Serves 4
(1½ cups per serving)
PREP TIME 15 minutes
COOK TIME 40 minutes

2 large carrots, peeled and finely chopped

3 celery ribs, finely chopped

5 cups low-sodium vegetable broth

1½ cups red lentils, picked over and rinsed

1 teaspoon ground coriander

1¼ teaspoons ground cumin

2½ tablespoons **tahini (sesame paste)**

2 cups finely chopped baby spinach or stemmed kale

Juice of 2 lemons

½ teaspoon kosher salt

¼ teaspoon freshly ground black pepper

2 tablespoons finely chopped fresh flat-leaf parsley

Dessert

With the exception of the Better-for-You Black Bean Brownies, this small collection of baby-friendly sweet treats is largely free of (or low in) added sugars and works well when offered at breakfast or lunch. I've found it's often nice to have a sweet treat to share with your baby on a holiday or at a gathering when other sweets will be served, so that your baby can feel included in the fun. Be forewarned, the brownies are downright decadent. You may not even be able to tell that they are made with black beans!

Cherry Almond BLF Cookies **227**

Mango Surprise Smoothie **228**

Peanut Butter Banana Baby Cookies **229**

Cherry Chocolate Ice Pops **230**

Pumpkin Spice Cookies **231**

Toasted Coconut Pumpkin Pudding **232**

Peanut Butter Power Pops **233**

Better-for-You Black Bean Brownies **234**

Cherry Almond BLF Cookies

PEANUTS   EGGS   **COW'S MILK**   FISH   **TREE NUTS**   WHEAT   SOY   SHELLFISH   SESAME
<1 g   2 g

Soft in texture, gluten-free, and with no added sugar or salt, these baby-friendly cookies are made with wholesome, minimally processed ingredients and work equally well as a dessert, snack, or nutritious breakfast component. *Note: To make this recipe, you will need a high-speed blender or food processor.*

YIELD Makes 12 cookies
(2 cookies per serving)
PREP TIME 10 minutes
COOK TIME 20 minutes

1 cup pitted sweet cherries

1 large, ripe banana

½ cup **almond flour**

¼ cup melted **ghee** or coconut oil

1 teaspoon vanilla extract

½ cup old-fashioned oats

1. Preheat the oven to 350°F. Line a rimmed baking sheet with parchment paper.

2. In a food processor or high-speed blender, combine the cherries, banana, almond flour, ghee, and vanilla and blend until smooth, stopping to scrape down the sides as needed.

3. Fold in the oats and mix by hand with a silicone spatula.

4. Using a 2-tablespoon (or 1-ounce) cookie scoop, scoop the dough into your hands, roll into 1-inch balls, and place on the prepared baking sheet. If needed (to prevent sticking), apply flour to your hands first, or spray with nonstick cooking spray.

5. Bake for 15 minutes. Using a nonstick spatula, press each cookie flat, then bake for another 5 minutes.

6. Cool on the baking sheet on a cooling rack for at least 10 minutes before serving. Store in an airtight container in the refrigerator for up to 1 week or in the freezer for up to 3 months.

RECIPE NOTE I always use thawed frozen pitted sweet cherries for this recipe. Not having to remove the pits saves a ton of time, and when you use frozen, there's no need to wait until cherries are in season.

MAKE IT A MEAL Serve with smashed blueberries and a dollop of plain, full-fat yogurt for a balanced baby meal.

DESSERT

Mango Surprise Smoothie

PEANUTS 2 g   EGGS   **COW'S MILK** 4 g   FISH   **TREE NUTS** 3 g   WHEAT   **SOY** 2 g   SHELLFISH   SESAME

YIELD Serves 2
(1½ cups per serving)
PREP TIME 5 minutes

1 large navel orange, peeled

2 cups frozen mango chunks

1 tablespoon smooth **peanut butter**

¼–½ teaspoon minced fresh ginger

¼ cup **silken tofu**

⅓ cup halved raw **walnuts**

1 cup **whole milk**

Peanuts and walnuts taste surprisingly delicious when blended with tropical fruits! If you are sensitive to the strong flavor of fresh ginger, feel free to adjust the level in this recipe by starting with ¼ teaspoon ginger and tasting before deciding whether to add more. You can also change up the flavor and nutrients in this smoothie by using ripe pear instead of mango (leave the skin on for extra fiber and nutrients). *Note: To make this recipe, you will need a blender.*

1. Combine all of the ingredients in a blender and blend until smooth.

2. For BLF, use thicker beverages like this smoothie as a helpful way to strengthen your baby's open-cup drinking skills. The thickness of the fluid doesn't flow as quickly toward the throat as water or milk and gives babies more time to manage fluid in the mouth, building familiarity and confidence around the process of drinking from a cup. If you have a baby who tends to cough and sputter a lot when drinking from an open cup, this tip is especially helpful! This smoothie does not keep well in the refrigerator and is best enjoyed right away as a beverage. If you have leftovers, you can pour them into ice pop molds and enjoy within 3 months.

MAKE IT A MEAL Serve with buttered toast strips and hard-boiled egg for a balanced baby breakfast.

Peanut Butter Banana Baby Cookies

PEANUTS **EGGS** **COW'S MILK** FISH **TREE NUTS** WHEAT SOY SHELLFISH SESAME
4 g <1 g <1 g 2 g

With no added sugar and tons of nutrient-rich ingredients, these cookies may look like a dessert but also work well for breakfast. They are beloved by babies and kids alike. Whenever I make a batch, they disappear quickly because my girls love grabbing a few on their way to after-school sports and activities. My favorite way to enjoy them is with a layer of raspberry jam on top, alongside my morning coffee or tea. *Note: To make this recipe, you will need an electric mixer.*

1. Preheat the oven to 350°F. Line two rimmed baking sheets with parchment paper.

2. In a medium bowl, use an electric mixer to beat the peanut butter, bananas, and ghee on medium speed until the mixture is smooth and there are no lumps. Add the eggs and vanilla and beat until well combined.

3. In a small bowl, whisk together the flour, oats, baking soda, cinnamon, and salt. Fold the dry ingredients into the wet.

4. Using a 1-tablespoon cookie scoop or measuring spoon, measure out the dough and roll into a ball with your hands. Place on the prepared baking sheets and flatten in a crisscross pattern with the flat side of a fork.

5. Bake until the cookies are lightly browned, 12–13 minutes.

6. Cool the baking sheets on cooling racks for 10 minutes before serving. Store in an airtight container at room temperature for up to 2 days, in the refrigerator for up to 1 week, or in the freezer for up to 3 months. Once refrigerated or frozen, the cookies taste best when gently reheated in a toaster oven.

YIELD Makes 28 cookies (2 cookies per serving)
PREP TIME 15 minutes
COOK TIME 13 minutes

1 cup smooth **peanut butter**

1 cup mashed ripe bananas (about 2 bananas)

¼ cup melted **ghee**

2 large **eggs**

2 teaspoons vanilla extract

1 cup **almond flour**

½ cup quick-cooking oats

1 teaspoon baking soda

1 teaspoon ground cinnamon

½ teaspoon kosher salt

RECIPE NOTE To make measuring peanut butter less messy, try spraying your measuring cup first with a little nonstick cooking spray.

MAKE IT A MEAL Serve with some cottage cheese and smashed blueberries for a balanced baby meal.

DESSERT

Cherry Chocolate Ice Pops

PEANUTS   EGGS   **COW'S MILK**   FISH   **TREE NUTS**   WHEAT   **SOY**   SHELLFISH   **SESAME**
                        4 g   1 g   1 g   1 g

SAFE & SIMPLE FOOD ALLERGY PREVENTION

YIELD Makes 6 ice pops
(1 ice pop per serving)
PREP TIME 5 minutes
INACTIVE PREP TIME 4 hours

1 cup plain, unsweetened
soy milk

1 (5-ounce) container plain,
full-fat Greek yogurt

1½ cups frozen pitted sweet
cherries

1½ tablespoons unsweetened
cocoa powder

1½ tablespoons **tahini
(sesame paste)**

1 tablespoon smooth
almond butter

1½ teaspoons vanilla extract

Cooling smoothie pops are soothing on sore, teething gums and so refreshing during the warmer months. Chocolaty, nutty, and naturally sweet, these pops are sure to keep your baby occupied for a spell. They have no added sugars and come together with minimal effort. Feel free to use bananas instead of cherries or a mix of both for a different flavor profile. *Note: To make this recipe, you will need a blender and six 3-ounce ice pop molds.*

1. Combine all of the ingredients in a blender and blend until smooth, stopping to scrape down the sides as needed.

2. Pour into ice pop molds and freeze for at least 4 hours.

3. Serve cold and store leftovers in the freezer for up to 4 months.

MAKE IT A MEAL Serve with strips of buttered waffle and scrambled egg for a balanced baby breakfast.

Pumpkin Spice Cookies

PEANUTS   **EGGS**   **COW'S MILK**   FISH   **TREE NUTS**   **WHEAT**   SOY   SHELLFISH   SESAME
1 g   1 g   <1 g   1 g   1 g

Packed with pumpkin flavor and bursting with nutrients, these cookies can be customized to include your child's favorite mix-ins. Best of all, they are easy to make, take only 45 minutes from start to finish, and include 5 different allergens. *Note: To make this recipe, you will need a high-speed blender or food processor.*

1. Preheat the oven to 350°F. Line a rimmed baking sheet with parchment paper or spray with nonstick cooking spray.

2. In a blender or food processor, combine the ground pecans, eggs, milk, pumpkin puree, peanut butter, oats, bananas, flour, flaxseeds, pumpkin pie spice, and salt. Pulse until the mixture forms a dough. Fold in the chocolate chips (if using) using a silicone spatula.

3. Use a 2-tablespoon (1-ounce) cookie scoop to scoop the dough into your hands and roll into 1-inch balls. Place on the prepared baking sheet and flatten into 2-inch-wide cookies. If needed (to prevent sticking), apply flour to your hands first, or spray with nonstick cooking spray.

4. Bake until light golden brown, about 25 minutes.

5. Transfer the cookies to a cooling rack and cool for 10 minutes before serving. Store in an airtight container in the refrigerator for up to 5 days or in the freezer for up to 3 months.

RECIPE NOTE If desired, stir in ¼ cup ground walnuts, ground almonds, or shredded coconut once the dough is formed.

MAKE IT A MEAL Serve with scrambled egg and applesauce for a balanced baby breakfast.

YIELD Makes 30 cookies (2 cookies per serving)
PREP TIME 15 minutes
COOK TIME 25 minutes

¾ cup ground **pecans**

2 large **eggs**, beaten

½ cup **whole milk**

½ cup canned pure pumpkin puree

¼ cup smooth **peanut butter**

1 cup quick-cooking oats

1 cup mashed extra-ripe bananas (about 2 bananas)

1 cup **all-purpose flour**

2 tablespoons ground flaxseeds

2 teaspoons pumpkin pie spice

¼ teaspoon fine sea salt

½ cup mini **chocolate chips** (optional; consider omitting for babies younger than 2 years)

DESSERT

231

Toasted Coconut Pumpkin Pudding

PEANUTS   EGGS   **COW'S MILK**   FISH   TREE NUTS   WHEAT   SOY   SHELLFISH   SESAME
4 g   1 g

YIELD Serves 4
(¼ cup per serving)
PREP TIME 5 minutes

4 teaspoons unsweetened shredded coconut

½ cup vanilla **full-fat yogurt**

½ cup canned pure pumpkin puree

¼ cup smooth **peanut butter**

½ teaspoon ground cinnamon

¼ teaspoon ground nutmeg

Fans of pumpkin spice will love this easy-to-make pudding that is subtly tart and sweet and loaded with vitamins, fiber, and probiotics. For a dairy-free version, swap out the dairy yogurt for vanilla coconut or soy yogurt. For a more robust, peanutty flavor, add an additional tablespoon of peanut butter. You can also add pumpkin seed or almond butter.

1. Toast the coconut, if desired, by spreading in an even layer on a small piece of aluminum foil and gently toasting in a toaster oven until lightly browned and fragrant, about 3 minutes. Or spread in an even layer in a medium skillet and toast over medium-low heat, stirring occasionally, until lightly brown, about 4 minutes.

2. Mix the yogurt, pumpkin puree, peanut butter, cinnamon, and nutmeg in a small bowl until smooth.

3. Top the mixture with the coconut and serve cold. Store in an airtight container in the refrigerator for up to 3 days or freeze in ice pop molds and enjoy within 3 months.

MAKE IT A MEAL Serve with plain oat O's cereal and a wedge of ripe, soft pear for a balanced baby meal.

Peanut Butter Power Pops

PEANUTS   EGGS   **COW'S MILK**   FISH   TREE NUTS   WHEAT   SOY   SHELLFISH   SESAME
4 g   2 g

Banana isn't the only fruit that pairs well with peanut butter! These sweet, creamy ice pops are made with no added sugars and sweetened with dates and blackberries. The recipe is easy to make in a high-speed blender, but if you don't have one, you can soak the pitted dates in hot water for about 5 minutes to help soften them up and then use a regular blender. Room-temperature dates will generally blend much more efficiently than refrigerated. *Note: To make this recipe, you will need a high-speed blender and six 3-ounce ice pop molds.*

1. Combine all of the ingredients in a high-speed blender and blend until smooth, stopping to scrape down the sides as needed.

2. Pour the mixture evenly into six ice pop molds and freeze until completely frozen, 4–6 hours.

3. Serve cold. If you can't budge the pops out of their molds, run the mold under a little hot water and they'll pop right out. Another pro tip is to poke the handle of the popsicle through the bottom of a paper muffin liner before handing it over to your baby—the paper liner will catch the melting drips! Store pops in the freezer and enjoy within 3 months.

MAKE IT A MEAL Serve with strips of toast topped with cream cheese and smashed blackberries for a balanced meal.

YIELD Makes 6 ice pops (1 ice pop per serving)
PREP TIME 8 minutes
INACTIVE PREP TIME 4–6 hours

⅓ cup plus 1 tablespoon smooth **peanut butter**

⅔ cup plain, **full-fat Greek yogurt**

12 large blackberries

6 Medjool dates, pitted

¼ teaspoon vanilla extract

⅛ teaspoon ground cinnamon

DESSERT

233

Better-for-You Black Bean Brownies

PEANUTS   **EGGS**   **COW'S MILK**   FISH   **TREE NUTS**   WHEAT   **SOY**   SHELLFISH   SESAME
           1 g   1 g   3 g   <1 g

YIELD Makes 12 brownies
(1 brownie per serving)
PREP TIME 10 minutes
COOK TIME 35 minutes

2 (15-ounce) cans low-sodium black beans, rinsed and drained

1½ cups **almond flour**

1¼ cups sugar

⅓ cup unsweetened cocoa powder

2 large **eggs**

⅔ cup plain, unsweetened **soy milk**

¼ cup melted **ghee**

1 tablespoon vanilla extract

1 teaspoon baking powder

½ teaspoon fine sea salt

1 cup **semisweet chocolate chips**

Rich in fiber, plant-based protein, iron, and other minerals that help support bone health, the black beans pack a strong nutritional punch in these brownies, but the experience of eating them is completely decadent. This is one of a small handful of recipes in this book that contains added sugars. You might want to hold off on serving these until your baby is older to help keep added sugar intake low, but if you want a few recipe options on hand for healthier treats, this one is a keeper. *Note: To make this recipe, you will need a blender.*

1. Preheat the oven to 350°F. Lightly oil a 9 × 13-inch baking pan.

2. Combine all of the ingredients except the chocolate chips in a blender and blend until the batter is smooth, stopping to scrape down the sides as needed.

3. Add the chocolate chips to the batter (reserving a handful to sprinkle over the top) and stir gently, but don't blend.

4. Transfer the batter to the prepared baking pan and smooth the top with a silicone spatula. Sprinkle the remaining chocolate chips evenly across the top.

5. Bake until the top is firm and set and does not jiggle, about 35 minutes.

6. Cool in the pan on a cooling rack before slicing. Store leftovers in an airtight container in the refrigerator for up to 5 days or in the freezer for up to 3 months.

SIGNING OFF

My friend, you are now ready to begin baby-led feeding and food allergy prevention! As you dive into the delicious journey that lies ahead, know that building trust with your baby is what matters most, as it does in all your parenting. Trust that your baby will follow their own appetite, meet nutrient needs, and explore new foods on their own timeline. And trust in yourself to perceive and respond to your baby's cues. When it comes to your baby, you are the expert.

In my mind, baby-led feeding isn't just a method of starting solids. It's part of a parenting style that helps foster more meaningful connectedness and mutual respect between you and your baby from the start.

How wonderful to give your little person—a tiny sponge—the lifelong gift of an appreciation for healthy foods, exciting flavors, recipe-related adventures, and the connectedness of family mealtimes and shared cultural cuisines with loved ones right from the very first few bites. Kudos to you for providing it. I wish you all the best as you begin.

xo Malina

ALLERGEN SWAPS

If your baby has been diagnosed with a food allergy or you are avoiding a particular allergen for another reason, here are some basic substitutions you can make in recipes and during food preparation.

Dairy Substitutes	How to use:
Plant-based milk alternatives	As a cow's milk replacement in cold and hot cereals, baked goods, smoothies, soups
Condensed coconut milk	As a condensed cow's milk replacement in recipes or to make dairy-free whipped cream
Vegan cheese or cashew cream	In recipes that require the creamy texture of soft dairy cheeses
Plant-based yogurts	As a cow's milk yogurt replacement in smoothies, in recipes as a substitute for buttermilk, as a meal or snack
Nutritional yeast	As a replacement for grated Parmesan cheese in foods that need a sprinkle of flavor (note—will not melt like cheese)
Coconut oil, almond milk–based butter substitute	As a replacement for butter in recipes

Egg action in recipes:	Substitutes (for 1 egg):	Use in which types of recipes:
Binding	1 tablespoon ground flaxseeds + 3 tablespoons water	Muffins, cakes, brownies, and cookies
Moisture	½ cup mashed banana ¼ cup unsweetened applesauce ½ cup pumpkin or squash puree ¼ cup pureed soft tofu or silken tofu	Muffins, cakes, brownies, and cookies
Thickening	2 tablespoons cornstarch	Sauces
Binding (savory)	2 tablespoons mashed potato flakes	Meatloaf, meatballs, and meat patties

Wheat Substitutes	How to use:
Finely ground tree nuts, almond flour, peanut flour, gluten-free rolled oats (pulsed in a food processor)	As a replacement for breadcrumbs when you need a crispy, bread-like coating
All-in-one blend (gluten-free flours)	As a replacement for all-purpose or whole wheat flour in quick bread recipes
Gluten-free all-purpose flour	As a replacement for all-purpose or whole wheat flour in yeast bread recipes
Cooked rice, mashed potato flakes	As a replacement binder in meatloaf or meatballs
Arrowroot flour, banana flour, tapioca flour	As a replacement for flour when thickening sauces
Sorghum flour	To make wheat-free porridge or flatbreads

Allergens	Substitutions
Tree nuts, peanuts, nut butters	Hemp seeds, sunflower seeds, pumpkin seeds, sesame seeds, chia seeds, roasted soybeans, peas, chickpeas; sunflower seed butter or mixed seed butters
Sesame	Peanuts, tree nuts, hemp seeds, sunflower seeds, pumpkin seeds, chia seeds, poppy seeds; sunflower seed butter or mixed seed butters made without sesame
Fish	Tofu, chicken, and turkey have a mild flavor and generally soft texture, making them a good substitute for fish.
Shellfish	Hearty white fish like cod has a similar consistency and holds up well in shellfish recipes; use tofu, chicken, or turkey if avoiding all seafood.
Soy	Peas, lentils, chickpeas, beans, dairy products

ACKNOWLEDGMENTS

I am deeply grateful to Claire Schulz, my magnificent editor; Amy Levenson, my agent extraordinaire; and the entire dream team at BenBella Books for believing in this project and helping me bring it to light.

Enormous thanks also go to my stellar advanced reader team, especially Carina Venter, PhD, RD; Marion Groetch, MS, RD, CDN; and Dr. Gideon Lack, MBBCh, FRCPch for helping deepen and expand my knowledge and understanding of this topic. And to Dr. Michael Pistiner, MD, MMSc; Sherry Coleman Collins, MS, RDN, LD; Leah Hackney, RD, LD, CSP; Melanie Potock, MA, CCC-SLP; Michael D. Wolf, PhD; Dr. Jennifer Gruen, MD; and Jill Castle, MS, RDN, to whom I am forever grateful for having contributed so much of their time, expertise, and insightful feedback to this manuscript.

Special shout-out to Chef Sara Haas, RDN, LDN, for sharing her cooking wisdom and experience with me, and for reviewing and editing these recipes with generosity, patience, and expertise. And to the wonderful team at ezpz for their partnership and for gifting me their thoughtful, beautifully designed products for my recipe photo shoots.

Sending appreciation and gratitude as well to my incredible team of Research Assistants, Beth Conlon, PhD, RDN; Amy Bryan, MS, RDN; and Gina Byers, MS, EP-C, who played such an important role in helping to conduct a review of the literature, as well as my 2023 Dietetic Interns, Amy Gionta, Susie Kice, Brittany Sito, Erica Jackson, Jessica Foung, Gabby Kirchner, Eva Lewandowski, and Alice Stejskal, for their creativity in the kitchen and help with recipe development.

Thank you also to the members of the Rye Moms Facebook Group who bravely volunteered to test recipes and graciously provided feedback. To my wonderful parents, Cynthia and Thomas Linkas, for their love, and for establishing within me early on an appreciation of the many ways food and meals knit families closer together. And to my friends and family for supporting me—especially my dietitian colleagues, dear friends, and mastermind partners who are always there when I need them: Mascha Davis, MPH, RDN; and Ginger Hultin, MS, RDN, CSO.

And of course, thank you to my three remarkable girls (and brutally honest recipe tasters): Alienna, Evangeline, and Solenne. You three paint my world in vibrant colors, you are my "why," and you will always be my babies.

NOTES

Chapter 1

1. Ruchi S. Gupta et al., "The Public Health Impact of Parent-Reported Childhood Food Allergies in the United States," *Pediatrics* 142, no. 6 (December 1, 2018): e20181235, https://doi.org/10.1542/peds.2018-1235.

2. Kate Roberts et al., "Parental Anxiety and Posttraumatic Stress Symptoms in Pediatric Food Allergy," *Journal of Pediatric Psychology* 46, no. 6 (July 1, 2021): 688–97, https://doi.org/10.1093/jpepsy/jsab012.

3. Bettina Holmberg Fagerlund et al., "Parental Concerns of Allergy or Hypersensitivity and the Infant's Diet," *Nursing Open* 6, no. 1 (August 19, 2018): 136–43, https://doi.org/10.1002/nop2.195.

4. Jodi Shroba et al., "Food Insecurity in the Food Allergic Population: A Work Group Report of the AAAAI Adverse Reactions to Foods Committee," *Journal of Allergy and Clinical Immunology: In Practice* 10, no. 1 (January 2022): 81–90, https://doi.org/10.1016/j.jaip.2021.10.058.

5. "American Academy of Pediatrics. Committee on Nutrition. Hypoallergenic Infant Formulas," *Pediatrics* 106, no. 2 Pt 1 (August 2000): 346–49; "Products - Data Briefs - Number 121 - May 2013," June 7, 2019, https://www.cdc.gov/nchs/products/databriefs/db121.htm.

6. George du Toit et al., "Randomized Trial of Peanut Consumption in Infants at Risk for Peanut Allergy," *New England Journal of Medicine* 372, no. 9 (February 26, 2015): 803–13, https://doi.org/10.1056/NEJMoa1414850.0/0/00 0:00:00 AM; Osamu Natsume et al., "Two-Step Egg Introduction for Prevention of Egg Allergy in High-Risk Infants with Eczema (PETIT): A Randomised, Double-Blind, Placebo-Controlled Trial," *Lancet (London, England)* 389, no. 10066 (January 21, 2017): 276–86, https://doi.org/10.1016/S0140-6736(16)31418-0.

7. Kirsty Logan et al., "Early Introduction of Peanut Reduces Peanut Allergy Across Risk Groups in Pooled and Causal Inference Analyses," *Allergy* 78, no. 5 (May 2023): 1307–18, https://doi.org/10.1111/all.15597.

8. U.S. Department of Agriculture and U.S. Department of Health and Human Services, "Dietary Guidelines for Americans, 2020–2025," December 2020, DietaryGuidelines.gov.

9. Michael Pollan, *In Defense of Food: An Eater's Manifesto* (New York: Penguin Publishing Group, 2008).

Chapter 2

1. Gill Rapley and Tracey Murkett, *Baby-Led Weaning: Helping Your Baby to Love Good Food* (London: Vermilion, 2008).

2. Erkan Dogan et al., "Baby-Led Complementary Feeding: Randomized Controlled Study," *Pediatrics International* 60, no. 12 (2018): 1073–80, https://doi.org/10.1111/ped.13671.

3. Veronique Gingras et al., "Timing of Complementary Feeding Introduction and Adiposity Throughout Childhood," *Pediatrics* 144, no. 6 (December 1, 2019): e20191320, https://doi.org/10.1542/peds.2019-1320.

4. Brittany J. Morison et al., "How Different Are Baby-Led Weaning and Conventional Complementary Feeding? A Cross-Sectional Study of Infants Aged 6–8 Months," *BMJ Open* 6, no. 5 (May 1, 2016): e010665, https://doi.org/10.1136/bmjopen-2015-010665; Rowan, H., M. Lee, and A. Brown, "Differences in Dietary Composition Between Infants Introduced to Complementary Foods Using Baby-Led Weaning and Traditional Spoon Feeding," *Journal of Human Nutrition and Dietetics* 32, no. 1 (2019): 11-20; S. Komninou, J. C. G. Halford, and J. A. Harrold, "Differences in Parental Feeding Styles and Practices and Toddler Eating Behaviour Across Complementary Feeding Methods: Managing Expectations Through Consideration of Effect Size," *Appetite* 137 (June 1, 2019): 198–206, https://doi.org/10.1016/j.appet.2019.03.001; Fu, Xiaoxi, Cathryn A. Conlon, Jillian J. Haszard, Kathryn L. Beck, Pamela R. von Hurst, Rachael W. Taylor, and Anne-Louise M. Heath, "Food Fussiness and Early Feeding Characteristics of Infants Following Baby-Led Weaning and Traditional Spoon-Feeding in New Zealand: An Internet Survey," *Appetite* 130 (2018): 110–16; Rachael W. Taylor et al., "Effect of a Baby-Led Approach to Complementary Feeding on Infant Growth and Overweight: A Randomized Clinical Trial," *JAMA Pediatrics* 171, no. 9 (September 1, 2017): 838–46, https://doi.org/10.1001/jamapediatrics.2017.1284.

5. Ellyn Satter, "The Satter Division of Responsibility in Feeding," n.d.

6. Dogan et al., "Baby-Led Complementary Feeding: Randomized Controlled Study."

7. Melanie Potock, *Responsive Feeding: The Baby-First Guide to Stress-Free Weaning, Healthy Eating, and Mealtime Bonding* (The Experiment, 2022).

Chapter 3

1. These include the American Academy of Pediatrics (AAP), Academy of Nutrition and Dietetics, United States Department of Agriculture (USDA), US Department of Health and Human Services (HHS), World Health Organization (WHO), UNICEF, American Academy of Family Physicians, Australian National Health and Medical Research Council, Health Canada, Canadian Paediatric Society, American College of Obstetricians and Gynecologists, and Academy of Breastfeeding Medicine.

2. Helen Coulthard, Gillian Harris, and Anna Fogel, "Exposure to Vegetable Variety in Infants Weaned at Different Ages," *Appetite* 78 (July 2014): 89–94, https://doi.org/10.1016/j.appet.2014.03.021.

3. Gillian Harris and Sarah Mason, "Are There Sensitive Periods for Food Acceptance in Infancy?," *Current Nutrition Reports* 6, no. 2 (2017): 190–96, https://doi.org/10.1007/s13668-017-0203-0; Marion M. Hetherington et al., "A Step-by-Step Introduction to Vegetables at the Beginning of Complementary Feeding: The Effects of Early and Repeated Exposure," *Appetite* 84 (January 2015): 280–90, https://doi.org/10.1016/j.appet.2014.10.014.

4. Andrea S. Maier et al., "Breastfeeding and Experience with Variety Early in Weaning Increase Infants' Acceptance of New Foods for up to Two Months," *Clinical Nutrition (Edinburgh, Scotland)* 27, no. 6 (December 2008): 849–57, https://doi.org/10.1016/j.clnu.2008.08.002.

Chapter 4

1. Alexandra R. Sitarik et al., "Infant Feeding Practices and Subsequent Dietary Patterns of School-Aged Children in a US Birth Cohort," *Journal of the Academy of Nutrition and Dietetics* 121, no. 6 (June 1, 2021): 1064–79, https://doi.org/10.1016/j.jand.2020.08.083; K. Northstone et al., "The Effect of Age of Introduction to Lumpy Solids on Foods Eaten and Reported Feeding Difficulties at 6 and 15 Months," *Journal of Human Nutrition and Dietetics: The Official Journal of the British Dietetic Association* 14, no. 1 (February 2001): 43–54, https://doi.org/10.1046/j.1365-277x.2001.00264.x; Helen Coulthard, Gillian Harris, and Pauline Emmett, "Delayed Introduction of Lumpy Foods to Children During the Complementary Feeding Period Affects Child's Food Acceptance and Feeding at 7 Years of Age," *Maternal & Child Nutrition* 5, no. 1 (December 16, 2008): 75–85, https://doi.org/10.1111/j.1740-8709.2008.00153.x.

2. Hannah Rowan, Michelle Lee, and Amy Brown, "Estimated Energy and Nutrient Intake for Infants Following Baby-Led and Traditional Weaning Approaches," *Journal of Human Nutrition and Dietetics: The Official Journal of the British Dietetic Association* 35, no. 2 (April 2022): 325–36, https://doi.org/10.1111/jhn.12981.

3. Peter J. Huth et al., "Major Food Sources of Calories, Added Sugars, and Saturated Fat and Their Contribution to Essential Nutrient Intakes in the U.S. Diet: Data from the National Health and Nutrition Examination Survey (2003–2006)," *Nutrition Journal* 12 (August 8, 2013): 116, https://doi.org/10.1186/1475-2891-12-116.

4. Arianna Giannetti et al., "Role of Vitamin D in Prevention of Food Allergy in Infants," *Frontiers in Pediatrics* 8 (August 18, 2020): 447, https://doi.org/10.3389/fped.2020.00447; Ashlyn Poole et al., "Cellular and Molecular Mechanisms of Vitamin D in Food Allergy," *Journal of Cellular and Molecular Medicine* 22, no. 7 (July 2018): 3270–77, https://doi.org/10.1111/jcmm.13607; Jenni Rosendahl et al., "High-Dose Vitamin D Supplementation Does Not Prevent Allergic Sensitization of Infants," *Journal of Pediatrics* 209 (June 2019): 139-145.e1, https://doi.org/10.1016/j.jpeds.2019.02.021.

5. Marion M. Hetherington et al., "A Step-by-Step Introduction to Vegetables at the Beginning of Complementary Feeding: The Effects of Early and Repeated Exposure," *Appetite* 84 (January 2015): 280–90, https://doi.org/10.1016/j.appet.2014.10.014; Valentina De Cosmi, Silvia Scaglioni, and Carlo Agostoni, "Early Taste Experiences and Later Food Choices," *Nutrients* 9, no. 2 (February 4, 2017): 107, https://doi.org/10.3390/nu9020107.

6. Julie A. Mennella, Coren P. Jagnow, and Gary K. Beauchamp, "Prenatal and Postnatal Flavor Learning by Human Infants," *Pediatrics* 107, no. 6 (June 2001): E88.

7. Joanne M. Spahn et al., "Influence of Maternal Diet on Flavor Transfer to Amniotic Fluid and Breast Milk and Children's Responses: A Systematic Review," *American Journal of Clinical Nutrition* 109 (March 1, 2019): 1003S–1026S, https://doi.org/10.1093/ajcn/nqy240.

8. De Cosmi, Scaglioni, and Agostoni, "Early Taste Experiences and Later Food Choices."

9. Jane Houlihan and Charlotte Brody, "What's in My Baby Food?," October 2019, https://www.healthybabyfood.org/sites/healthybabyfoods.org/files/2019-10/BabyFoodReport_FULLREPORT_ENGLISH_R5b.pdf, accessed February 17, 2023.

10. National Academies of Sciences, Engineering, and Medicine, *Dietary Reference Intakes for Sodium and Potassium* (National Academies Press, 2019), https://doi.org/10.17226/25353, accessed February 17, 2023.

11. Center for Food Safety and Applied Nutrition, "Sodium in Your Diet," *FDA*, February 25, 2022, https://www.fda.gov/food/nutrition-education-resources-materials/sodium-your-diet.

12. Crystal Smith-Spangler et al., "Are Organic Foods Safer or Healthier than Conventional Alternatives?: A Systematic Review," *Annals of Internal Medicine* 157, no. 5 (September 4, 2012): 348–66, https://doi.org/10.7326/0003-4819-157-5-201209040-00007; Alan D. Dangour et al., "Nutritional Quality of Organic Foods: A Systematic Review," *American Journal of Clinical Nutrition* 90, no. 3 (September 2009): 680–85, https://doi.org/10.3945/ajcn.2009.28041; Axel Mie et al., "Human Health Implications of Organic Food and Organic Agriculture: A Comprehensive Review," *Environmental Health: A Global Access Science Source* 16, no. 1 (October 27, 2017): 111, https://doi.org/10.1186/s12940-017-0315-4.

13. Anne Lise Brantsæter et al., "Organic Food in the Diet: Exposure and Health Implications," *Annual Review of Public Health* 38 (March 20, 2017): 295–313, https://doi.org/10.1146/annurev-publhealth-031816-044437.

14. Smith-Spangler et al., "Are Organic Foods Safer or Healthier Than Conventional Alternatives?"

15. Brantsæter et al., "Organic Food in the Diet"; Carl K. Winter and Sarah F. Davis, "Organic Foods," *Journal of Food Science* 71, no. 9 (2006): R117–24, https://doi.org/10.1111/j.1750-3841.2006.00196.x.

Chapter 5

1. Liz Williams Erickson et al., "Impact of a Modified Version of Baby-Led Weaning on Infant Food and Nutrient Intakes: The BLISS Randomized Controlled Trial," *Nutrients* 10, no. 6 (June 2018): 740, https://doi.org/10.3390/nu10060740; Hannah Rowan, Michelle Lee, and Amy Brown, "Estimated Energy and Nutrient Intake for Infants Following Baby-Led and Traditional Weaning Approaches," Journal of Human Nutrition and Dietetics: The Official Journal of the British Dietetic Association 35, no. 2 (April 2022): 325–36, https://doi.org/10.1111/jhn.12981.

2. Carina Venter et al., "Maternal Dietary Intake in Pregnancy and Lactation and Allergic Disease Outcomes in Offspring," *Pediatric Allergy and Immunology: Official Publication of the European Society of Pediatric Allergy and Immunology* 28, no. 2 (March 2017): 135–43, https://doi.org/10.1111/pai.12682; Carina Venter et al., "EAACI Position Paper on Diet Diversity in Pregnancy, Infancy and Childhood: Novel Concepts and Implications for Studies in Allergy and Asthma," *Allergy* 75, no. 3 (March 2020): 497–523, https://doi.org/10.1111/all.14051.

3. Lisa Daniels et al., "Baby-Led Introduction to SolidS (BLISS) Study: A Randomised Controlled Trial of a Baby-Led Approach to Complementary Feeding," *BMC Pediatrics* 15 (November 12, 2015): 179, https://doi.org/10.1186/s12887-015-0491-8.

Chapter 6

1. Betty Ruth Carruth et al., "Prevalence of Picky Eaters Among Infants and Toddlers and Their Caregivers' Decisions

About Offering a New Food," *Journal of the American Dietetic Association* 104, no. 1, Suppl 1 (January 2004): s57–64, https://doi.org/10.1016/j.jada.2003.10.024.

2. American Academy of Pediatrics, "How Can I Tell If My Baby Is Constipated?" HealthyChildren.org, updated May 12, 2022, https://www.healthychildren.org/English/ages-stages/baby/diapers-clothing/Pages/Infant-Constipation.aspx.

3. S. Komninou, J. C. G. Halford, and J. A. Harrold, "Differences in Parental Feeding Styles and Practices and Toddler Eating Behaviour Across Complementary Feeding Methods: Managing Expectations Through Consideration of Effect Size," *Appetite* 137 (June 1, 2019): 198–206, https://doi.org/10.1016/j.appet.2019.03.001.

4. Jennifer Utter et al., "Family Meals Among Parents: Associations with Nutritional, Social and Emotional Wellbeing," *Preventive Medicine* 113 (August 2018): 7–12, https://doi.org/10.1016/j.ypmed.2018.05.006.

5. Amber J. Hammons and Barbara H. Fiese, "Is Frequency of Shared Family Meals Related to the Nutritional Health of Children and Adolescents?," *Pediatrics* 127, no. 6 (June 1, 2011): e1565–74, https://doi.org/10.1542/peds.2010-1440.

6. Faye Powell et al., "The Importance of Mealtime Structure for Reducing Child Food Fussiness," *Maternal & Child Nutrition* 13, no. 2 (April 8, 2016): e12296, https://doi.org/10.1111/mcn.12296.

Chapter 7

1. Graham Roberts et al., "Defining the Window of Opportunity and Target Populations to Prevent Peanut Allergy," *Journal of Allergy and Clinical Immunology* 151, no. 5 (May 2023): 1329–36, https://doi.org/10.1016/j.jaci.2022.09.042.

2. Gideon Lack, "Update on Risk Factors for Food Allergy," *Journal of Allergy and Clinical Immunology* 129, no. 5 (May 2012): 1187–97, https://doi.org/10.1016/j.jaci.2012.02.036.

3. "Food Allergies | Causes, Symptoms & Treatment," ACAAI Public Website, accessed April 2, 2023, https://acaai.org/allergies/allergic-conditions/food/.

4. "Common Allergens—Peanut, Egg, and Sesame Allergies | FARE," accessed April 2, 2023, https://www.foodallergy.org/living-food-allergies/food-allergy-essentials/common-allergens.

5. Alkis Togias et al., "Addendum Guidelines for the Prevention of Peanut Allergy in the United States: Report of the National Institute of Allergy and Infectious Diseases–Sponsored Expert Panel," *World Allergy Organization Journal* 10, no. 1 (January 6, 2017): 1, https://doi.org/10.1186/s40413-016-0137-9.

6. David M. Fleischer et al., "A Consensus Approach to the Primary Prevention of Food Allergy Through Nutrition: Guidance from the American Academy of Allergy, Asthma, and Immunology; American College of Allergy, Asthma, and Immunology; and the Canadian Society for Allergy and Clinical Immunology," *Journal of Allergy and Clinical Immunology: In Practice* 9, no. 1 (January 2021): 22–43.e4, https://doi.org/10.1016/j.jaip.2020.11.002.

7. Roberts et al., "Defining the Window of Opportunity and Target Populations to Prevent Peanut Allergy."

8. Fleischer et al., "A Consensus Approach to the Primary Prevention of Food Allergy Through Nutrition."

9. Ruchi S. Gupta et al., "The Public Health Impact of Parent-Reported Childhood Food Allergies in the United States," *Pediatrics* 142, no. 6 (December 1, 2018): e20181235, https://doi.org/10.1542/peds.2018-1235.

10. Kirsty Logan et al., "Early Introduction of Peanut Reduces Peanut Allergy Across Risk Groups in Pooled and Causal Inference Analyses," *Allergy* 78, no. 5 (May 2023): 1307–18, https://doi.org/10.1111/all.15597.

11. Elizabeth Tepler, Katelyn H. Wong, and Gary K. Soffer, "Health Disparities in Pediatric Food Allergy," *Annals of Allergy, Asthma & Immunology* 129, no. 4 (October 1, 2022): 417–23, https://doi.org/10.1016/j.anai.2022.04.022.

Chapter 8

1. David M. Fleischer et al., "A Consensus Approach to the Primary Prevention of Food Allergy Through Nutrition: Guidance from the American Academy of Allergy, Asthma, and Immunology; American College of Allergy, Asthma, and Immunology; and the Canadian Society for Allergy and Clinical Immunology," *Journal of Allergy and Clinical Immunology: In Practice* 9, no. 1 (January 2021): 22-43.e4, https://doi.org/10.1016/j.jaip.2020.11.002; Alkis Togias et al., "Addendum Guidelines for the Prevention of Peanut Allergy in the United States: Report of the National Institute of Allergy and Infectious Diseases–Sponsored Expert Panel," *World Allergy Organization Journal* 10, no. 1 (January 6, 2017): 1, https://doi.org/10.1186/s40413-016-0137-9.

2. Tetsuhiro Sakihara et al., "Early Discontinuation of Cow's Milk Protein Ingestion Is Associated with the Development of Cow's Milk Allergy," *Journal of Allergy and Clinical Immunology: In Practice* 10, no. 1 (January 2022): 172–79, https://doi.org/10.1016/j.jaip.2021.07.053.

3. Carina Venter et al., "Different Measures of Diet Diversity During Infancy and the Association with Childhood Food Allergy in a UK Birth Cohort Study," *Journal of Allergy and Clinical Immunology: In Practice* 8, no. 6 (June 2020): 2017–26, https://doi.org/10.1016/j.jaip.2020.01.029; Enza D'Auria et al., "The Role of Diet Diversity and Diet Indices on Allergy Outcomes," *Frontiers in Pediatrics* 8 (September 15, 2020): 545, https://doi.org/10.3389/fped.2020.00545; Venter et al., "EAACI Position Paper on Diet Diversity in Pregnancy, Infancy and Childhood."

4. Fleischer et al., "A Consensus Approach to the Primary Prevention of Food Allergy Through Nutrition."

5. George Du Toit et al., "Randomized Trial of Peanut Consumption in Infants at Risk for Peanut Allergy," *New England Journal of Medicine* 372, no. 9 (February 26, 2015): 803–13, https://doi.org/10.1056/NEJMoa1414850; Natsume et al., "Two-Step Egg Introduction for Prevention of Egg Allergy in High-Risk Infants with Eczema (PETIT)"; Michael R. Perkin et al., "Enquiring About Tolerance (EAT) Study: Feasibility of an Early Allergenic Food Introduction Regimen," *Journal of Allergy and Clinical Immunology* 137, no. 5 (May 2016): 1477-1486.e8, https://doi.org/10.1016/j.jaci.2015.12.1322; Fleischer et al., "A Consensus Approach to the Primary Prevention of Food Allergy Through Nutrition."

6. Sakihara et al., "Early Discontinuation of Cow's Milk Protein Ingestion Is Associated with the Development of Cow's Milk Allergy."

7. Giulia Nuzzi, Maria Elisa Di Cicco, and Diego Giampietro Peroni, "Breastfeeding and Allergic Diseases: What's New?," *Children* 8, no. 5 (April 24, 2021): 330, https://doi.org/10.3390/children8050330.

8. Fleischer et al., "A Consensus Approach to the Primary Prevention of Food Allergy Through Nutrition."

9. Jane L. Holl et al., "A Randomized Trial of the Acceptability of a Daily Multi-Allergen Food Supplement for Infants," *Pediatric Allergy and Immunology: Official Publication of the European Society of Pediatric Allergy and Immunology* 31, no. 4 (May 2020): 418–20, https://doi.org/10.1111/pai.13223.

10. Amanda L. Cox et al., "Allergic Reactions in Infants Using Commercial Early Allergen Introduction Products," *Journal of Allergy and Clinical Immunology: In Practice* 9, no. 9 (September 2021): 3517-3520.e1, https://doi.org/10.1016/j.jaip.2021.04.068.

11. Vanessa Garcia-Larsen et al., "Diet During Pregnancy and Infancy and Risk of Allergic or Autoimmune Disease: A Systematic Review and Meta-Analysis," *PLoS Medicine* 15, no. 2 (February 2018): e1002507, https://doi.org/10.1371/journal.pmed.1002507.

12. Garcia-Larsen et al. "Diet During Pregnancy and Infancy and Risk of Allergic or Autoimmune Disease"; Alessandro Fiocchi et al., "World Allergy Organization-McMaster University Guidelines for Allergic Disease Prevention (GLAD-P): Probiotics," *World Allergy Organization Journal* 8, no. 1 (December 1, 2015): 1–13, https://doi.org/10.1186/s40413-015-0055-2; Waheeda Samady et al., "The Prevalence of Atopic Dermatitis in Children with Food Allergy," *Annals of Allergy, Asthma & Immunology: Official Publication of the American College of Allergy, Asthma, & Immunology* 122, no. 6 (June 2019): 656-657.e1, https://doi.org/10.1016/j.anai.2019.03.019.

13. Fleischer et al., "A Consensus Approach to the Primary Prevention of Food Allergy Through Nutrition."

14. Elissa M. Abrams et al., "Dietary Exposures and Allergy Prevention in High-Risk Infants," *Allergy, Asthma & Clinical Immunology* 18, no. 1 (April 30, 2022): 36, https://doi.org/10.1186/s13223-021-00638-y.

15. Caroline Roduit et al., "High Levels of Butyrate and Propionate in Early Life Are Associated with Protection Against Atopy," *Allergy* 74, no. 4 (April 2019): 799–809, https://doi.org/10.1111/all.13660.

16. Carina Venter et al., "EAACI Position Paper: Influence of Dietary Fatty Acids on Asthma, Food Allergy, and Atopic Dermatitis," *Allergy* 74, no. 8 (2019): 1429–44, https://doi.org/10.1111/all.13764.

17. Mark Messina, "Soy and Health Update: Evaluation of the Clinical and Epidemiologic Literature," *Nutrients* 8, no. 12 (November 24, 2016): 754, https://doi.org/10.3390/nu8120754.

18. Xiao Ou Shu et al., "Soy Food Intake and Breast Cancer Survival," *JAMA* 302, no. 22 (December 9, 2009): 2437–43, https://doi.org/10.1001/jama.2009.1783; Gianluca Rizzo et al., "The Role of Soy and Soy Isoflavones on Women's Fertility and Related Outcomes: An Update," *Journal of Nutritional Science* 11 (ed. 2022): e17, https://doi.org/10.1017/jns.2022.15; Ilaria Testa et al., "Soy-Based Infant Formula: Are Phyto-Oestrogens Still in Doubt?," *Frontiers in Nutrition* 5 (November 23, 2018): 110, https://doi.org/10.3389/fnut.2018.00110; Jill M. Hamilton-Reeves et al., "Clinical Studies Show No Effects of Soy Protein or Isoflavones on Reproductive Hormones in Men: Results of a Meta-Analysis," *Fertility and Sterility* 94, no. 3 (August 2010): 997–1007, https://doi.org/10.1016/j.fertnstert.2009.04.038.

Chapter 9

1. A. Brown, "No Difference in Self-Reported Frequency of Choking Between Infants Introduced to Solid Foods Using a Baby-Led Weaning or Traditional Spoon-Feeding Approach," *Journal of Human Nutrition and Dietetics: Official Journal of the British Dietetic Association* 31, no. 4 (August 2018): 496–504, https://doi.org/10.1111/jhn.12528; Louise J. Fangupo et al., "A Baby-Led Approach to Eating Solids and Risk of Choking," *Pediatrics* 138, no. 4 (October 2016): e20160772, https://doi.org/10.1542/peds.2016-0772.

2. CDC, "Fast Facts About Food Poisoning," Centers for Disease Control and Prevention, March 24, 2023, https://www.cdc.gov/foodsafety/food-poisoning.html.

Chapter 10

1. Alkis Togias et al., "Addendum Guidelines for the Prevention of Peanut Allergy in the United States: Report of the National Institute of Allergy and Infectious Diseases–Sponsored Expert Panel," *World Allergy Organization Journal* 10, no. 1 (January 6, 2017): 1, https://doi.org/10.1186/s40413-016-0137-9; David M. Fleischer et al., "A Consensus Approach to the Primary Prevention of Food Allergy Through Nutrition: Guidance from the American Academy of Allergy, Asthma, and Immunology; American College of Allergy, Asthma, and Immunology; and the Canadian Society for Allergy and Clinical Immunology," *Journal of Allergy and Clinical Immunology: In Practice* 9, no. 1 (January 2021): 22-43.e4, https://doi.org/10.1016/j.jaip.2020.11.002.

2. Fleischer et al., "A Consensus Approach to the Primary Prevention of Food Allergy Through Nutrition."

3. Fleischer et al., "A Consensus Approach to the Primary Prevention of Food Allergy Through Nutrition."

4. "Food Allergies | Causes, Symptoms & Treatment," ACAAI Public Website, accessed April 2, 2023, https://acaai.org/allergies/allergic-conditions/food/.

5. PALISADE Group of Clinical Investigators et al., "AR101 Oral Immunotherapy for Peanut Allergy," *New England Journal of Medicine* 379, no. 21 (November 22, 2018): 1991–2001, https://doi.org/10.1056/NEJMoa1812856.

INDEX

African Peanut Stew, 222

allergens. *see also food allergies*
  FAQs about, 73–83
  swaps for, 236–238
  top nine, 5, 60–61

allergic reactions, 96–102
  other symptoms vs., 100–101
  of parents, 101–102
  signs and symptoms of, 97–99

almond(s)
  Almond Cardamom Pancakes, 135
  Almond Cherry BLF Cookies, 227
  Walnut-Crusted Butternut French Toast, 144

almond butter
  Apple Oat Baby Bars, 136
  Cherry Chocolate Ice Pops, 230
  Sweet Potato Almond Butter Mash, 168

almond flour
  Almond Cardamom Pancakes, 135
  Apple Oat Baby Bars, 136
  Cast-Iron Skillet Corn Bread, 209
  Cinnamon Oat Breakfast Bars, 139
  Nutty French Toast Casserole, 137
  Seafood Sliders with Lemon Aioli, 158
  6-Allergen Blender Pancakes, 134

Apple
  Apple Oat Baby Bars, 136
  Butternut Apple Muffin Cakes, 142

Avgolemono, 194

avocado, 36
  Avocado Crab Quesadillas, 186
  Sardine Avotoasts, 154

Baby Back Ribs, Easy Maple Pecan, 206
baby-led feeding, 14–15, 49–57, 106–112
baby-led weaning, 11–12, 29–30
baby sign language, 16–19
balanced meals, 45–48
banana, 36
  Banana Peanut Butter Baby Cookies, 229

Peanut Butter Banana Mini Muffins, 131
beans, 36
beef, 36
  Fall-Apart Slow Cooker Beef Stew, 204
  Skillet Macaroni with Veggies and Beef, 208
Beet Hummus, Pinkalicious, 171
Benadryl, 98
bibs, 25
Black Bean Brownies, 234
black sea bass, Fishies Wearing Bow Ties, 184
bowls, 24
bread(s), 41, 79–80
  Cast-Iron Skillet Corn Bread, 209
  Zucchini Walnut Bread, 132
breast milk, solids and, 47–48
broccoli, 36
  Shrimp and Broccoli Croquettes, 160
Brownies, Black Bean, 234
butter, 78
  African Peanut Stew, 222
  Almond Cardamom Pancakes, 135
  Cast-Iron Skillet Corn Bread, 209
  Memere's Shepherd's Pie, 202
  Peanut Butter and Jelly Muffins, 138
  Savory Scones, 150
  Sheet Pan Salmon Dinner, 176
  Shrimp and Broccoli Croquettes, 160
  6-Allergen Blender Pancakes, 134
buttermilk, Cast-Iron Skillet Corn Bread, 209
butternut squash
  Butternut Apple Muffin Cakes, 142
  Walnut-Crusted Butternut French Toast, 144
butyrate, 78

candies, 41
carrots, 41
  Shells and Cheese with Carrots and Peas, 169
cashew butter, Nutty French Toast Casserole, 137
cashews
  Baby-Friendly Cashew Dip, 166

Cashew Tartar Sauce, 180
  Coconut Curry Lentil Stew, 210
  Easy Slow Cooker Chicken Korma, 195
celiac disease, 102
cetirizine, 98
cheddar cheese
  Cheesy Crab Dip, 156
  Huevos Rancheros Eggs, 149
  Oyster Noodle Casserole, 187
  Shells and Cheese with Carrots and Peas, 169
  Shrimp and Tofu Fajitas, 188
  Shrimpy Grits, 152
  Skillet Macaroni with Veggies and Beef, 208
  Turkey and Tempeh Slow Cooker Chili, 198
  Veggie Strata, 146
cheese, 40, 77, 79. *see also specific types*
cherry(-ies), 41
  Cherry Almond BLF Cookies, 227
  Cherry Chocolate Ice Pops, 230
cherry tomatoes, 41
Chia Seed Pudding, Strawberry Mango, 140
chicken, 35
  Easy Slow Cooker Chicken Korma, 195
  Tarragon Chicken Salad, 162
  Za'atar Chicken Drumsticks, 196
Chili, Turkey and Tempeh, 198
chocolate
  Better-for-You Black Bean Brownies, 234
  Chocolate Cherry Ice Pops, 230
  Peanut Butter Banana Mini Muffins, 131
  Pumpkin Spice Cookies, 231
  Zucchini Walnut Bread, 132
choking, 41, 88–90
choline, 33
Cinnamon Oat Breakfast Bars, 139
Clam Chowder, Herbed, 192
coconut, 75
  Coconut Curry Lentil Stew, 210
  Toasted Coconut Pumpkin Pudding, 232

cod
  Cod Tacos with Lime Sauce, 182
  Macadamia-Crusted Fish, 181
Colby Jack cheese
  Cast-Iron Skillet Corn Bread, 209
  Turkey and Tempeh Slow Cooker Chili, 198
combined feeding approach, 16
contact dermatitis, 100
Cookies
  Cherry Almond BLF, 227
  Peanut Butter Banana Baby, 229
  Pumpkin Spice, 231
Corn Bread, Cast-Iron Skillet, 209
cottage cheese
  Cottage Cheese Mash, 170
  Zucchini Boats, 219
cow's milk, 40, 115
  African Peanut Stew, 222
  Almond Cardamom Pancakes, 135
  an Za'atar Chicken Drumsticks, 196
  Apple Oat Baby Bars, 136
  Avocado Crab Quesadillas, 186
  Baked PB Oatmeal Sticks, 141
  Better-for-You Black Bean Brownies, 234
  BLF Saag Paneer, 224
  Butternut Apple Muffin Cakes, 142
  Cast-Iron Skillet Corn Bread, 209
  Cheesy Crab Dip, 156
  Cherry Almond BLF Cookies, 227
  Cherry Chocolate Ice Pops, 230
  Coconut Curry Lentil Stew, 210
  Cod Tacos with Lime Sauce, 182
  Cottage Cheese Mash, 170
  Easy Slow Cooker Chicken Korma, 195
  English Muffin Baby Pizzas, 165
  Fish Fingers, 179
  Herbed Clam Chowder, 192
  Huevos Rancheros Eggs, 149
  Lasagna Roll-Ups, 212
  Macadamia-Crusted Fish, 181
  Mango Surprise Smoothie, 228
  Many Nut Pesto Pasta, 214
  Mascarpone Peanut Butter Melts, 133
  Memere's Shepherd's Pie, 202
  Nutty French Toast Casserole, 137
  Oyster Noodle Casserole, 187

Peanut Apple Fritters, 167
Peanut Butter and Jelly Muffins, 138
Peanut Butter Banana Baby Cookies, 229
Peanut Butter Banana Mini Muffins, 131
Peanut Butter Power Pops, 233
Peanut Butter Sweet Potato Casserole, 215
Presto Pressed Pesto Grilled Cheese, 173
Pumpkin Spice Cookies, 231
Rainbow Egg Bites, 147
Roasted Zucchini Sticks, 218
Salmon Salad with Pickled Red Onion, 155
Savory Scones, 150
Sheet Pan Salmon Dinner, 176
Shrimp and Broccoli Croquettes, 160
Shrimp and Tofu Fajitas, 188
Shrimp and Vegetable Fritters, 157
Shrimpy Grits, 152
6-Allergen Blender Pancakes, 134
Skillet Macaroni with Veggies and Beef, 208
Spaghetti Squash Quinoa Bake, 220
Spinach Manchego Frittata, 148
Strawberry Mango Chia Seed Pudding, 140
Tarragon Chicken Salad, 162
Toasted Coconut Pumpkin Pudding, 232
  as top allergen, 5, 61
Turkey and Tempeh Slow Cooker Chili, 198
Veggie Strata, 146
Walnut-Crusted Butternut French Toast, 144
Zucchini Boats, 219
Zucchini Walnut Bread, 132
crab
  Avocado Crab Quesadillas, 186
  Cheesy Crab Dip, 156
  Crab Linguine with Lemon and Basil, 190
crackers, 41
cream cheese
  Butternut Apple Muffin Cakes, 142
  Cheesy Crab Dip, 156
  Spaghetti Squash Quinoa Bake, 220
crème fraîche, Peanut Butter and Jelly Muffins, 138
Croquettes, Shrimp and Broccoli, 160
cups, 24–25

dairy products, 34, 40. see also specific products
dairy substitutes, 236

Date Tahini Shake, 145
daycare, baby-led feeding at, 52–53
DHA, 33
diphenhydramine, 98
dried fruits, 41
drool rash, 100

eczema, 61–62
edamame, 83
  Edamame Tahini Dip, 164
  Fishies Wearing Bow Ties, 184
egg(s), 114
  African Peanut Stew, 222
  Almond Cardamom Pancakes, 135
  Apple Oat Baby Bars, 136
  Avgolemono, 194
  Baked PB Oatmeal Sticks, 141
  Better-for-You Black Bean Brownies, 234
  Butternut Apple Muffin Cakes, 142
  Cast-Iron Skillet Corn Bread, 209
  Cheesy Crab Dip, 156
  Cinnamon Oat Breakfast Bars, 139
  Cod Tacos with Lime Sauce, 182
  Crab Linguine with Lemon and Basil, 190
  Fall-Apart Slow Cooker Beef Stew, 204
  Fish Fingers, 179
  Greek Meatballs with Tomato Sauce and Orzo, 200
  Herbed Clam Chowder, 192
  Huevos Rancheros Eggs, 149
  Lasagna Roll-Ups, 212
  Macadamia-Crusted Fish, 181
  Miso Mushroom Soup with Egg, 216
  Nutty French Toast Casserole, 137
  offering for first time, 76–77
  Oyster Noodle Casserole, 187
  Peanut Apple Fritters, 167
  Peanut Butter and Jelly Muffins, 138
  Peanut Butter Banana Baby Cookies, 229
  Peanut Butter Banana Mini Muffins, 131
  Peanut Butter Sweet Potato Casserole, 215
  Presto Pressed Pesto Grilled Cheese, 173
  Pumpkin Spice Cookies, 231
  Rainbow Egg Bites, 147
  Roasted Zucchini Sticks, 218
  Salmon Salad with Pickled Red Onion, 155

Sardine Avotoasts, 154
Seafood Sliders with Lemon Aioli, 158
Shrimp and Broccoli Croquettes, 160
Shrimp and Vegetable Fritters, 157
6-Allergen Blender Pancakes, 134
Spinach Manchego Frittata, 148
Tahini Egg Salad, 172
Tarragon Chicken Salad, 162
as top allergen, 5, 61
Veggie Strata, 146
Walnut-Crusted Butternut French Toast, 144
Zucchini Boats, 219
Zucchini Walnut Bread, 132
Eggplant Sesame Dip, 163
egg substitutes, 237
English Muffin Baby Pizzas, 165
epinephrine, 98
EpiPen, 99

Fajitas, Shrimp and Tofu, 188
family meals, 56–57
fat, 33–34
feeding-related items/equipment, 23–25
feta cheese, Zucchini Boats, 219
finger foods, 29–30
first foods, 28–44
    added sugars, 43–44
    to avoid, 40–41
    finger food size and texture, 29–30
    flavors of, 37
    ideal options for, 35–37
    infant rice cereal, 37–38
    key nutrients in, 30–34
    organic vs. nonorganic, 42–43
    sodium in, 38–39
fish, 40, 116. see also specific types
    Cod Tacos with Lime Sauce, 182
    Easy Foil-Grilled Haddock, 178
    Fish Fingers, 179
    Fishies Wearing Bow Ties, 184
    Macadamia-Crusted Fish, 181
    Memere's Shepherd's Pie, 202
    offering for first time, 80–81
    Salmon Salad with Pickled Red Onion, 155
    Sardine Avotoasts, 154
    Seafood Sliders with Lemon Aioli, 158

Sheet Pan Salmon Dinner, 176
shellfish (see shellfish)
Skillet Macaroni with Veggies and Beef, 208
    as top allergen, 5, 61
fish substitutes, 238
flavors of first foods, 37
flavor training, 22
food allergies, 58–63. see also allergens; introducing
    allergenic foods
    allergic reactions, 96–102
    anxiety about, 3–4
    described, 59
    development of, 60
    and food intolerances, 102–104
    lack of cure for, 95
    maintenance meal plans for, 119–128
    outgrowing, 95
    prevention of, 2–8
    risk for, 61–63, 92
    screening for, 92–94
    treatment for, 95
food intolerances, 102–104
food protein-induced allergic proctocolitis (FPIAP),
    102
food protein-induced enterocolitis syndrome
    (FPIES), 96–97
food/reaction tracker, 103–104
food safety, 86–91
foods to avoid, 40–41
footrest, 23
formula, solids and, 47–48
French Toast
    Nutty French Toast Casserole, 137
    Walnut-Crusted Butternut, 144
Frittata, Spinach Manchego, 148
Fritters
    Peanut Apple, 167
    Shrimp and Vegetable, 157
fruit juice, 41, 51, 55
fruits, 41
fullness, signals of, 16–19

gagging, 88–90
ghee, 78
    African Peanut Stew, 222
    Apple Oat Baby Bars, 136

Better-for-You Black Bean Brownies, 234
BLF Saag Paneer, 224
Butternut Apple Muffin Cakes, 142
Cherry Almond BLF Cookies, 227
Coconut Curry Lentil Stew, 210
Nutty French Toast Casserole, 137
Oyster Noodle Casserole, 187
Peanut Butter and Jelly Muffins, 138
Peanut Butter Banana Baby Cookies, 229
Sheet Pan Salmon Dinner, 176
Shells and Cheese with Carrots and Peas, 169
Shrimp and Vegetable Fritters, 157
Shrimpy Grits, 152
6-Allergen Blender Pancakes, 134
Skillet Macaroni with Veggies and Beef, 208
Spaghetti Squash Quinoa Bake, 220
Walnut-Crusted Butternut French Toast, 144
Zucchini Boats, 219
Gouda cheese, Veggie Strata, 146
grapes, 41
grape tomatoes, 41
Greek Egg and Lemon Soup, 194
Greek Meatballs with Tomato Sauce and Orzo, 200
green beans, 36
Grilled Cheese, Presto Pressed Pesto, 173
Grits, Shrimpy, 152

haddock
    Cod Tacos with Lime Sauce, 182
    Easy Foil-Grilled Haddock, 178
    Macadamia-Crusted Fish, 181
half-and-half
    Memere's Shepherd's Pie, 202
    Oyster Noodle Casserole, 187
hard candies, 41
hazelnuts, Butternut Apple Muffin Cakes, 142
heavy cream
    BLF Saag Paneer, 224
    Butternut Apple Muffin Cakes, 142
highchair, 23
high-mercury fish, 40
honey, 40
hotdogs, 41
Hummus, Pinkalicious Beet, 171
hunger, signals of, 16–19

Ice Pops, Cherry Chocolate, 230
infant rice cereal, 37–38
introducing allergenic foods, 2–8, 64–83
    animal-based, if you are vegan or vegetarian, 70–72
    and commercial multiple-allergen products, 69
    FAQs about, 73–83
    for the first time, 72–73
    9-day plan for, 112–118
    parents' allergies when, 101–102
    what to focus on when, 64–65
    what to ignore when, 65–68, 70
iron, 31–32

kefir, Strawberry Mango Chia Seed Pudding, 140

labneh, Za'atar Chicken Drumsticks, 196
lamb, 35
Lasagna Roll-Ups, 212
lemon
    Lemon Tahini Lentil Stew, 225
    Seafood Sliders with Lemon Aioli, 158
lentil
    Coconut Curry Lentil Stew, 210
    Lemon Tahini Lentil Stew, 225
Lime Sauce, Cod Tacos with, 182
Linguine, Crab, 190

macadamia nuts
    Macadamia-Crusted Fish, 181
    Strawberry Mango Chia Seed Pudding, 140
Macaroni, Veggies and Beef, 208
maintenance meal plans, 119–128
    food preparation for, 120
    suggested recipes for, 121–128
Manchego Spinach Frittata, 148
mango
    Mango Surprise Smoothie, 228
    Strawberry Mango Chia Seed Pudding, 140
mango pit, 36
Many Nut Pesto
    Many Nut Pesto Pasta, 214
    Pressed Grilled Cheese with, 173
mascarpone cheese
    Mascarpone Peanut Butter Melts, 133

Peanut Butter and Jelly Muffins, 138
Shells and Cheese with Carrots and Peas, 169
mayonnaise
    Cheesy Crab Dip, 156
    Cod Tacos with Lime Sauce, 182
    Presto Pressed Pesto Grilled Cheese, 173
    Salmon Salad with Pickled Red Onion, 155
    Sardine Avotoasts, 154
    Seafood Sliders with Lemon Aioli, 158
    Tarragon Chicken Salad, 162
meals
    balanced, 45–48
    family, 56–57
    maintenance meal plans, 119–128
Meatballs with Tomato Sauce and Orzo, Greek, 200
Memere's Shepherd's Pie, 202
Miso Mushroom Soup with Egg, 216
modified baby-led weaning, 14–15
moist white breads, 41
Monterey Jack cheese
    Avocado Crab Quesadillas, 186
    Shrimp and Tofu Fajitas, 188
mozzarella cheese
    English Muffin Baby Pizzas, 165
    Lasagna Roll-Ups, 212
    Shrimp and Broccoli Croquettes, 160
Muenster cheese, Presto Pressed Pesto Grilled
    Cheese, 173
Muffin Cakes, Butternut Apple, 142
Muffins
    Peanut Butter and Jelly, 138
    Peanut Butter Banana Mini, 131
Mushroom Miso Soup with Egg, 216

9-day allergen introduction plan, 112–118
noodles
    Fall-Apart Slow Cooker Beef Stew, 204
    Miso Mushroom Soup with Egg, 216
nut butters, 41, 74, 76, 117. see also specific types
nut butter substitutes, 238
nutrients, 30–34
nuts, 41. see also tree nuts
    offering for first time, 74–76
    as top allergen, 5, 61
nut substitutes, 238

Oat
    Apple Oat Baby Bars, 136
    Baked PB Oatmeal Sticks, 141
    Cinnamon Oat Breakfast Bars, 139
oat cereal, 38
Onion, Pickled Red, 155
open cups, 24–25
oral allergy syndrome (OAS), 103
organic foods, 42–43
orzo
    Avgolemono, 194
    Greek Meatballs with Tomato Sauce and Orzo, 200
outgrowing food allergies, 95
Oyster Noodle Casserole, 187

palmar grasp, 29
Pancakes
    Almond Cardamom Sheet Pan Pancakes, 135
    6-Allergen Blender Pancakes, 134
Paneer, BLF Saag Paneer, 224
panko breadcrumbs
    Fish Fingers, 179
    Greek Meatballs with Tomato Sauce and Orzo, 200
    Peanut Butter Sweet Potato Casserole, 215
    Seafood Sliders with Lemon Aioli, 158
    Sheet Pan Salmon Dinner, 176
    Zucchini Boats, 219
parent-led weaning, 13
parents, food allergies of, 101–102
Parmesan cheese
    Fish Fingers, 179
    Lasagna Roll-Ups, 212
    Many Nut Pesto Pasta, 214
    Memere's Shepherd's Pie, 202
    Rainbow Egg Bites, 147
    Roasted Zucchini Sticks, 218
    Savory Scones, 150
    Spaghetti Squash Quinoa Bake, 220
pasta
    Crab Linguine with Lemon and Basil, 190
    Fishies Wearing Bow Ties, 184
    Greek Meatballs with Tomato Sauce and Orzo, 200
    Lasagna Roll-Ups, 212
    Many Nut Pesto Pasta, 214

Oyster Noodle Casserole, 187
Shells and Cheese with Carrots and Peas, 169
Skillet Macaroni with Veggies and Beef, 208
peanut butter, 115
    African Peanut Stew, 222
    Baked PB Oatmeal Sticks, 141
    Fishies Wearing Bow Ties, 184
    Mango Surprise Smoothie, 228
    Mascarpone Peanut Butter Melts, 133
    Nutty French Toast Casserole, 137
    Peanut Butter and Jelly Muffins, 138
    Peanut Butter Banana Baby Cookies, 229
    Peanut Butter Banana Mini Muffins, 131
    Peanut Butter Power Pops, 233
    Peanut Butter Sweet Potato Casserole, 215
    Pumpkin Spice Cookies, 231
    6-Allergen Blender Pancakes, 134
    Toasted Coconut Pumpkin Pudding, 232
peanuts, 115
    African Peanut Stew, 222
    Baked PB Oatmeal Sticks, 141
    Fishies Wearing Bow Ties, 184
    Mango Surprise Smoothie, 228
    Mascarpone Peanut Butter Melts, 133
    Nutty French Toast Casserole, 137
    offering for first time, 74
    Peanut Apple Fritters, 167
    Peanut Butter and Jelly Muffins, 138
    Peanut Butter Banana Baby Cookies, 229
    Peanut Butter Banana Mini Muffins, 131
    Peanut Butter Power Pops, 233
    Peanut Butter Sweet Potato Casserole, 215
    Pumpkin Spice Cookies, 231
    6-Allergen Blender Pancakes, 134
    Toasted Coconut Pumpkin Pudding, 232
    as top allergen, 5, 61
peanut substitutes, 238
Peas, Shells and Cheese with Carrots and, 169
pecans
    Butternut Apple Muffin Cakes, 142
    Easy Maple Pecan Baby Back Ribs, 206
    Pumpkin Spice Cookies, 231
    Walnut-Crusted Butternut French Toast, 144
pediatrician, talking with, 20–21
Pickled Red Onion, 155

pincer grasp, 29
Pineapple Ginger Glaze, 181
pine nuts, Many Nut Pesto Pasta, 214
pistachios, Many Nut Pesto Pasta, 214
Pizzas, English Muffin, 165
plates, 24
pollock, Cod Tacos with Lime Sauce, 182
popcorn, 41
Pops, Peanut Butter Power, 233
pork, Easy Maple Pecan Baby Back Ribs, 206
portion sizes, 47
potato chips, 41
Presto Pressed Pesto Grilled Cheese, 173
protein, 34
Pudding
    Strawberry Mango Chia Seed, 140
    Toasted Coconut Pumpkin, 232
pumpkin
    Pumpkin Spice Cookies, 231
    Toasted Coconut Pumpkin Pudding, 232

Quesadillas, Avocado Crab, 186
Quinoa Spaghetti Squash Bake, 220

rainbow trout, Macadamia-Crusted Fish with
    Pineapple Ginger Glaze, 181
rashes, 100–101
raw fruits or vegetables, 41
readiness for solids, 21–23
recipes, 29. see also specific recipes
    breakfast, 130–152
    desserts, 226–234
    dinner and sides, 174–225
    lunch, 153–173
    in maintenance meal plans, 121–128
    using, 110–111
responsive feeding, 15–16
rice cereal, 37–38
ricotta cheese, Lasagna Roll-Ups, 212
rigatoni, Many Nut Pesto Pasta, 214

Saag Paneer, BLF, 224
Salad
    Salmon Salad with Pickled Red Onion, 155
    Tahini Egg, 172

Tarragon Chicken, 162
salmon
    Salmon Salad with Pickled Red Onion, 155
    Seafood Sliders with Lemon Aioli, 158
    Sheet Pan Salmon Dinner, 176
Sardine Avotoasts, 154
sausage rounds, 41
Scones, Savory, 150
screening for food allergies, 92–94
seed butters, 41
seeds, 41
    sesame, 83, 184, 196, 216
    Strawberry Mango Chia Seed Pudding, 140
sesame, 118
    Cherry Chocolate Ice Pops, 230
    Edamame Tahini Dip, 164
    Fishies Wearing Bow Ties, 184
    Lemon Tahini Lentil Stew, 225
    Miso Mushroom Soup with Egg, 216
    offering for first time, 83
    Pinkalicious Beet Hummus, 171
    Sesame Eggplant Dip, 163
    Tahini Date Shake, 145
    Tahini Egg Salad, 172
    as top allergen, 5, 61
    Za'atar Chicken Drumsticks, 196
sesame seeds
    Fishies Wearing Bow Ties, 184
    Miso Mushroom Soup with Egg, 216
    Za'atar Chicken Drumsticks, 196
sesame substitutes, 238
Shake, Tahini Date, 145
shapes of foods, 41
shellfish, 118
    Avocado Crab Quesadillas, 186
    Cheesy Crab Dip, 156
    Crab Linguine with Lemon and Basil, 190
    Herbed Clam Chowder, 192
    offering for first time, 81–82
    Oyster Noodle Casserole, 187
    Seafood Sliders with Lemon Aioli, 158
    Shrimp and Broccoli Croquettes, 160
    Shrimp and Tofu Fajitas, 188
    Shrimp and Vegetable Fritters, 157
    Shrimpy Grits, 152

INDEX

shellfish (continued)

Squid Stew, 191

as top allergen, 5, 61

shellfish substitutes, 238

Shells and Cheese with Carrots and Peas, 169

Shepherd's Pie, Memere's, 202

shrimp

Seafood Sliders with Lemon Aioli, 158

Shrimp and Broccoli Croquettes, 160

Shrimp and Tofu Fajitas, 188

Shrimp and Vegetable Fritters, 157

Shrimpy Grits, 152

6-Allergen Blender Pancakes, 134

size of finger foods, 29–30

Sliders, Seafood Sliders with Lemon Aioli, 158

Smoothie, Mango Surprise, 228

sodium, 38–39

soup

Avgolemono, 194

Herbed Clam Chowder, 192

Miso Mushroom Soup with Egg, 216

sour cream

Avocado Crab Quesadillas, 186

Cheesy Crab Dip, 156

Cod Tacos with Lime Sauce, 182

Memere's Shepherd's Pie, 202

Peanut Butter and Jelly Muffins, 138

Shells and Cheese with Carrots and Peas, 169

Shrimp and Broccoli Croquettes, 160

Shrimp and Tofu Fajitas, 188

Tarragon Chicken Salad, 162

Turkey and Tempeh Slow Cooker Chili, 198

sourdough bread

Cheesy Crab Dip, 156

Nutty French Toast Casserole, 137

Sardine Avotoasts, 154

Veggie Strata, 146

Walnut-Crusted Butternut French Toast, 144

soy, 117

Almond Cardamom Pancakes, 135

Apple Oat Baby Bars, 136

Baked PB Oatmeal Sticks, 141

Better-for-You Black Bean Brownies, 234

Cast-Iron Skillet Corn Bread, 209

Cherry Chocolate Ice Pops, 230

Cinnamon Oat Breakfast Bars, 139

Coconut Curry Lentil Stew, 210

Easy Slow Cooker Chicken Korma, 195

Edamame Tahini Dip, 164

Fishies Wearing Bow Ties, 184

Herbed Clam Chowder, 192

Huevos Rancheros Eggs, 149

Macadamia-Crusted Fish, 181

Mango Surprise Smoothie, 228

Memere's Shepherd's Pie, 202

Miso Mushroom Soup with Egg, 216

Nutty French Toast Casserole, 137

offering for first time, 82–83

Rainbow Egg Bites, 147

Savory Scones, 150

Shells and Cheese with Carrots and Peas, 169

Shrimp and Tofu Fajitas, 188

Shrimpy Grits, 152

Spaghetti Squash Quinoa Bake, 220

Strawberry Mango Chia Seed Pudding, 140

Tahini Date Shake, 145

as top allergen, 5, 61

Turkey and Tempeh Slow Cooker Chili, 198

Veggie Strata, 146

soy milk, 117

Almond Cardamom Pancakes, 135

Apple Oat Baby Bars, 136

Baked PB Oatmeal Sticks, 141

Cast-Iron Skillet Corn Bread, 209

Easy Slow Cooker Chicken Korma, 195

Herbed Clam Chowder, 192

Huevos Rancheros Eggs, 149

Nutty French Toast Casserole, 137

Savory Scones, 150

Shells and Cheese with Carrots and Peas, 169

Shrimpy Grits, 152

6-Allergen Blender Pancakes, 134

Strawberry Mango Chia Seed Pudding, 140

Tahini Date Shake, 145

Veggie Strata, 146

soy sauce

Fishies Wearing Bow Ties, 184

Macadamia-Crusted Fish, 181

Miso Mushroom Soup with Egg, 216

soy substitutes, 238

Spaghetti Squash Quinoa Bake, 220

Spinach Manchego Frittata, 148

splat mats, 25

spoon-feeding with purees, 13

spoons, 24

Squid Stew, 191

starting solids, 9–19

with baby-led weaning, 11–12

combined approach to, 16

foods for (see first foods)

with modified baby-led weaning, 14–15

options for, 9–10

preparation for, 20–25

with responsive feeding, 15–16

safety when, 86–91

signals of hunger/fullness, 16–19

by spoon-feeding with purees, 13

steak, 35

Stew

African Peanut, 222

Coconut Curry Lentil, 210

Fall-Apart Slow Cooker Beef, 204

Lemon Tahini Lentil, 225

Squid, 191

stocking the kitchen, 106–110

stone fruits, 41

Strata, Veggie, 146

Strawberry Mango Chia Seed Pudding, 140

straw cups, 24–25

substitutes for allergens, 236–238

suction-bottom bowls and plates, 24

sugars, 41, 43–44

sweet potato, 36

Peanut Butter Sweet Potato Casserole, 215

Sweet Potato Almond Butter Mash, 168

Tacos, Cod with Lime Sauce, 182

tahini, 83, 118

Cherry Chocolate Ice Pops, 230

Edamame Tahini Dip, 164

Fishies Wearing Bow Ties, 184

Lemon Tahini Lentil Stew, 225

Pinkalicious Beet Hummus, 171

Sesame Eggplant Dip, 163

Tahini Date Shake, 145

Tahini Egg Salad, 172

Za'atar Chicken Drumsticks, 196

Tartar Sauce, Cashew, 180

tempeh, 82
    Memere's Shepherd's Pie, 202
    Turkey and Tempeh Slow Cooker Chili, 198
texture of foods, 29–30
Toasted Coconut Pumpkin Pudding, 232
toast toppings, 79
tofu, 31, 82, 117
    Cinnamon Oat Breakfast Bars, 139
    Coconut Curry Lentil Stew, 210
    Mango Surprise Smoothie, 228
    Miso Mushroom Soup with Egg, 216
    Rainbow Egg Bites, 147
    Shrimp and Tofu Fajitas, 188
    Spaghetti Squash Quinoa Bake, 220
Tomato Sauce, Greek Meatballs with Orzo and, 200
tortilla chips, 41
treatment for food allergies, 95
tree nuts, 117. see also specific types
    Apple Oat Baby Bars, 136
    Baby-Friendly Cashew Dip, 166
    Better-for-You Black Bean Brownies, 234
    Butternut Apple Muffin Cakes, 142
    Cashew Tartar Sauce, 180
    Cast-Iron Skillet Corn Bread, 209
    Cherry Almond BLF Cookies, 227
    Cherry Chocolate Ice Pops, 230
    Cinnamon Oat Breakfast Bars, 139
    Coconut Curry Lentil Stew, 210
    Easy Maple Pecan Baby Back Ribs, 206
    Easy Slow Cooker Chicken Korma, 195
    Lasagna Roll-Ups, 212
    Macadamia-Crusted Fish, 181
    Mango Surprise Smoothie, 228
    Many Nut Pesto Pasta, 214
    Nutty French Toast Casserole, 137
    offering for first time, 74–76
    Peanut Butter Banana Baby Cookies, 229
    Presto Pressed Pesto Grilled Cheese, 173
    Pumpkin Spice Cookies, 231
    Seafood Sliders with Lemon Aioli, 158
    Shrimp and Tofu Fajitas, 188
    6-Allergen Blender Pancakes, 134
    Strawberry Mango Chia Seed Pudding, 140
    Sweet Potato Almond Butter Mash, 168
    Tarragon Chicken Salad, 162
    as top allergen, 5, 61

Walnut-Crusted Butternut French Toast, 144
    Zucchini Walnut Bread, 132
tree nut substitutes, 238
turkey, 35
    Turkey and Tempeh Slow Cooker Chili, 198

unpasteurized milk, 40

Veggie Strata, 146
vitamin D, 34

walnut(s)
    Butternut Apple Muffin Cakes, 142
    Mango Surprise Smoothie, 228
    Many Nut Pesto Pasta, 214
    Tarragon Chicken Salad, 162
    Walnut-Crusted Butternut French Toast, 144
    Zucchini Walnut Bread, 132
washcloths, 25
wheat, 116
    Almond Cardamom Pancakes, 135
    Apple Oat Baby Bars, 136
    Avgolemono, 194
    Butternut Apple Muffin Cakes, 142
    Cast-Iron Skillet Corn Bread, 209
    Cheesy Crab Dip, 156
    Cinnamon Oat Breakfast Bars, 139
    Cottage Cheese Mash, 170
    Crab Linguine with Lemon and Basil, 190
    Easy Maple Pecan Baby Back Ribs, 206
    English Muffin Baby Pizzas, 165
    Fall-Apart Slow Cooker Beef Stew, 204
    Fish Fingers, 179
    Fishies Wearing Bow Ties, 184
    Greek Meatballs with Tomato Sauce and Orzo, 200
    Herbed Clam Chowder, 192
    Macadamia-Crusted Fish, 181
    Many Nut Pesto Pasta, 214
    Memere's Shepherd's Pie, 202
    Miso Mushroom Soup with Egg, 216
    Nutty French Toast Casserole, 137
    Oyster Noodle Casserole, 187
    Peanut Butter Banana Mini Muffins, 131
    Peanut Butter Sweet Potato Casserole, 215
    Presto Pressed Pesto Grilled Cheese, 173
    Pumpkin Spice Cookies, 231

Rainbow Egg Bites, 147
Roasted Zucchini Sticks, 218
Sardine Avotoasts, 154
Savory Scones, 150
Seafood Sliders with Lemon Aioli, 158
Sheet Pan Salmon Dinner, 176
Shells and Cheese with Carrots and Peas, 169
Shrimp and Broccoli Croquettes, 160
Shrimp and Vegetable Fritters, 157
6-Allergen Blender Pancakes, 134
Skillet Macaroni with Veggies and Beef, 208
    as top allergen, 5, 61
Veggie Strata, 146
Walnut-Crusted Butternut French Toast, 144
Zucchini Boats, 219
Zucchini Walnut Bread, 132
wheat substitutes, 237
Worcestershire sauce
    Memere's Shepherd's Pie, 202
    Skillet Macaroni with Veggies and Beef, 208

yogurt
    Almond Cardamom Pancakes, 135
    Apple Oat Baby Bars, 136
    Cherry Chocolate Ice Pops, 230
    Easy Slow Cooker Chicken Korma, 195
    offering for first time, 77
    Peanut Butter Power Pops, 233
    Salmon Salad with Pickled Red Onion, 155
    Savory Scones, 150
    6-Allergen Blender Pancakes, 134
    Toasted Coconut Pumpkin Pudding, 232
    Za'atar Chicken Drumsticks, 196

Za'atar Chicken Drumsticks, 196
zinc, 32–33
zucchini
    Roasted Zucchini Sticks, 218
    Zucchini Boats, 219
    Zucchini Walnut Bread, 132
Zyrtec, 98

ABOUT THE AUTHOR

Photo by Oleksandr Radomskyi

Malina Malkani, MS, RDN, CDN, is a pediatric registered dietitian nutritionist, top nutrition influencer, sought-after speaker, and trusted nutrition expert in local and national media outlets, publications, and organizations, including *Sirius XM Doctor Radio, Food Allergy Research and Education, The Doctors* (CBS), *U.S. News and World Report, Newsweek, Babylist, Well + Good, Health, Insider, Eating Well, Everyday Health, New York* magazine, CNN, and Food Network.

A single mother of three behind the Instagram, TikTok, and YouTube handle @healthy.mom.healthy.kids, Malkani is dedicated to educating her audience of over 140,000 followers about infant and childhood nutrition. She owns a nutrition consulting company and private practice at MalinaMalkani.com that helps caregivers feed their babies and kids with confidence, and loves partnering with brands (including Mission MightyMe and ezpz), commodity boards, and organizations that share her mission and dedication to public health.

Malkani is the best-selling author of *Simple & Safe Baby-Led Weaning: How to Integrate Foods, Manage Portion Sizes, and Identify Allergies* and the creator of two popular online courses for parents: *Safe & Simple Baby-Led Feeding* and *Solve Picky Eating,* both designed to help parents grow adventurous, intuitive eaters. A member of the Forbes Health Advisory Board since 2022, she served a three-year term as a national media spokesperson for the Academy of Nutrition and Dietetics and is currently serving as an Advisory Council Member for the Robert Wood Johnson Foundation's "Reframing Child Health and Obesity Project."

Having completed her undergraduate degrees at Northwestern University, master's degree in clinical nutrition at New York University, and dietetic internship at the accredited James J. Peters Bronx VA Medical Center, Malkani subsequently worked at the Bronx VA as an outpatient weight loss and bariatric surgery dietitian. Her overarching mission is to reshape the nutritional habits and behaviors of our next generation, to optimize their long-term health, and to reduce the likelihood of the development of food allergies, cancer, and other chronic diseases.

When not working, Malkani can usually be found singing, running around with her girls, developing new recipes, hiking, or hanging out with her giant Maine coon cat, Tasha.

Stay on top of Malkani's current offerings by joining her email list at MalinaMalkani.com /join-malina-malkani-email-list.